Blacks and Whites

SOCIAL
TRENDS
IN THE
UNITED
STATES

Editors
James A. Davis
John Modell

Committee on Social Indicators
Social Science Research Council

BLACKS and WHITES

Narrowing the Gap?

Reynolds Farley

Harvard University Press
Cambridge, Massachusetts, and London, England   1984

Library of Congress Cataloging in Publication Data

Farley, Reynolds, 1938–
     Blacks and whites : narrowing the gap?

     (Social trends in the United States)
     Bibliography: p.
     Includes index.
     1. Afro-Americans—Economic conditions. 2. Afro-
Americans—Social conditions. 3. Afro-Americans—Eco-
nomic conditions—Statistics. 4. Afro-Americans—Social
conditions—Statistics. I. Title. II. Series.
E185.8.F35 1984   305.8'96073   84-638
ISBN 0-674-07631-1

Foreword

For much of the first half of this century, American social science was actively engaged in overcoming what Walter Lippmann in 1922 identified as "the central difficulty of self-government" in the modern world, namely, the difficulty of creating a public competent to confront complexity and change without retreating into political passivity. Quantitative social scientists set out to devise ways of tracking and analyzing change that would make it comprehensible to the public. Social "reporting," as originally conceived, was integral to the underlying political purpose of social science: the accommodation of a plurality of interests in the context of expanding popular expectations.

The classic monument to this commitment was the two-volume *Recent Social Trends*, prepared by the President's Research Committee on Recent Social Trends and published in 1933. The blending of science and public information characteristic of the day is expressed in the summary of the committee's findings: "in the formulation of . . . new and emergent values, in the construction of the new symbols to thrill men's souls, in the contrivance of the new institutions and adaptations useful in the fulfillment of new aspirations, we trust that this review of recent social trends may prove of value to the American public."

Optimism about the role of empirical social science continued into the era of the Great Depression, although it came to emphasize the problems introduced by change rather than progressive improvements. This work nonetheless reflected engaged, hopeful concern, as did the contributions of American social scientists to the war effort that followed. When social science emerged from World War II, however, its characteristic posture was far more ironic than formerly, less confident in the meaning of its indicators, more hermetic, more specialized. The task of systematic description and analysis of recent social change fell further away from the ordinary activities of academic social scientists.

As editors of the series Social Trends in the United States, we contend that social science has a collective responsibility to report findings about society to the public, in order to contribute to the informed choices that are necessary in a democracy. If the reports of social scientists are to be useful to citizens, their authors must define questions for educational and political relevance and must translate technical terminology into the language of common discourse. Modern statistical methods make it possible to trace change along a large number of dimensions in which the pattern of change over time is rarely visible to people directly involved in it, and to discern how change in one dimension may affect change in others. Such information, in compact and comprehensible form, can make a useful contribution to political discussion.

This is the rationale of the series, which is sponsored by the Committee on Social Indicators of the Social Science Research Council. The committee invites authoritative scholars to contribute manuscripts on particular topics and has other scholars review each manuscript with attention to both the scientific and the broadly educational purposes of the series. Nevertheless, the volumes in the series are the authors' own, and thus far from uniform. Each is free-standing, but we hope that the effect of the series will be cumulative. Taken together, these volumes will not constitute an overall contemporary history: historical accounts evoke context rather than extract single dimensions of change. The series, however, will provide insights into interconnected aspects of contemporary society that no contemporary history—and no one interested in understanding our present condition—should ignore.

The Social Indicators Committee of the Social Science Research Council consists of Kenneth C. Land (Chair), University of Texas; Richard A. Berk, University of California, Santa Barbara; Martin H. David, University of Wisconsin; James A. Davis, Harvard University; Graham Kalton, University of Michigan; Kinley Larntz, University of Minnesota; John Modell, Carnegie-Mellon University; John F. Padgett, University of Chicago; and Stephen H. Schneider, National Center for Atmospheric Research, Boulder, Colorado. Richard C. Rockwell, Staff Associate at the Social Science Research Council, made indispensable contributions to the production of this volume.

James A. Davis
John Modell

Acknowledgments

This is the second book in the series Social Trends in the United States, sponsored by the Social Science Research Council. I appreciate the encouragement and assistance of Richard Rockwell and of his colleagues at the SSRC, Robert Parke and David E. Myers. James A. Davis and John Modell provided useful advice. I received helpful comments on the manuscript from Fred L. Bookstein, Andrew J. Cherlin, Philip E. Converse, Greg J. Duncan, Nathan Glazer, Robert B. Hill, Robert Mare, Douglas S. Massey, Howard Schuman, Finis Welch, and William J. Wilson, and valuable editorial help from Camille Smith. This investigation was partially supported by a grant made by the National Science Foundation's Program in Measurement Methods and Data Resources to the Social Science Research Council's Committee on Social Indicators.

James R. Wetzel invited me to spend a sabbatical at the Census Bureau's Center for Demographic Studies during 1981 and 1982. Jim and his colleagues Suzanne M. Bianchi, Michael J. Fortier, Larry H. Long, and Daphne G. Spain helped me to appreciate both the merits and the complexities of data gathered in the decennial censuses and the Current Population Survey.

This book was largely written at the University of Michigan's Population Studies Center, and the computations were made there also. I thank Albert I. Hermalin, Director of the Center, for his support and for providing the needed facilities. The completion of this work depended upon his assistance and that of Albert F. Anderson, Kathleen F. Duke, Lisa J. Neidert, and Judith A. Mullin.

Contents

Blacks and Whites

1

Introduction

When he wrote about race relations in the early 1940s, Gunnar Myrdal described a fundamental dilemma. Americans endorsed the principles that all persons were created equal and endowed by God with inalienable rights, that the government existed to protect these rights, and that, before the law, all persons had exactly the same status. And yet the ideals of equality, fair treatment, and democracy were only abstract principles so far as blacks were concerned. In many areas of the South, blacks had almost no civil rights that whites respected. They could not hope to hold public office, to vote, or even to serve on juries. They could be capriciously arrested by the white police force. If they were accused of criminal acts, they were tried by white judges and white juries in racially segregated courts. The segregated system of education often provided nothing but deficient grammar school training for southern blacks. In the North, explicit practices and legal agreements designated where blacks could live and set strict limits on their occupational achievements, and *de facto* segregation in urban areas ensured that blacks and whites attended different schools.

In the period following World War II, America confronted the basic issue of whether the principles of equality and democracy extended to blacks. The pace of racial change increased after 1960, but there is a very long history of struggle for civil rights in the United States. Many of the laws and court decisions of the 1960s and 1970s resembled similar measures that were enacted during Reconstruction but then lay dormant for nine decades.

The Civil Rights Movement

The civil rights movement of the period since World War II has six distinct but overlapping aspects. The first is the litigation strategy of the National Association for the Advancement of Colored People (NAACP), which laid the groundwork for challenging state-imposed racial discrimination. For decades, NAACP lawyers filed suit when blacks were denied the right to vote, kept off juries, denied accommodations on interstate trains, or provided with separate and unequal schools. They were sometimes victorious in the federal courts. In 1940, for example, courts ruled that equally qualified black and white teachers in segregated systems must be paid similar amounts. In the early 1950s NAACP litigation succeeded in getting one black student into a graduate program in education at the University of Oklahoma and another admitted to the law school of the University of Texas. Many of these decisions involved a small number of plaintiffs, plaintiffs who could be harassed if they fought too diligently for their civil rights. Furthermore, southern states frequently established new barriers to racial equality when the federal courts eliminated the old ones. Nevertheless, the litigation strategy, which was based upon the American ideal of equal opportunity, achieved some important victories. The key decision, *Brown v. Board of Education of Topeka* (1954), greatly strengthened the civil rights movement by upholding the principles of democracy and, theoretically, overturning state-imposed racial discrimination.

The second aspect of the movement was a massive increase in the number of blacks actively involved in the struggle for rights. The bus boycott in Montgomery, Alabama, initiated by Rosa Parks in 1957 and the Greensboro, North Carolina, lunch-counter sit-in of Joseph McNeil, Izell Blair, Franklin McCain, and David Richmond in 1960 mark the beginning of this phase. There was nothing new about these protests. The Congress of Racial Equality (CORE) had been organizing peaceful demonstrations in northern and border cities for two decades. In Baltimore and St. Louis, for example, their picketing and sit-ins made it possible for blacks to eat at the lunch counters and cafeterias of the downtown stores. It was only after 1960, however, that civil rights demonstrations became widespread in the deep South, where racial discrimination was most blatant. New organizations such as the Student Nonviolent Coordinating Committee and the Southern Christian Leadership Conference mobilized many blacks. In 1963 the civil rights organizations assembled more than half a million people for their March on Washington. Two years later a series of marches in Alabama led to the passage of the Voting Rights Bill.

Third, as the black protests made more white Americans aware of the dilemma Myrdal had described, the attitudes and actions of whites changed. Such changes are not easy to document, but there are several types of evidence. In national opinion polls, the proportion of whites who said they would object if a Negro with an education and income similar to their own moved next door diminished from 62 percent in 1942 to 39 percent in 1963 and 15 percent in 1972 (Pettigrew, 1973). In 1942 only 44 percent of whites approved of racially integrated public transportation, but this rose to 60 percent in 1956, and by the mid-1960s approval was almost universal (Sheatsley, 1966). Similar changes occurred in white views about integrated public education: between 1963 and 1972 the proportion endorsing integrated schooling went from 62 to 82 percent (Taylor, Sheatsley, and Greeley, 1978). A growing number of whites also participated in the protest movement in the South by marching with blacks, organizing freedom schools, or helping blacks register to vote.

The fourth aspect of the movement involved the elected officials of the federal government, who gradually, by the mid-1960s, came to support effective civil rights laws, laws overturning the principle of states' rights. In 1945 the Congress spurned President Truman's efforts to extend the Fair Employment Practices Commission, but twelve years later it enacted a modest civil rights law, which was followed by much more encompassing legislation. The Twenty-Fourth Amendment, ratified in 1964, ended the poll tax requirement for federal elections. The Civil Rights Act of 1964 outlawed racial discrimination in public accommodations, provided assistance for integration of schools, put the Justice Department on the side of plaintiffs in civil rights litigation, banned racial discrimination in the use of federal funds, and outlawed discrimination in employment. The Voting Rights Act of 1965 was effective in bringing blacks into the electoral process: it called for the appointment of federal registrars if local ones persisted in keeping blacks off the voting rolls. After the assassination of Dr. Martin Luther King, Jr., the Congress passed the Civil Rights Act of 1968, which banned racial discrimination in the sale or rental of most housing units.

Fifth, the Supreme Court joined the executive and legislative branches in protecting the rights of black citizens. Throughout the twentieth century the Court had been issuing rulings that seemed to defend the rights of blacks, but all too often southern states had developed strategies that voided the intent of the rulings. For example, the Supreme Court declared it unconstitutional to use grandfather clauses to determine who could vote. (These clauses waived literacy requirements for those whose forebears had voted before the Civil War, effectively granting the vote to illiterate whites and denying it to blacks.) But several southern states then decided that political parties were private organizations and as such could establish their own racist rules. After 1960 there was a change in the pace and scope of federal court rulings concerning civil rights. Rather than focusing upon the theoretical legal rights of individual blacks, the courts began to protect the interests of blacks as a class and to consider their actual status compared to that of whites. The Supreme Court approved the use of federal powers to eliminate discrimination in areas that had been subject to state law only, including public accommodations, the assignment of pupils to local schools, the registration of voters, and the private sale of real estate.

After years of delays and inaction, the Court finally insisted upon the actual integration of public schools. In a series of decisions beginning in 1968, it outlawed the ineffective freedom-of-choice plans used in southern states, overturned the "all deliberate speed" principle, the use of racial ratios and busing to integrate urban school systems, and declared that northern school districts were under the same requirement to operate racially integrated schools as southern districts. The Court also gradually came to endorse affirmative action programs designed to increase educational and employment opportunities for blacks. In the 1978 *Bakke* decision it ruled that universities might use race as one of a number of criteria when deciding whom to admit; in 1979 it upheld a quota system that reserved some of the better-paying jobs for blacks even if they had less seniority than similarly qualified whites; and the next year it endorsed a law requiring that 10 percent of federal construction funds be spent with minority contractors.

The sixth aspect was the high level of racial violence that marked the 1960s. Many of the early black protesters in the South lost their jobs, were shot at, or were harassed in other ways. In the summers of 1963 and 1964 more than two dozen black churches in Alabama and Mississippi were burned or bombed (Franklin, 1967; Meier and Rudwick, 1975). Civil rights protesters in Birmingham were attacked by police with German Shepherds and fire hoses. Numerous civil rights activists were slain by white racists. Some of the victims were whites, such as Andrew Goodman and Michael Schwerner, who died in Mississippi, or Viola Liuzzo, who was killed while helping blacks register to vote in Alabama. Other victims were black leaders, including Medgar Evers and Martin Luther King, Jr. The 1960s were also a decade of urban racial violence. In 1967 alone, some 164 incidents of racial disorders were recorded in American cities. Black protesters fought with white policemen or firemen or attacked white-owned stores. In most cases these were minor events that were quickly quelled, but in Los Angeles, Newark, and Detroit dozens of lives were lost. In the summer of 1967, eighty-three people died in urban racial riots (U.S. National Advisory Commission on Civil Disorders, 1968).

It is extremely difficult to assess the consequences of this violence. Myrdal noted in 1944 that getting publicity was of highest strategic importance for blacks. He predicted that whites in the North would be shaken when they learned the facts about the treatment of blacks in the South. And apparently the nightly television reports showing peaceful protesters clubbed by policemen and mauled by snarling dogs dramatically increased the support of whites for strong civil rights legislation such as the Voting Rights Act of 1965 (Garrow, 1978).

The National Advisory Commission on Civil Disorders, known as the Kerner Commission, studied the riots of 1967 and helped to publicize the discriminatory treatment of blacks. Its report pointed out that this was a national issue, not just a southern one. The Commission did not legitimate the violence of the late 1960s, but it stressed civil rights abuses and the immense racial differences in housing, job opportunities, education, and income found in northern cities. Rather than blaming blacks for their own poverty and for the urban violence or attributing the problem to communist agitators, the commission pointed out that "What white Americans have never fully understood—but what the Negro can never forget—is that white society is deeply implicated in the ghetto. White institutions created it, white institutions maintain it, and white society condones it" (U.S. National Advisory Commission on Civil Disorders, 1968:2).

These conclusions strengthened the civil rights movement and helped to bring about the War on Poverty which was designed to provide educational and employment opportunities to the poor. The Head Start program was created to prepare poor children to do well in school. The low-income population received food stamps. Laid-off workers were given job training or were employed in newly created public-sector jobs. Since a large proportion of the poor population was black, the War on Poverty was expected not only to reduce poverty but to help blacks catch up with whites in economic status.

Looking back from the vantage point of the 1980s, we see many areas of racial change and others in which the situation has not changed much. Blacks are now voting throughout the nation, and some are elected to office even in those counties of the South where in 1964 no black dared approach the polling booth. It is now quite common to find blacks in professional occupations and in managerial positions. In the early 1960s the federal government used troops to admit James Meredith to the University of Mississippi; by 1980 blacks were enrolled in almost all universities.

And yet other perspectives suggest that the nation has made only modest racial progress. The Kerner Commission warned of a geographic polarization of U.S. society. Although a detailed assessment of racial residential segregation awaits analysis of 1980 Census data, it is clear that the basic pattern of neighborhood segregation in metropolitan areas has not been altered. Public schools in many large cities remain highly segregated, and efforts to integrate them still generate intense controversy.

What has happened to the status of blacks in the United States in the last two decades? Has there been a great reduction in discrimination, perhaps so great a change that within a few years blacks will achieve equality with whites in social and economic status? Or have the changes been superficial ones? Are just a few exceptional blacks now succeeding in white society while a much greater number of blacks find their status little changed from twenty years ago?

The Optimistic View

Some social scientists and essayists believe we have made much progress toward racial equality and that racial discrimination has been significantly reduced or perhaps even eliminated. This view can be traced to a controversial paper published in 1973 by Ben Wattenberg and Richard Scammon, who argued that a remarkable change took place in American society after 1960 as blacks increased their educational attainment, moved into skilled blue-collar or white-collar jobs, and began earning salaries close to those of whites. Wattenberg and Scammon believed that in the early 1970s, for the first time in the nation's history, a majority of blacks could be called middle class.

At about the same time, Daniel Patrick Moynihan (1972) observed that young, black, husband-wife families living outside the South had incomes almost as high as those of comparable white families. Nathan Glazer (1975) also analyzed the incomes of black and white husband-wife families and concluded that there was a trend toward convergence of income in all regions. These statistics are often used to bolster the argument that racial differences and discrimination are disappearing from American society.

Richard Freeman focused on the employment and earnings of college-educated blacks and found that they were comparable to those of similar whites. Reporting that by the mid-1970s college-educated black men entering the labor force could expect to earn at least as much as white men, he concluded that there had been "a dramatic collapse in traditional discriminatory patterns in the market for highly qualified black Americans" (Freeman, 1976:33). Although Freeman restricted his investigation to one component of the black population, his findings are often cited as evidence of substantial black gains in the labor market.

Several investigators used data from the decennial censuses and from the Census Bureau's monthly Current Population Survey to determine if black and white men with similar amounts of education earned similar amounts of money. In general, their findings suggest that the earnings associated with educational attainment in the mid-1970s were greater for white men than for black men but that racial differences declined substantially after 1960 (Weiss and Williamson, 1972; Freeman, 1973; Welch, 1973; Masters, 1975; Farley, 1977; Smith and Welch, 1977; Featherman and Hauser, 1978).

William Wilson (1978), who provided an overview of racial change in post–World War II America, noted that blacks made unprecedented progress in the government and corporate sectors. He argued that by the 1970s an individual's skill or ability, rather than skin color, determined economic success or failure. Indeed, Wilson entitled his book *The Declining Significance of Race*.

On the policy front, the gains made by blacks led Moynihan to circulate a memorandum to the White House in 1970 recommending a program of "benign neglect" because he believed court decisions and civil rights laws had dramatically reduced discrimination (Plotski and Marr, 1976). Because these racial gains were so extensive, Moynihan argued, no further governmental efforts were required.

George Gilder (1981:128), whose ideas influenced policymaking in the Reagan administration, called a chapter on racial issues "The Myths of Discrimination." In his view, "The last thirty years in America have seen a relentless and thoroughly successful advance against the old prejudices, to the point that it is now virtually impossible to find in a position of power a serious racist. Gaps in income between truly comparable blacks and whites have nearly closed . . ."

The Pessimistic View

Many other investigators of racial trends challenge these optimistic conclusions. The annual report of the National Urban League for 1980 begins with a summary by Vernon Jordan (1980:i): "For black Americans, the decade of the 1970s was a time in which many of their hopes, raised by the civil rights victories of the 1960s, withered away, a time in which they saw the loss of much of the momentum that seemed to be propelling the nation along the road to true equality for all its citizens . . . The 70s . . . brought forth in Black America a mood of disappointment, frustration and bitterness at promises made and promises unkept." Elsewhere Jordan (1979) noted that the income gap between blacks and whites had actually widened during the 1970s, that the unemployment rate for blacks was at a historical peak, and that the gap in joblessness between blacks and whites was the widest it had ever been.

Robert Hill, in *Economic Policies and Black Progress: Myths and Realities* (1981), observed that during the 1970s the simultaneous impact of periodic recessions and double-digit inflation hit the black community disproportionately hard. He presented a number of indicators showing that the status of blacks relative to whites declined in that decade. For example, the unemployment rate increased 61 percent among black men and only 40 percent among white men, and the number of blacks below the poverty line rose by 300,000 while the number of whites fell by 800,000.

Several other economists have speculated that the policies of the 1960s either were ineffective or had at best a temporary impact upon racial differences. Michael Reich (1981) argued that the incomes of blacks relative to those of whites improved largely because of urbanization and structural change in the economy. That is, blacks moved away from low-wage southern agriculture and into higher-paying industrial jobs. After controlling for such structural changes in employment, Reich found a persistence of substantial racial differences in income.

Edward Lazear (1979) observed that the earnings of white and black men tended to converge in the early 1970s, but he did not believe this heralded real racial gains. Employers responded to affirmative action requirements by equalizing the wages paid to entry-level blacks and whites, but firms would eventually compensate for this by promoting whites more rapidly than blacks. Pay rates then would increase with seniority much more rapidly for whites than for blacks. Thus Lazear saw the gains of the 1970s as illusory and predicted a persistent or even a widening gap between the races in the future.

Thomas Sowell (1981) and Walter Williams (1981) also presented a picture of the status of blacks that contrasts sharply with the optimistic one. They noted the high levels of deprivation among blacks and the substantial differences between blacks and whites on most indicators of status. These problems came about in large part, they contended, because of government programs and requirements. The War on Poverty encouraged blacks to stay out of the competitive labor market and to survive on welfare or other benefit programs. Blacks were thereby locked into dependency and discouraged from obtaining the skills needed to escape poverty. These economists also argued that government regulations, unnecessarily restrictive job requirements, and minimum wage laws prevented blacks from entering business or taking jobs.

The Polarization Thesis

A third perspective on the current racial situation stresses that the black community is becoming economically polarized. Commentators report that many young blacks are completing college educations and moving into the kinds of prestigious jobs that guarantee economic security, a prosperous standard of living, perhaps a home in the suburbs. They have taken advantage of the opportunities opened up by the civil rights revolution of the 1960s. At the same time, it is argued, many other blacks are trapped within central city ghettos where schools are poor, where opportunities for employment or advancement are limited, and where they are likely to be victims of

crime. Some writers see these blacks as highly dependent upon welfare programs. Increasingly, the term "underclass" is used to refer
to this component of the black population (Auletta, 1982).

The idea that blacks are becoming polarized by economic status can
be traced at least back to 1965, when Moynihan wrote: "There is
considerable evidence that the Negro community is, in fact, dividing
between a stable middle class group that is steadily growing stronger
and more successful and an increasingly disorganized and disadvantaged lower class group" (U.S. Department of Labor, 1965:5–6). Five
years later Andrew Brimmer defended the polarization hypothesis in
a paper subtitled "The Deepening Schism" (1970:58):

> During the 1960s, Negroes as a group did make significant
> economic progress. This can be seen in terms of higher em-
> ployment and occupational upgrading as well as in lower un-
> employment and a narrowing of the income gap between
> Negroes and Whites.
>
> However, beneath these overall improvements, another—
> and disturbing—trend is also evident: within the Negro com-
> munity there appears to be a deepening schism between the
> able and the less able, between the well-prepared and those
> with few skills.

More recently, Wilson (1978) has argued that the economic split
within the black community will be the nation's major racial issue in
the future, and Gilder (1981:12) has endorsed this view: "Although
intact black families are doing better than ever and discrimination has
vastly diminished, the condition of poor blacks has radically worsened." In the words of Ken Auletta (1982:259), "there are at least two
distinct minority communities—one, consisting mainly of female-
headed households, slips more deeply into poverty; the other moves
forward, albeit too slowly, toward the economic middle class."

A Demographic Approach

To determine which of these views most accurately describes recent
racial change, I will examine trends in the social and economic status
of blacks between 1960 and 1980. In analyzing these trends I will
employ demographic methods and measures. This demographic ap-

proach makes it possible to describe changes over time in the status of blacks. The data used in this investigation are the most comprehensive available: from the decennial censuses and from the Census Bureau's Current Population Survey, a monthly national sample that obtains responses from the residents of approximately sixty thousand households. Most of the questions and procedures used to gather information about educational attainment, employment status, occupational achievement, and earnings have been used repeatedly over the years. This continuity facilitates the study of time trends as well as the comparison of blacks and whites.

Another advantage of this approach is that demographic data can throw light on some of the *causes* of racial change. For example, as I will discuss in Chapters 3 and 4, wage rates are typically higher in the North and West than in the South. If we find that the wages of black workers rose in a certain period and that in the same period there was a movement of blacks away from the South, we can determine how much of the change in wages was due to the geographic shift and how much came about because wages increased within each region. In other words, we can disaggregate trends into their demographic components.

A dramatic example of this is described in Chapter 6: the ratio of black to white income for all families declined during the 1970s, suggesting that the economic status of blacks relative to that of whites deteriorated. However, for the two most common types of families, namely husband-wife families and those headed by women, the ratio of black to white family income rose for much of the decade, suggesting that the status of blacks improved. During the 1970s the number of families headed by black women increased much more than the number of black husband-wife families. Husband-wife families have average incomes considerably higher than those of families headed by women. Thus when the proportion of husband-wife families fell, the overall ratio of black to white family income decreased. In this manner, a demographic analysis moves beyond a simple plotting of trends to detect reasons behind the changes in the status of blacks.

An issue that cannot be fully explored in a demographic study is racial discrimination. Is it declining in the United States? If so, by how much and why? It is important to specify the meaning of the term *discrimination*. By racial discrimination I mean behavior toward people that is dictated by their skin color, rather than by their talents, accomplishments, or qualifications. A demographic analysis can provide useful information about this issue and may reveal evidence of racial discrimination, but it can seldom prove the presence or absence of discrimination.

I must stress that racial differences on measures of status do not necessarily indicate discrimination, although they may have come about because of past or present discrimination. In the United States there is consensus that it is better to get more education than less. There is also agreement about which jobs are desirable, and almost everyone believes that high earnings are better than low earnings. Individuals differ in their abilities, their willingness to stay in school, their diligence to achieve in the occupational sphere, and the amount of time they devote to earning money. Thus it makes sense that there would be variation in educational attainment, occupational achievement, and income. But there is no good reason to believe that the races differ substantially in abilities or in tastes. Thus, if there were no racial discrimination, blacks and whites would probably be quite similar in average levels of educational attainment, occupational success, and earnings.

As Chapters 2 and 3 report, racial differences in these indicators of status declined considerably after 1960. This strongly suggests that racial discrimination in education and in the labor market decreased, but it is not proof. Even if, for example, blacks and whites have the same occupational distributions or identical family incomes, it may be that blacks have to spend more time on the job to get promotions or that black wives work more hours per year than white wives. A thorough examination of the data can yield reasons for racial differences but will seldom isolate the specific effects of racial discrimination.

Similarly, even large differences between the races may not directly result from current discrimination. Suppose that blacks earn less money than whites, that at every educational attainment level blacks earn just about as much as comparably educated whites, and that blacks typically complete fewer years of schooling than whites. The gross difference in earnings does not prove discrimination. Indeed, the fact that blacks and whites with similar educations earn about the same amount of money implies there is little discrimination against black workers when wage rates are set. The finding that blacks and whites attain different amounts of education may reflect discrimination in the educational system. But it may not reflect current discrimination as much as discrimination in the past that limited educational opportunities for the parents of the black men and women whose earnings are being analyzed. Past discrimination may account for present racial differences.

In several places in this book I discuss racial discrimination as the most plausible explanation for a racial difference. I do this cautiously and with awareness of the constraints of the analysis.

Another limitation of a demographic study is that it can provide only partial answers to questions about the underlying causes of racial change. Why did the status of blacks change more in the 1960s than in the 1920s or the 1930s? Was it because of Martin Luther King's leadership of the civil rights movement, a change in the attitudes of whites, the Civil Rights Act of 1964, economic growth, or other causes? A demographic analysis can assess the amount and rapidity of change and may rule out some explanations, but it cannot often lead to conclusive proof about causes of large-scale social change.

Relative versus Absolute Change

It is possible for two investigators to examine identical racial data and draw opposite conclusions about whether the status of blacks improved or deteriorated, depending on whether they focus on relative or absolute changes. This issue will arise many times in this book and needs to be explained at the outset.

Consider the median income of black and white families. By the definition of *median*, half of all families have incomes below the median and the other half have incomes above it. Table 1.1 shows median

Table 1.1. Median income of black and white families (in constant 1979 dollars), 1959 and 1982.

Year	White families	Black families	Racial gap in income	Black income as % of white
1959	$14,301	$ 7,587	$6,714	53.1%
1982	$18,502	$10,277	$8,275	55.3%
Change in income	$ 4,201	$ 2,640		
Average annual rate of change	+1.1%	+1.3%		

Source: U.S. Bureau of the Census, *Census of Population: 1960*, PC(2)-1C, table 14; *Current Population Survey*, ser. P-60, no. 140, tables 2 and A-1.

income figures for black and white families in 1959 and 1982. Incomes are shown in constant dollars; that is, the dollar amounts families reported were adjusted so that the year-to-year changes in incomes are not affected by inflation but measure actual differences in purchasing power.

According to the table, the median income of white families rose from $14,301 in 1959 to $18,502 in 1982, and that of black families rose from $7,587 to $10,227. Does this mean black families gained on whites during this period, or did they fall further behind? Unfortunately, we cannot give an unambiguous answer to this question. During the period 1959–1982 the median income of black families grew by an average of 1.3 percent each year and that of white families by 1.1 percent each year. In 1959 black families had incomes that averaged about 53 percent of those of white families. Because of the difference in growth rates, the incomes of black families became larger relative to those of whites, so that by 1982 they averaged 55 percent of the incomes of white families. In this sense, the incomes of black families gained on those of whites.

But the actual, *absolute* increase in family income in this period was considerably larger for whites than for blacks. Income, or purchasing power, went up about $4,200 for the typical white family but only $2,600 for the typical black family. Thus the gap between the races in median income widened: the average white family had about $6,700 more purchasing power than the average black family in 1959, but $8,300 more in 1982. In this sense blacks fell further behind whites: the absolute racial gap in family income expanded.

This puzzling situation occurs because the higher rate of income growth for blacks was applied to a smaller base amount. The 1.3 percent annual growth rate for blacks led to a smaller actual increase in purchasing power over this twenty-three year interval than did the 1.1 percent growth rate for whites. Thus, depending on whether relative or absolute change is considered, these data lead to very different conclusions about the direction of racial change.

There is no guiding principle to tell us whether it is better to look at rates of change or at absolute change. The optimists who believe racial discrimination is disappearing will focus on rates of change which often indicate that blacks are catching up with whites. The pessimists are likely to stress absolute change, since these statistics often show that whites are widening the advantage they already enjoy. In this book I will present a balanced perspective, but the reader should be aware of this ambiguity in social science analysis. We can be sure of one thing: if the rate of change for blacks exceeds that for whites, racial parity will eventually be reached. But achieving this goal may take a long time. In the example of family income, if the growth rates of 1959–1982 persist without interruption, the median incomes of black and white families in the United States will be equal in about three centuries.

2

Education, Employment, and Occupation

If racial change is occurring rapidly and if barriers limiting the achievement of blacks have been eliminated, blacks and whites should be much more alike now than in the past on indicators of social and economic status such as educational attainment, employment, and occupation. If racial differences are now as large as they were twenty or thirty years ago, we may conclude that little progress has been made in improving the status of American blacks.

Educational Attainment

After the Civil War, southern states established public schools, but they often provided for the education of white children long before they got around to building schools for blacks. The Supreme Court's *Plessy v. Ferguson* decision in 1896 permitted states to organize separate but equal systems of education; however, schools for blacks and whites were seldom equal. Well into the twentieth century, black children in the South—and the majority of blacks lived in that region—were less likely than white children to attend school. In 1910, for example, about 85 percent of the nation's white children aged 6–14 but only 60 percent of the black children were enrolled in school (U.S. Bureau of the Census, 1918, table 24). Southern schools for blacks were open fewer days each year than those for whites, their classes were larger, and their teachers were less well paid (Bond, 1934; Bullock, 1973; Myrdal, 1944). In the South, especially in rural areas, the first real efforts to provide black and white children with comparable schools, with free transportation to school, and with similarly paid teachers occurred after World War II.

The Census of 1940 was the first to ask about educational attainment, that is, the number of years of schooling a person has completed. Although a few will later finish college or get an advanced degree, most people in the United States have completed their formal education by the time they reach their late twenties. For this reason, the educational attainment of persons aged 25–29 is a sensitive indicator of recent trends. Figure 2.1 shows the average educational attainment reported by persons in this age group between 1940 and 1982. Note the steady convergence in attainment. Among men who finished their education on the eve of World War II, blacks completed three and one-half fewer years of school than whites. This difference decreased to about two years in 1960 and to about half a year in 1982. Racial differences in the amount of education are reduced

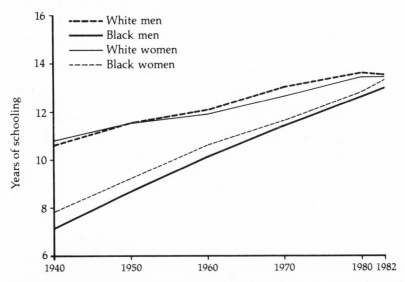

Figure 2.1. Average years of schooling completed by persons aged 25–29, by race and sex, 1940–1982.

Source: U.S. Bureau of the Census, *Sixteenth Census of the United States: 1940*, vol. IV, *Characteristics by Age*, table 18; *Census of Population: 1960*, vol. 1, pt. 1, table 173; *Census of Population: 1970*, vol. 1, pt. 1, table 199; *Current Population Reports*, ser. P-20, no. 356, table 1. (Data through 1960 refer to whites and nonwhites.)

primarily not because older blacks go back to school, but because black and white young people who are more similar in attainment become adults and replace older people whose attainments were dissimilar.

The trends for women are quite similar to those for men: young black women were about three years behind white women in educational attainment in 1940 but only half a year behind in 1982. Traditionally, black women remained enrolled in school longer than black men, while the average attainment of white women was just about equal to that of white men. By the end of the 1970s this sexual difference disappeared among blacks, as black men caught up with black women in average educational attainment.

Blacks have also caught up with whites in secondary-school enrollment. Back in 1940, over 70 percent of the whites aged 16–17 but less than 55 percent of the blacks were attending school (U.S. Bureau of the Census, 1943a, table 14). By 1970 the proportion of 16- and 17-year-olds in school exceeded 90 percent for whites and was just a little less—87 percent—for blacks (U.S. Bureau of the Census, 1973a, table 197). Since the mid-1970s there has been no racial difference in enrollment rates at these ages: among both blacks and whites about nine out of ten of those aged 16–17 attend school.

This convergence of enrollment rates does not mean that the racial difference in the completion of high school has been eliminated. Black children are much more likely than whites to be enrolled below the grade that is typical for their age. For example, the typical 17-year-old is in the twelfth grade. In the fall of 1979 about 54 percent of the black men age 17 who attended school, but only 26 percent of their white counterparts, were below this grade (U.S. Bureau of the Census, 1981a, table 16). At all ages and for both sexes, blacks are more likely than whites to fall behind their age-mates in their level of schooling. As a result, there is still a sizable racial difference in the completion of high school: among persons who were 20 and 21 at the end of the 1970s, approximately 85 percent of the whites but only 70 percent of the blacks had finished secondary school. This is, however, a major improvement from 1960, when about 70 percent of the whites and 40 percent of the blacks were finishing high school (U.S. Bureau of the Census, 1981a, table 1; 1963a, table 173).

For much of the period after World War II, college enrollment rates increased more rapidly among whites than among blacks, and thus racial differences in the proportion of young people with a college education grew larger at the very time differences at the high school level contracted. Information about this for the recent period is shown in Figure 2.2. In 1960 about 16 percent of the white men and 5 percent of the black men aged 25–29 were college graduates; by 1982 25 percent of the white men and only 12 percent of the black men in this age group had completed college. Women showed a similar pattern: the proportion finishing college increased for both races but the rise was more substantial among white women, leading to a larger racial difference.

Many of those writers who stressed that blacks made impressive economic gains, such as Richard Freeman (1976) and William Wilson (1978), observed that college-educated blacks fared quite well in the labor market, competing successfully with whites for prestigious jobs and high incomes. These writers devoted less attention to the proportion of young people graduating from college. If differences in the percentages of blacks and whites who complete college increase, differences in economic status will not soon disappear.

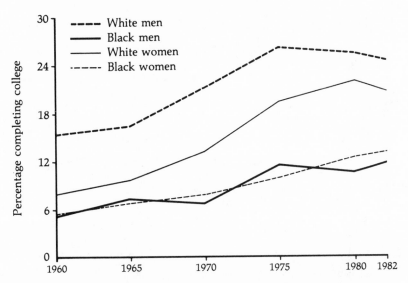

Figure 2.2. Percentage of persons aged 25–29 who completed four or more years of college, by race and sex, 1960–1982.
Source: U.S. Bureau of the Census, *Census of Population: 1960*, vol. 1, pt. 1, table 173; *Census of Population: 1970*, vol. 1, pt. 1, table 199; *Current Population Reports*, ser. P-20, no. 158, table 4; no. 294, table 1; no. 356, table 1. (Data for 1960 refer to whites and nonwhites.)

Evidence from the 1970s suggests that racial differences in the completion of college may decline in the future because of changing rates of college enrollment. Figure 2.3 shows the proportion of blacks and whites aged 18–24 who were enrolled in college, either full-time or part-time, each year from 1960 to 1981. This figure, like many others in this book, presents age-standardized data in order to eliminate the confounding effects of changes in the age distribution. For example, young people at ages 18 and 19 are more likely to attend college than are people at age 24. In the entire age group 18–24, the proportion of those who are, say, 18 changes from year to year, reflecting previous fluctuations in birth rates. Even if the enrollment rates at all specific ages remain exactly the same over time, the overall proportion of those aged 18–24 who are in college will fluctuate because of changes in the age distribution. To assess the real trends in college attendance, we take the enrollment rate for each specific age group and adjust it by a standard set of weights that does not change from year to year.

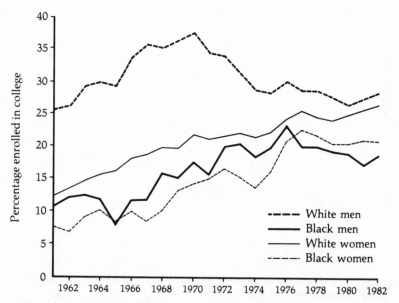

Figure 2.3. College enrollment of persons aged 18–24, by race and sex, 1960–1982.

Source: U.S. Bureau of the Census, *Current Population Reports,* ser. P-20, nos. 110, 117, 126, 129, 148, 162, 167, 190, 206, 222, 241, 260, 272, 286, 303, 319, 333, 346, 360, 362.

Throughout the 1960s enrollment rates rose for all groups, and for this reason there was no racial convergence. The enrollment rates of white men began to fall after 1969, however, while those of women and black men continued to increase at least through 1976. Consequently, racial differences in college enrollment rates were somewhat smaller in the early 1980s than a decade earlier. Just as the enrollment rates of blacks and whites at the secondary-school level converged during earlier decades, so too enrollment rates at the college level may eventually converge if the trends of the 1970s persist. As of the fall of 1981, however, there was still a substantial racial difference in college attendance, especially among men: about 28 percent of the white men aged 18–24 and only 19 percent of the black were going to college.

One of the major reasons for the convergence of college enrollment rates among men has been the drop in the proportion of white men attending college. At first glance, one might assume that this drop came about because of the absence of a military draft. During the Viet Nam war years, college attendance often justified a deferment from military service; as Figure 2.3 shows, enrollment rates for young white men peaked in 1969 and generally declined thereafter. But these data refer to the civilian population. If we take into account the changing number of young men serving in the armed forces, college enrollment rates for white men still decreased in the 1970s. In 1969 about 30 percent of white men aged 18–24 attended college: a decade later this had declined to 25 percent (U.S. Bureau of the Census, 1981a, table A-3).

There is a large sexual difference in this pattern of racial convergence. Racial differences in college attainment are decreasing more rapidly among women than among men. In other words, black women will catch up with white women in college completion long before black men catch up with white men.

Among whites there has always been a large sexual difference in college attendance, with men being much more likely than women to get their degrees. This is changing, and by the mid or late 1980s there will be no sexual difference in the proportion of young whites who graduate from college. The situation has been quite different among blacks: the proportion finishing college has been similar for men and women.

Much progress has been made in eliminating racial differences in education. Throughout the period after World War II, local governments and federal agencies spent large amounts of money to build schools and to improve old ones. Many new educational programs were initiated, such as schools for handicapped children, Head Start, junior and community college systems, and bilingual programs. Total educational expenditures per pupil in public elementary and secondary schools (measured in constant 1979 dollars) rose from $450 in 1940 to $1,500 in 1970 and $2,100 in 1981 (U.S. Bureau of the Census, 1975, ser. H, 505–507; 1982a, table 213).

One important consequence of this investment in education was a rise in attainment. The typical person who reached age 25 in the early 1980s spent about three more years in school than did a person who reached the same age four decades earlier. Blacks, whose access to educational facilities had been restricted by discrimination in many states, particularly increased their attainment. Another important consequence was the equalization of black and white schools. In 1965 James Coleman and his colleagues (U.S. Department of Health, Education and Welfare, 1966) found that blacks and whites were going to schools that were quite similar in physical facilities and instructional staffs. The schools black children attended were actually somewhat newer than those of white children, and in all regions and at both elementary and secondary levels, schools for blacks had laboratories, libraries, and extracurricular activities similar to those of the schools white children attended. A third consequence, as we have seen, was that the enrollment rates of blacks came closer to those of whites.

Despite this progress, there are persisting racial differences. Blacks are much more likely than whites to be behind the grade appropriate for their age, meaning that their enrollment rates will have to exceed those of whites if there is to be racial parity in educational attainment. There is also evidence that—on average—black children score less well on standardized tests of learning or achievement than do white children who have gone to school for the same number of years (U.S. Bureau of the Census, 1977, tables 7/20 and 7/22). Blacks and whites apparently choose different majors in college: blacks tend to elect education and commerce courses, while whites are more likely than blacks to choose majors in the biological sciences, engineering, or the physical sciences (U.S. Bureau of the Census, 1976, table 1).

Integration of Public Schools

Although Coleman found in 1965 that racial differences in school facilities were small, he reported one large difference: blacks and whites generally went to different schools. The struggle to integrate public schools has been among the most important and divisive domestic issues in the period since World War II. Many civil rights leaders placed the integration of schools high on their list of goals. By the early 1970s the majority of whites came to endorse the principle of racial integration in public education, but many whites strongly opposed steps, such as busing, that would be necessary to bring it about.

In 1954 the Supreme Court unanimously declared in its *Brown vs. Board of Education of Topeka* decision, that racially separate schools were inherently unequal and that the state-imposed separation of black children from white marked blacks as inferior. This symbolized a fundamental change in racial issues in the United States and was a precedent for numerous encompassing civil rights decisions. Indeed, most historians of the civil rights movement consider the *Brown* decision the key change of the period after World War II. But did this ruling, and the extensive activities on the part of civil rights groups, actually lead to the integration of public schools?

There is impressive and unambiguous evidence of some reductions in segregation in education. At the college level, a rapidly growing proportion of blacks attend predominantly white institutions. Although comparable figures are difficult to assemble, it appears that in 1950 about two-thirds of all black college students enrolled in traditionally black colleges or universities (U.S. Bureau of the Census, 1963a, table 183; 1953, table 112). By 1975, however, about 70 percent of black college students attended predominantly white schools (U.S. Bureau of the Census, 1978a, tables 260, 263).

In small and medium-sized cities throughout the country, public elementary and secondary schools generally are racially integrated. The gains in the South have been particularly impressive, because federal courts in that region mandated the thorough integration of schools in many cities. Since the mid-1970s schools have been more thoroughly integrated in the South than in other regions (Farley, 1978; Wurdock and Farley, 1980).

But in the nation's largest cities—especially those outside the South— the picture is mixed. In some cities federal courts identified policies of *de jure* segregation and ordered integration. In others the legal responsibility for racial segregation in the schools is still being litigated, while in still others segregation exists because most black children attend largely black central-city schools while whites go to largely white suburban schools. Attempts to integrate schools by merging black central-city districts with white suburban districts—in Detroit, Indianapolis, Louisville, Richmond, and St. Louis—were strongly opposed by most suburban residents.

The integration of public elementary and secondary schools in large cities can be investigated quite thoroughly, because the Civil Rights Act of 1964 called for the collection of data about enrollment trends and racial segregation.

Such data for the nation's twenty largest cities are shown in Table 2.1. Because the legal history of segregation and the rulings of federal courts differ greatly by region, the ten largest cities in the South are distinguished from those in other regions. In addition, legal questions about the segregation and education of Hispanic students differ from those regarding blacks. This analysis is restricted to blacks and to those whites who are not of Hispanic origin. It is helpful to remember that Hispanic enrollment has grown rapidly in recent years. By the late 1970s, about one public school student in twelve was of Hispanic origin while about one in six was black (U.S. Bureau of the Census, 1981a, table 1). In cities such as New York, Los Angeles, and San Antonio, Hispanic students are now more numerous than either white or black students.

The first two columns in Table 2.1 show changes in enrollment between 1967—the first year in which data were collected—and 1978. The decrease in white enrollment in this interval was substantial in many of these cities. In Atlanta the number of white students fell by 85 percent; in Detroit, by 75 percent. In thirteen other cities, white enrollment declined by more than half. Nationally, the number of white students in public elementary and secondary schools dropped by only 7 percent in this interval (U.S. Bureau of the Census, 1978b, table 1; 1981a, table 1).

This change in white enrollment is not primarily the result of "white flight" to avoid racially mixed schools. To be sure, there tends to be an unusually large loss of white enrollment during the year in which a city's schools are racially integrated (Coleman, Kelly, and Moore, 1975; Rossell, 1975–76; Farley, Richards, and Wurdock, 1980). However, the loss of white enrollment attributable to white flight is small compared to the decline produced by long-run demographic trends such as the fall in the white birth rate, the aging of the white population of cities, and the continuing movement of whites away from older central cities. Cities in which judges have not issued integration orders, such as Chicago, New York, and Philadelphia, have lost white students at a rate comparable to cities involved in court-ordered integration.

Several different criteria can be used to measure the racial integration of public schools. Some judges have interpreted the *Brown* ruling to mean that within a given school district there should be no identifiably black or identifiably white schools. One way to accomplish this is to insist that every school within a district have just about the same racial composition. If racial segregation is thought of in this manner, the *index of dissimilarity* is an extremely useful measure (Taeuber and Taeuber, 1965). If all black students in a district attend exclusively black schools and all white students attend exclusively white schools, this index takes on its maximum value of 100, indicating the complete segregation of the two races in that school system. If all schools within a district have exactly the same racial composition, the index of dissimilarity equals zero, indicating the absence of segregation. The numerical value of this index reports the minimum proportion of either black or white students who would have to switch from one school to another to achieve an index of zero.[1] This measure of segregation was calculated from data for individual schools using information about blacks and non-Hispanic whites. Columns 3–5 of Table 2.1 report these segregation indexes and the change from 1967 to 1978.

Trends in segregation in central-city school systems may be readily summarized. In 1967 the indexes were high in all southern cities except Washington, reflecting the dual systems that persisted for many years after the *Brown* decision. In the North, segregation varied depending on the extent of racial residential segregation in a city and the city's own history of school integration. Changes after 1967 were almost entirely dependent upon the presence and scope of court orders. In Jacksonville, Milwaukee, and Nashville, judges ordered the shifting of many black and white students and thereby reduced those cities' segregation indexes. In Dallas, Indianapolis, Los Angeles, Memphis, and San Diego more modest integration plans were ordered by courts, and school segregation decreased less sharply. In Chicago, Philadelphia, New York, and Washington, where no integration orders were issued, segregation did not decrease; in three of these cities it actually increased.

By 1978 there was a wide range in the extent of racial segregation in the schools of these large cities. In Chicago and Cleveland, segregation levels were similar to those of southern cities in the early

Table 2.1. Changes in enrollment and racial segregation in school districts of largest U.S. cities, by region, 1967–1978.

	Change in enrollment, 1967–1978		Index of dissimilarity			% white in school of typical black			% black in school of typical white		
	White (1)	Black (2)	1967 (3)	1978 (4)	Change (5)	1967 (6)	1978 (7)	Change (8)	1967 (9)	1978 (10)	Change (11)
North and West											
New York	−45%	+16%	62	70	+ 8	26%	14%	−12%	16%	19%	+ 3%
Chicago	−56	− 1	90	90	—	6	4	− 2	7	11	+ 4
Los Angeles	−54	− 4	91	71	−20	7	15	+ 8	3	13	+10
Philadelphia	−32	− 7	75	79	+ 4	14	10	− 4	21	20	− 1
Detroit	−74	+ 8	75	60	−15	15	11	− 4	21	62	+41
San Diego	−21	+27	80	51	−29	24	39	+15	4	10	+ 6
Indianapolis	−48	− 1	78	46	−32	22	36	+14	10	32	+22
San Francisco	−67	−30	54	35	−19	27	18	− 9	15	25	+10
Milwaukee	−48	+31	86	39	−47	16	38	+22	6	32	+26
Cleveland	−48	−23	89	89	—	7	5	− 2	9	11	+ 2
South											
Houston	−57%	+ 7%	93	75	−18	5%	12%	+ 7%	3%	18%	+15%
Dallas	−55	+39	93	64	−29	7	17	+10	3	25	+22
Baltimore	−52	− 7	82	67	−15	10	12	+ 2	18	40	+22
San Antonio	−63	−15	86	67	−19	8	11	+ 3	4	14	+10
Memphis	−50	+29	95	60	−35	4	16	+12	4	45	+41
Washington	−62	−25	75	85	+10	4	2	− 2	44	40	− 4

Table 2.1 continued

	Change in enrollment, 1967–1978		Index of dissimilarity			% white in school of typical black			% black in school of typical white		
	White (1)	Black (2)	1967 (3)	1978 (4)	Change (5)	1967 (6)	1978 (7)	Change (8)	1967 (9)	1978 (10)	Change (11)
New Orleans	−66	+2	85	74	−11	9	8	−1	17	45	+28
Jacksonville	−23	+6	92	40	−52	7	49	+42	3	26	+23
Nashville	−29	+6	83	40	−43	19	53	+34	6	25	+19
Atlanta	−84	+2	94	75	−19	5	6	+1	7	55	+48

Sources: U.S. National Center for Educational Statistics, *Directory, Public Schools in Large Districts with Enrollment and Staff by Race: Fall, 1967;* U.S. Office for Civil Rights, "Directory of Public Elementary and Secondary Schools in Selected Districts, Enrollment and Staff by Racial/Ethnic Groups" (tape file of 1978 data).

Note: The Census of 1980 showed that Phoenix, San Jose, and El Paso were among the twenty largest cities. Phoenix is not listed here because its central city contains many school districts; San Jose and El Paso, because less than 3 percent of their enrollment was black in 1967. The school district for Indianapolis does not include the entire central city. Data for Houston and Dallas refer to 1968 and 1978. The school district for Jacksonville includes all of Duval County; that for Nashville, all of Davidson County.

1960s: to eliminate segregation it would have been necessary to shift a minimum of 90 percent of the white or black students. Segregation was at a low level in Milwaukee, San Francisco, and the two districts that included entire counties—Jacksonville and Nashville.

The criterion I have been discussing for defining segregation is racial balance: Is the racial composition similar in all schools in a district, or are there all-black schools and all-white schools? The index of dissimilarity answers this question. But many of the efforts to integrate schools sought to end the isolation of black students from whites. From this viewpoint, an integrated system might be one in which black students attend schools that enroll many whites and whites go to schools with sizable black enrollments.

Using data gathered by the Office for Civil Rights, I calculated the average proportion of students who are white in the school of the typical black student and the average proportion black in the school of the typical white student. These statistical indicators, of course, do not reveal whether black and white children are in the same classroom or whether they interact in the cafeteria or on the playground.

This measure of segregation differs greatly from the index of dissimilarity, as an example will illustrate. Public schools in Washington, D.C., are approximately 95 percent black and 5 percent white. If a federal court ruled that the schools should be integrated, it might insist that every school in the district have the same racial composition. If such a ruling were implemented, the index of dissimilarity would equal zero, suggesting that the schools were racially integrated. However, both black children and the few whites in the system would attend predominantly black schools; that is, schools that were about 95 percent black and 5 percent white. Undoubtedly, this is not the kind of integration the Supreme Court envisioned in its 1954 ruling. The measure I am now describing assesses racial isolation, and, unlike the index of dissimilarity, it is influenced by the racial composition of the school district (Zoloth, 1976).

Columns 6–8 of Table 2.1 show the proportion of students who are white in the school of the typical black and the changes in this measure between 1967 and 1978. In 1967, for example, the typical black student in New York City attended a school where 26 percent of the students were white. Some black students, of course, went to schools where almost all their classmates were white, while a few others went to schools with hardly any white students. But on average black students attended schools where 26 percent of the students were white. (The other 74 percent were black, Asian, or Hispanic.) By 1978 the proportion white in the school of the typical black in New York fell to 14 percent: the isolation of blacks from whites increased.

In more than half of these twenty cities, black students became less isolated from whites between 1967 and 1978: the proportion white in their schools rose. The biggest reductions in isolation were in the two country-wide districts, Jacksonville and Nashville. In eight cities, including New York, blacks became *more* racially isolated as the proportion white for the typical black student went down. Even where court orders mandated integration and thereby reduced the index of dissimilarity—in Detroit and San Francisco, for instance—black students attended schools that enrolled proportionally fewer whites in 1978 than in 1967. This came about largely because of the sharp decline in white enrollment. At the very time when many districts were moving toward racial balance, their white enrollments were falling, and thus the representation of whites in the schools blacks attended became smaller.

The relatively few white students who remained in the public schools of these large cities increasingly attended schools with black classmates, as reported in the final three columns of Table 2.1, which show the average proportion of students who are black in the school of the typical white student. In Houston, for instance, in 1967 whites went to schools where only 3 percent of the students were black; in 1978, 18 percent were black. In Dallas the change was from 3 to 35 percent black. The increases in proportion black in the school of the typical white student were greatest in the cities with the largest declines in the index of dissimilarity. By 1978 there was substantial city-to-city difference in the racial composition of the public schools whites attended: in Chicago, Cleveland, and San Diego whites went to schools where about one-tenth of their classmates were black; in Atlanta and Detroit they went to schools with black majorities.

It is important to stress that changes in enrollment and segregation vary by region, by size of city, and by the racial composition of the school district. Table 2.2 presents data about the central-city districts of the nation's 100 largest metropolitan areas. Some metropolitan areas include two or more central cities, so data are shown for a total of 116 school districts. Fourteen of these—all but one in the South— include an entire county, so that students from the city and from much of the suburban ring live in the same school district. These are called county-wide or metropolitan districts. Since white opposition

Table 2.2. Changes in enrollment and racial segregation in central-city school districts, by region, size or type, and minority enrollment, 1967–1978.

	N (1)	% change in enrollment, 1967–1978		Index of dissimilarity			% white in school of typical black			% black in school of typical white		
		White (2)	Black (3)	1967 (4)	1978 (5)	Change (6)	1967 (7)	1978 (8)	Change (9)	1967 (10)	1978 (11)	Change (12)
All districts	116	−39%	+ 4%	72	46	− 26	30%	39%	+9%	10%	24%	+14%
Districts by region												
North	51	− 45	+ 2	65	49	− 16	37	36	− 1	14	25	+11
South	39	− 26	+ 6	86	45	− 41	11	38	+27	8	32	+24
West	26	− 41	0	65	41	− 24	44	48	+ 4	5	10	+ 5
Districts by size or type												
City <150,000	36	− 22	+12	64	38	− 26	40	45	+ 5	12	23	+11
City 150,000–399,999	37	− 37	+ 5	70	46	− 24	34	41	+ 7	9	23	+14
City 400,000 or more	29	− 51	+ 1	79	60	− 19	19	24	+ 5	11	27	+16
County-wide district	14	− 10	+19	85	38	− 47	15	51	+36	5	24	+19
Districts by minority enrollment in 1967												
<15%	19	− 36	+36	65	38	− 27	63	65	+ 2	4	10	+ 5
15.0–29.9%	34	− 23	+18	72	36	− 36	32	52	+20	8	22	+14
30.0–44.9%	28	− 42	+ 6	76	46	− 30	22	33	+11	8	26	+18
≥45%	35	− 48	0	73	60	− 13	16	17	+ 1	17	31	+14

Sources: same as Table 2.1.

to integrating a school system is linked to the racial composition of the district, cities are also classified by their school district's racial mix in 1967.

Columns 2 and 3 of Table 2.2 indicate that these 116 districts lost an average of 39 percent of their white enrollment and gained 4 percent in black enrollment. Nationally, the comparable figures were a loss of 7 percent for whites and a gain of 5 percent for blacks (U.S. Bureau of the Census, 1978b, table 1; 1981a, table 1). Declines in white enrollment were much greater outside the South, reflecting regional migration patterns as well as the fact that thirteen of the southern districts are metropolitan. White enrollment declined more in larger cities than in smaller ones, but the metropolitan districts did not experience large losses; their loss of white students was close to the national average. Enrollment change was also linked to the racial composition of the school district: the greater the representation of minorities in 1967, the greater the decline in white enrollment.

The index of dissimilarity decreased much more in southern school districts than elsewhere (columns 4–6). Federal judges held many southern districts responsible for racial segregation and ordered extensive integration plans. Outside the South, there is continuing litigation about who bears responsibility for school segregation, and even where courts have found unconstitutional segregation the remedies ordered have generally been more modest than in the South.

The extent of progress toward integration—as measured by changes in the index of dissimilarity—was greater in small cities and those with a small proportion minority than in large cities and those where a high proportion of the students were black. The physical and political problems associated with desegregation are least in small cities and in those with relatively few blacks because integration there may not require long-distance busing or the assignment of white children to schools in large black ghettos. The county-wide, metropolitan districts stand out once again because of their unusually large declines in segregation.

Black children in the nation's large cities attend schools with increasing proportions of white students (columns 7–9): in 1967 they went to schools where, on average, 30 percent of the students were white; by 1978 this number was 39 percent. Changes in this kind of racial isolation differed by type of school district. In northern cities, the schools blacks attended enrolled proportionally fewer white students in 1978 than in 1967, so blacks became more racially isolated in that region. Elsewhere this did not happen. In the South, in county-wide districts, and in districts with relatively small black enrollments, the proportion of white students in the school of the typical black student increased.

White children in these large-city school districts increasingly go to school with blacks (columns 10–12). This trend results from the changing racial composition of central-city schools and the desegregation activities of the last decade.

It is impossible to conclude either that the school integration efforts and litigation of the past thirty years were very successful or that they were failures. Most of the nation's colleges and universities became integrated as black students chose to attend schools with predominantly white enrollments. At the elementary and secondary level, substantial progress was made in integrating schools in many southern districts, in small and medium-sized cities, and in cities with moderate minority enrollments. The few metropolitan school districts are unique in that they reduced racial segregation by all of the criteria I have used but did not lose an unusually large fraction of their white enrollment. This occurred because they include spacious suburban rings and because they are located in rapidly growing areas of the South.

Thirty years ago, schools were segregated in the South because of state laws and in the North because of neighborhood segregation. But most school districts enrolled both whites and blacks, so some integration could be accomplished by transferring white and black students. Today public schools are segregated because blacks and whites live in separate school districts. In most of the largest cities, the public school district enrolls few whites but many black and Hispanic students. Nationally, about 76 percent of the students in public elementary and secondary schools in 1978 were non-Hispanic whites (U.S. Bureau of the Census, 1981b, table 1), but in Washington, D.C., only 5 percent were white; in Atlanta 10 percent, in San Antonio 13 percent, and in Detroit and New Orleans 14 percent. By 1980 only three of the country's twenty largest cities had a majority of white students in their public schools. Within these metropolises there are many white students, but they live in the suburban ring, often in small districts with few minority students.

Unless there are changes in the current policies that separate city and suburban students into different school districts, the persistence of racial residential segregation will combine with demographic trends to produce public schools almost as racially segregated as those which were constitutionally permitted before the 1954 *Brown* decision. In the largest metropolises, a central-city district that enrolls mostly blacks and Hispanics will be surrounded by numerous suburban districts, most of them enrolling just a few blacks.

Racial Residential Segregation

Public schools in many metropolitan areas will be integrated only if the traditional pattern of black cities and white suburbs is altered. We do not yet know whether the residential segregation of blacks from whites decreased during the 1970s. The Civil Rights Act of 1968, which banned discrimination in the sale or rental of housing, was in effect for the entire decade and may have provided opportunities for blacks who wished to move into formerly white neighborhoods. In addition, the long-run trend toward more liberal racial attitudes on the part of whites may have lessened segregation. Perhaps blacks are now entering the suburbs and those many central-city neighborhoods which once were reserved for whites.

The black population of the nation's suburbs grew rapidly during the 1970s: an annual rate of 4.0 percent per year for blacks compared to 1.5 percent for whites (Long and DiAre, 1981). This is the first time the black suburban population has grown substantially faster than the white. As a result, the black proportion of suburban population rose from 4.8 percent in 1970 to 6.1 percent in 1980.[2] Until data from the Census of 1980 are thoroughly analyzed, we will know little about the implications of this suburbanization for residential segregation. This trend may mean that blacks are now spread throughout the suburban ring, or that central-city black ghettos are now crossing city limits and older industrial suburbs are undergoing a white-to-black transition like the one that occurred in central cities after World War II. One preliminary study suggests that black suburban population growth was not restricted to older suburbs near the central city (Long and DiAre, 1981), but another analysis found that almost all of the increase in black suburban population in New Jersey occurred in or near existing black neighborhoods (Lake, 1981).

One study of trends in residential segregation within central cities during the 1970s looked at changes in those cities that have the largest black populations (Taeuber, 1983), using the index of dissimilarity. Recall that this index takes on its maximum value of 100 in a situation of total apartheid such that all city blocks are exclusively black or exclusively white, and that its value approaches the minimum of zero

when blacks and whites are randomly distributed across all neighborhoods in a city (Massey, 1978). The indexes of residential segregation for the twenty-five cities with the largest black populations in
1980, shown in Table 2.3, are based upon city-block data for the black
and nonblack populations.

There was a mixed pattern of change in residential segregation in
the 1970s. In five cities—including Houston and Dallas—segregation
declined by ten or more points on this 100-point scale, and on average
there was a drop of six points. The Civil Rights Act of 1968 may have
been at least partly effective; the decrease in segregation in the 1970s
seems quite substantial compared to the changes of the three previous
decades (Taeuber and Taeuber, 1965; Sørensen, Taeuber, and Hollingsworth, 1975). This decrease in the neighborhood segregation of
blacks from whites, however, was far from universal. In three cities
the scores did not change, and in Philadelphia and Cleveland residential segregation apparently increased. Despite decades of racial
change and numerous civil rights laws, Chicago, St. Louis, and Cleveland were almost as segregated as they would have been if a law
mandated that all blacks must live in exclusively black blocks and
whites in exclusively white ones. If the findings from a wider array
of metropolitan areas and cities parallel these, residential segregation
will be another mixed indicator of racial progress.

Employment and Unemployment

Blacks in the United States have traditionally had a much more difficult time than whites in finding employment, so civil rights organizations have always stressed the need for jobs. Blacks have made
consistent gains in educational attainment, but it is much more difficult to summarize trends in employment. One reason for this is that
the proportion of the population that is out of work is closely linked
to the economic circumstances at a given time, making it hard to
distinguish real trends from short-run fluctuations. The employment
situation for blacks was much better in the prosperous 1960s than in
the Depression decade, but less good in 1982 than in the 1960s. This
largely reflects national economic changes rather than a different status for blacks in the labor market. Another reason it is not easy to
summarize employment trends is that there is disagreement about
whether the Bureau of Labor Statistics correctly defines employment
or unemployment. Nevertheless, we can determine some trends, and

Table 2.3.   Racial residential segregation scores for central cities with large black populations, 1970 and 1980.

	1970	1980	Change 1970–1980
New York	77	75	−2
Chicago	93	92	−1
Detroit	82	73	−9
Philadelphia	84	88	+4
Los Angeles	90	81	−9
Washington	79	79	0
Houston	93	81	−12
Baltimore	89	86	−3
New Orleans	84	76	−8
Memphis	92	85	−7
Atlanta	92	86	−6
Dallas	96	83	−13
Cleveland	90	91	+1
St. Louis	90	90	0
Newark	76	76	0
Oakland	70	59	−11
Birmingham	92	85	−7
Indianapolis	90	83	−7
Milwaukee	88	80	−8
Jacksonville	94	82	−12
Cincinnati	84	79	−5
Boston	84	80	−4
Columbus	86	75	−11
Kansas City	90	86	−4
Richmond	91	79	−12
Average for 25 central cities	84	78	−6

Source: K. Taeuber, "Racial Residential Segregation, 28 Cities, 1970–1980," CDE-Working Paper 87–12 (Madison: University of Wisconsin, Center for Demography and Ecology).

Note: Cities are ranked by their black population in 1980.

they suggest that, so far as employment is concerned, blacks are falling further behind whites.

Gunnar Myrdal observed in 1944 that employment opportunities for blacks in the South decreased throughout the first four decades of this century. Blacks once worked at some industrial jobs in the South and on the railroads, but this situation deteriorated after 1900. The legalization of Jim Crow practices allowed employers to avoid hiring blacks or to confine them to the lowest-paying jobs. The emerging union movement also had the effect of reducing the employment chances of blacks. On the railroads, for example, many blacks were employed in the late nineteenth century. Unions had organized northern rail workers by the late 1800s and began to recruit southern members in the early 1900s. To thwart their efforts, the railroads tried to replace white workers—particularly striking white workers—with blacks. After years of struggle, the unions were successful, and they maintained white-only memberships throughout the nation until after World War II (Harris, 1982). New industries such as chemicals and textiles came to the South in the 1920s, but they generally hired blacks only to do manual work. Several of the New Deal's agricultural programs also increased unemployment among blacks by encouraging farm owners to reduce their output, thereby cutting employment for laborers or sharecroppers.

Prior to Pearl Harbor, U.S. defense industries expanded, but civil rights leaders feared that blacks would not be hired for such jobs. In one of the most successful early efforts of the civil rights movement, A. Philip Randolph threatened to bring fifty to one hundred thousand black marchers to Washington to protest employment discrimination. Fearing that such a demonstration would weaken efforts to mobilize for World War II, President Roosevelt issued an executive order in 1941 that established a Fair Employment Practices Committee (FEPC) and prohibited racial discrimination in employment in defense industries. Following World War II, President Truman favored an extension of FEPC, but Congress refused this request. Shortly after taking office in 1961, President Kennedy issued an executive order that prohibited racial discrimination in employment by government contractors. For the first time in a government document, the term "affirmative action" was used; employers were encouraged to make special efforts to see that workers were treated fairly without regard to race, creed, color, or national origin. Three years later Congress passed the Civil Rights Act of 1964, which outlawed all types of racial discrimination in employment. The Supreme Court upheld this law and defined its implication; for example, the Court ruled that some seniority programs and many testing procedures unfairly denied blacks a chance to get a job or to be promoted.

The data described in this section, as well as the information in the previous section about school enrollment and educational attainment, come from the Census Bureau's Current Population Survey. Each month since the mid 1940s, interviewers have gone to or telephoned a national sample of homes and asked questions about who is working and who is looking for a job. From time to time, other questions have been asked about people in these households, such as their educational attainment, their school enrollment, or how many children they expected to have. The sample size has changed over the years; by the late 1970s interviewers contacted approximately 68,000 households every month.

In this book I am investigating racial differences; that is, differences between blacks and whites. In some circumstances, however, data are available only for whites and for nonwhites. Data on employment and occupation, for example, were not presented for blacks until 1979. At one time a very high proportion of nonwhites in the United States were black: in 1950, 96 out of every 100 nonwhite persons gave Negro as their racial identity. The Asian and Indian populations have grown more rapidly than the black, so that in 1980 only 85 out of every 100 nonwhites were black (U.S. Bureau of the Census, 1975; ser. A, 100–101; 1982b, table B).

It is not always easy to define who has a job or who is looking for work. At present, people are counted as employed if they worked for pay for any amount of time during the survey week or if they were unpaid workers in a family business such as a teenager who pumps gas in his mother's filling station or a young man who works on his father's farm. People are also considered employed if they have jobs but did not work during the survey week because of illness or bad weather. This means that people in many different situations are in the employed category, including some who work just a few hours each week and others who hold down two full-time jobs.

A person is classified as unemployed if he does not have a job but made a specific effort to find work within the last four weeks. Such efforts are broadly defined and include checking with friends or answering help-wanted advertisements in the newspaper. People are also unemployed if they are waiting to be recalled to their jobs or if they intend to begin a new job within a month.

There is much controversy about these definitions. According to current definitions, the labor force consists of those who are working and those who are seeking work. The unemployment rate indicates the proportion of the labor force that is currently not working but looking for work. Some analysts believe that unemployment is vastly overestimated. They point out that people would be called unemployed if they made only sporadic efforts to locate jobs or if they were only willing to take a narrow range of high-paying, part-time jobs close to home. Others argue that the unemployment rate substantially underestimates the true number of people who want to work but cannot find jobs. A person who spends six months earnestly searching for a job, finds nothing, and then gives up the search will be classified as out of the labor force rather than as unemployed. (Not all people who are out of the labor force are discouraged workers; some are retirees, persons with disabilities, and homemakers or students who are neither working nor looking for work.)

Robert Hill of the National Urban League claims that many blacks are so discouraged about their employment prospects that they have given up the search for a job and that the official unemployment rate is thus unrealistically low. The Bureau of Labor Statistics reported an unemployment rate of 13 percent for blacks in 1980. Hill (1981) asserts that, if all discouraged workers had been included, the actual unemployment rate for blacks would have been about 24 percent.

Although several presidential commissions (President's Committee to Appraise Employment and Unemployment Statistics, 1962; National Commission on Employment and Unemployment Statistics, 1979) have proposed new definitions for employment and unemployment, no consensus has been reached about better measures. As a result we are restricted to the concepts that have been used since World War II. In addition to discussing trends in the unemployment rate, that is, the proportion of the labor force that is out of work, I will look at rates of employment, defined as the proportion of all adults currently at work. In an investigation of racial differences in economic status, it is particularly appropriate to consider the proportion of adults who hold jobs. Economists call this the employment-population ratio.

Do blacks still have a much more difficult time than whites in getting and keeping jobs? One way to answer this question is to look at trends in the proportion of men who are out of work. Figure 2.4 shows the unemployment rate for men for the years 1950–1982. Since unemployment varies by age—men in their teens or early twenties, for instance, are much more likely to be out of work than are those in

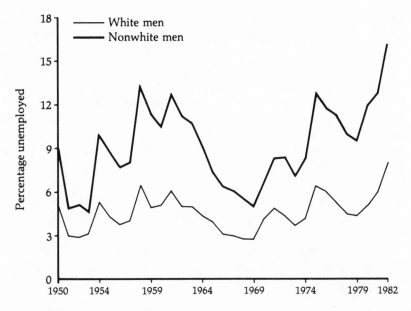

Figure 2.4. Unemployment rates for men, by race, 1950–1982 (data standardized for age).
Source: U.S. Bureau of Labor Statistics, *Handbook of Labor Statistics: 1978*, tables 3 and 60; *Employment and Earnings*, vols. 26–29, no. 1 for each vol.

their thirties or forties—these data are standardized for age. In 1950 about 9 percent of the nonwhite and 5 percent of the white men were unemployed; in 1982 it was 16 percent of the nonwhite and 8 percent of the white men.

For both races, unemployment rates fluctuated with general economic conditions. They sank to low levels during the late 1960s, when the nation had a booming domestic economy and carried out a war in Asia. In the mid-1970s and again at the start of the 1980s, the nation experienced a recession and unemployment rose to high levels. Looking at year-to-year changes in the Gross National Product (GNP), I have calculated that a real increase of 1 percent in the GNP reduced unemployment among nonwhite men by about six-tenths of a percentage point and among white men by about three-tenths of a point.[3] This means that a rapidly growing economy will reduce unemployment for blacks more than for whites. A real increase of 5 percent in the GNP may reduce black unemployment by three percentage points while the white rate will go down by only one and a half points. Conversely, a declining economy has an especially adverse effect upon blacks.

As Figure 2.4 indicates, there has been no racial convergence in unemployment rates. At all dates, the rate for nonwhite men was about twice that for whites, and the racial discrepancy was at least as large at the end of this period as at the beginning. In fact, a closer look at the data reveals that unemployment rates have risen more over time among nonwhites than among whites. In the early 1950s the unemployment rate for nonwhite men was about 76 percent higher than that for white men; in the late 1970s and early 1980s it was about 118 percent higher. There is a long-term trend toward a larger racial difference in the proportion of men who cannot find work.

Figure 2.5 shows the proportion of persons aged 16 and over who were employed for the years 1950–1982. Since rates of employment and unemployment differ substantially from one age group to an-

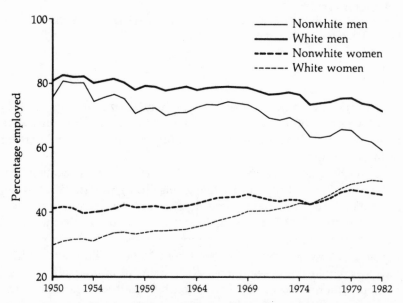

Figure 2.5. Proportion of the population aged 16 and over employed, by race and sex, 1950–1982 (data standardized for age).

Source: same as for Figure 2.4.

other, these trends are also standardized for age. For men, the proportion with jobs in 1950 was about five percentage points greater for whites than for nonwhites. The proportion holding jobs fluctuated a bit in the 1950s and 1960s, but the racial difference was no greater in 1970 than twenty years earlier. Since 1970 there has been a falling-off in the proportion of men with jobs, and the decrease has been much greater among nonwhites than among whites, so that by 1982 the racial difference in the proportion of adult men with jobs was 12 percentage points. Black men are falling further behind white men not only in the proportion of those who are out of work but also in the proportion employed.

As Figure 2.5 indicates, smaller proportions of both white and nonwhite men were employed in 1980 than thirty years earlier. It is important to know why this change occurred. Do men in the 1980s retire earlier, do they remain in school longer, or do they simply have a more difficult time finding work?

Among white men the proportion at work has declined largely because fewer men aged 55 and over hold jobs. The proportion of adult white men who were employed fell about ten percentage points between 1950 and 1982; and approximately two-thirds of that drop came about because of less employment after age 54. The expansion of Social Security benefits and the development of better private pension programs provide many older men with an attractive alternative to working.

There has also been a substantial drop in employment of nonwhite men at ages over 54, but this accounts for only one-third of the decrease in the proportion of men at work. Below age 55, the proportion of men employed has decreased much more for nonwhites than for whites.

Since 1967 federal agencies have provided some information about people who are not in the labor force: that is, who are neither working nor looking for a job. Such people are asked what their major activity was during the week of the survey. Their responses are coded as "going to school," "unable to work," "keeping house," or not working for "other reasons." Presumably, those individuals who have been out of work for so long that they have given up the search for a job will be classified as not working for "other reasons."

Most of the decline in the employment rates among adult men occurred after 1970. Table 2.4 shows post–1970 trends in employment, unemployment, and the activities of men who are not in the labor

Table 2.4. Labor force activities of white and nonwhite men aged 25–54, 1970 and 1982 (data standardized for age.).

Major activity	Nonwhite men			White men		
	1970	1982	Change	1970	1982	Change
In labor force						
At work (employed)[a]	88%	77%	−11%	94%	89%	−5%
Looking for work					—	
(unemployed)	4	11	+7	2	6	+4
Out of labor force						
Going to school	1	2	1	1	1	0
Unable to work	3	3	0	1	1	0
Other reasons	4	7	+3	2	3	+1

a. Includes military labor force.

Source: U.S. Bureau of Labor Statistics, *Employment and Earnings*, 17, no. 7, table A-1; 30, no. 1, table 3.

force. This information is restricted to men at the peak years of employment, 25–54, to eliminate the confounding effects of early retirement; these data are also standardized for age.

For white men, the decrease in the proportion employed between 1970 and 1981 was largely accounted for by a rise in unemployment; there was almost no change in the percentage of white men going to school, unable to work, or keeping house. For nonwhite men, the decrease in proportion employed is not accounted for by the rise in unemployment; there has been an increase in the proportion of nonwhite men who are not in the labor force for other reasons. Although we cannot be certain, this change strongly suggests that declining employment prospects and the resulting discouragement that cause some men to drop out of the labor force account for the decline in the proportion of nonwhite men aged 25–54 who have jobs.

This finding is corroborated by other data from the monthly surveys. For about 15 years, people who were neither working nor looking for work were asked if they wanted a job. If they said yes, they were asked why they were not looking. Throughout the 1970s there was a rise in the proportion of nonwhite men who said they were not looking for jobs because they thought they could not find them. In 1970, for every 1,000 employed nonwhite men there were 103 who were looking for jobs and 11 who said they had given up because work was not available; in 1982, 222 were looking for jobs and 35 had given up (U.S. Bureau of Labor Statistics, 1971; 1983).

Racial differences in unemployment are quite similar for women and men. Every year since 1950, the proportion unemployed has been greater for nonwhite women than for whites, and this disparity has grown larger: in 1950 the unemployment rate of nonwhite women was about 60 percent higher than that of white women; by the early 1980s it was about 90 percent higher.

In the rates of employment, by contrast, a major change has occurred. Traditionally, a higher proportion of black women than white women were employed, but this is no longer true. In 1950 about four out of ten nonwhite women and three out of ten white women held jobs. White women caught up with nonwhite women on this indicator of economic activity by the mid-1970s, and in 1982 about half of all white women aged 16 and over held jobs compared to about 45 percent of nonwhite women. Thus among both men and women the proportion at work is now substantially higher for whites than for blacks.

Employment Opportunities for the Young

Each month the Bureau of Labor Statistics reports unemployment rates for different age groups. Quite often reporters focus their attention on teenagers and proclaim that a record proportion of young blacks are out of work. To determine whether this is true, I will look closely at the employment and activities of persons aged 16–24. For this age group, it is important to consider military service. The data presented thus far in this chapter have referred only to the civilian population (this does not confound the analysis, since few women and only a small proportion of adult men serve in the armed forces).

Figure 2.6 presents information about the activities of men in the age group 16–24: the proportions with civilian jobs, in the military, unemployed, out of the labor force because of school, and out of the labor force for other reasons. The figure does not show the small percentage of young men—less than 1 percent in 1982—who were out of the labor force because they were keeping house or unable to work.

It is apparent that young blacks and whites are becoming less alike in their activities. For white men, the proportion with civilian jobs tended to increase, but this was offset by a decline in the proportion

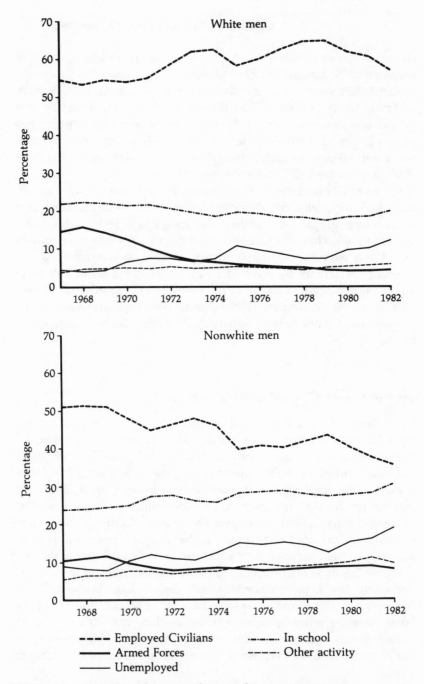

Figure 2.6. Activities of men aged 16–24, by race, 1967–1982.
Source: U.S. Bureau of Labor Statistics, *Employment and Earnings*, vols. 14–23, no. 7 for each vol.; vols. 24–29, no. 1 for each vol.

serving in the armed forces. As a result, a nearly constant proportion
—about 65–70 percent—of young white men held either civilian or
military jobs. Among nonwhite men, both the proportion with civilian
jobs and the proportion in the military declined, and thus there was
a clear trend toward less employment. In 1967 about 63 percent had
jobs; in the early 1980s this was down to 43 percent.

For both races, the proportion of men who were unsuccessfully
searching for work—the percentage unemployed—fluctuated with
the economic conditions, but at all dates the unemployment rate for
nonwhite men was much larger than that for whites. The proportion
of young men who were not in the labor force for other reasons also
increased throughout the period for both races. This suggests that
young men of both races are finding it more difficult to get jobs.
However, the increase for white men was very slight, and for much
of the period the proportion who were out of the labor force for other
reasons was about twice as high for nonwhites as for whites.

Racial differences in school attendance have also grown larger. The
proportion of men who neither worked nor sought a job because they
were enrolled in school declined for whites but increased for nonwhites. Young nonwhite men are much more likely than young whites
to say they are out of the labor force because they are in school. This
may mean that a larger share of black men are putting off taking a
job until they gain skills and complete their training. There is an
alternative explanation, however. Going to school and working are
not exclusive activities, and it may be that young white men who
attend school find it easier to get part-time jobs than do black men.

The activities of young women (not shown in the figure) follow
similar trends for both races. Since 1967, women have increasingly
delayed getting married and bearing children, and the proportion
who report that keeping house is their major activity has declined.
For both races, both the proportion unemployed and the proportion
out of the labor force for other reasons have gone up, reflecting the
increasing difficulties young women face when they seek employment.

Among women there is a growing racial difference in both employment and schooling. The proportion of white women with jobs
has increased: even during the recessionary years 1975 and 1982, the
percentage of young white women with jobs was greater than in 1967,
a year of prosperity. For nonwhite women, by contrast, the share
who held jobs generally declined even during periods of economic
growth. Education shows the opposite pattern: a decreasing share of

white women and an increasing share of nonwhite women report that their major activity is attending school.

On most indicators of status, I assume that racial progress is made when blacks catch up with whites and differences between the races decline. The activities of young people show no such racial convergence but rather increasing differences: young blacks and young whites allocate their time to work, education, military service, and homemaking in increasingly different ways. It is difficult to interpret these trends in terms of racial progress. An optimistic interpretation of these trends would focus on the rising proportion of young blacks who stay out of the labor force because they are attending school or college. Compared to their white age-mates, they are getting a slower start on careers, but once they finish their education they may be able to catch up. A pessimistic view would focus on the general increase in unemployment among the young. A declining share of those who look for jobs find them. At later ages, blacks have much higher unemployment rates than whites: typically about twice as high. Young blacks are also much less successful than young whites in finding work. Perhaps this is the reason they remain students and are classified as out of the labor force. It may be a dearth of employment opportunities for young blacks that explains why blacks and whites are becoming less alike in their activities.

Occupation

Although racial differences in educational attainment are gradually declining, blacks do not seem to have made much progress in employment. A close look at the occupations of those who hold jobs, however, reveals that by this measure progress has been made and racial differences are much smaller now than in the past.

Throughout the twentieth century the occupational structure of the United States has been upgraded as the industrial composition of the economy has changed. The proportion of people working as unskilled laborers or domestic servants has decreased while the proportion employed as skilled craftsmen, white-collar workers, or managers or professionals has grown. In the future there is likely to be a shift away from manufacturing and into service industries and the new fields of high technology. This will mean a further upgrading of the occupations of workers.

Traditionally, blacks were relegated to the lowest-paying and least desirable jobs for at least three reasons. First, few blacks obtained the educational credentials and skills needed for high-paying jobs. Second, until World War II the majority of blacks lived in rural areas of the South, where there were few factories or offices. Third, unions and management discriminated against blacks. I have described Myrdal's finding that job opportunities for blacks did not improve during the early decades of this century. As a result, in 1940 a much larger proportion of blacks than of whites were at the bottom of the occupational ladder: 41 percent of the employed black men worked as laborers on farms or in factories, compared to 14 percent of the employed white men.

The Bureau of the Census classified jobs into several major categories. White-collar occupations—jobs as professionals, managers, clerical workers, or sales workers—are typically more highly regarded and better paid than blue-collar jobs. There are exceptions; many skilled craftsworkers earn more than clerical workers, and some managers of small businesses report long hours and low pay. Nevertheless, white-collar jobs are usually the most desirable ones.

Figure 2.7 shows the percentage of employed white and nonwhite men and women who held white-collar jobs in the years 1960–1982. In 1960 this proportion was about twenty-five percentage points higher for white men than for nonwhite men: 39 percent compared to 14 percent. By 1970 this racial difference had declined to about twenty-one percentage points, and in 1982 it was only fourteen percentage points. The proportion of white men with white-collar jobs has risen only slightly in the last two decades, while the proportion of nonwhite men with such jobs has more than doubled. Thus the difference between the races on this indicator is much smaller than it used to be.

An examination of the entire occupational distribution, instead of just white-collar jobs, also shows movement toward a racial convergence. This is indicated in Figure 2.7 by trends in the index of occupational dissimilarity, which measures whether whites and nonwhites work at similar jobs. This index would have its maximum value of 100 in an apartheid-like situation in which white workers were employed only in certain job categories and nonwhites were confined to separate categories that included no whites. It would take on its minimum value of zero in a society in which skin color was not relevant to occupation, so that the ratio of white to nonwhite workers was similar in all job categories. The numerical value of this index is the minimum percentage of either whites or nonwhites who would

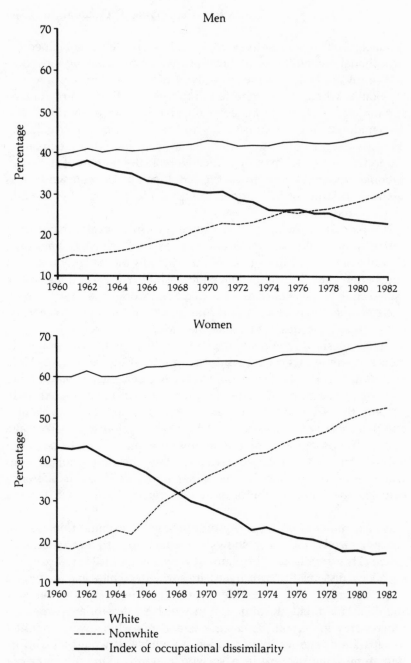

Figure 2.7. Proportion of employed workers with white-collar jobs, by race and sex.

Source: U.S. Bureau of Labor Statistics, *Employment and Earnings*, vols. 14–23, no. 7 for each vol.; vols. 24–29, no. 1 for each vol.

have to switch from one job category to another to produce an index of zero. The indexes shown in Figure 2.7 were calculated from data about eleven broad occupational categories. If more occupational categories had been included, the trend over time would be the same but the numerical values of the index of occupational dissimilarity would be greater.

The first year for which it is possible to calculate this measure of occupational segregation is 1950, when its value was 37. In 1960 it was also 37, implying that no change occurred in the 1950s. It began to fall after 1962; in 1970 its value was 30; by 1982 it had fallen to 23. The occupational distributions of white and nonwhite men are becoming more similar as occupational segregation declines.

Changes in occupational distribution have been even more dramatic for nonwhite women than for nonwhite men. Traditionally, a high proportion of urban black women cleaned the homes, washed the laundry, and cooked the food of whites, while rural black women worked as farm laborers. This pattern continued long after World War II; in 1960 more than a third of the black women with jobs were domestic servants and another 15 percent labored on farms or operated machines in factories (U.S. Bureau of the Census, 1963b, table 32). As Figure 2.7 indicates, in 1960 fewer than 20 percent of employed nonwhite women but more than 60 percent of employed white women had white-collar jobs. This changed quickly as black women moved into offices or into the professions. The racial difference in the proportion of women with white-collar jobs, which had been forty-one points in 1960, declined to only seventeen points in 1982. The index of occupational dissimilarity for women fell by almost two-thirds in this period.

It is clear that racial progress has been made on the occupational front during both the prosperous 1960s and the leaner 1970s. The improvement came about largely because the number of blacks working at prestigious jobs increased much more rapidly than the number of whites. For example, during the 1970s the number of nonwhite men employed as professionals or managers increased by about 5 percent each year while the number of white men increased by approximately 2 percent. Also in the 1970s, for the most highly paid of the manual jobs—craftsworkers—the annual increase in the number employed was about 3 percent for nonwhite men and only 1 percent for whites. At the other end of the occupational distribution, nonwhites moved away from farm jobs much more rapidly than whites. The barriers that once confined blacks to manual labor and domestic service have been removed. With regard to the occupations of employed workers, there is unambiguous evidence that blacks are gradually catching up with whites. Furthermore, this improvement, which apparently began in the 1960s, continued in the 1970s and early 1980s even though the economy experienced two major recessions.

Despite this substantial improvement, a very large gap still distinguishes the occupational distribution of blacks from that of whites. In 1982 about three out of ten employed nonwhite men held white-collar jobs—approximately the same proportion as white men in 1940. The situation is similar for women: in 1982 about 52 percent of employed nonwhite women were working at white-collar jobs; in 1940 the figure for white women was about 50 percent (U.S. Bureau of the Census, 1943b, table 62).

Blacks are still greatly overrepresented at the lowest rungs of the occupational distribution. At the start of the 1980s, about one employed nonwhite woman in sixteen was a domestic servant compared to about one white woman in fifty, and approximately one employed nonwhite man in eight was an unskilled laborer compared to about one white man in fifteen (U.S. Bureau of Labor Statistics, 1982, table 22). The occupational distribution of blacks will catch up with that of whites only if there are several more decades of change similar to the 1960s and 1970s.

Conclusions

The racial changes described in this chapter indicate the success of some efforts to bring about equal opportunities for blacks and the failure of others. Education is one of the successes. By the early 1960s blacks and whites attended public schools with similar physical characteristics and curricular programs. A decade later the racial discrepancy in enrollment through the high school ages disappeared.

Blacks have been coming closer to completing as many years of schooling as whites, and this seems likely to continue. How quickly the remaining gap in educational attainment will be eliminated depends upon a variety of factors. At present, the proportion of teenage students who are behind the grade level appropriate for their age is much higher among blacks than among whites. If this difference is reduced, there may be racial equality in the completion of high school. At the college level, enrollment rates are still higher among whites than among blacks, but during the 1970s this gap narrowed. While the relationship is not a strong one, the number of years individuals spend in school is linked to their parents' attainment (Duncan, 1969; Featherman and Hauser, 1978). Previous gains in attainment mean that forthcoming generations of blacks will have more extensively educated parents than the blacks who are now in school, and this will hasten the convergence of levels of attainment.

Several types of racial segregation in public education have been reduced or eliminated since the Supreme Court gave its *Brown* ruling in 1954. A high proportion of blacks now attend formerly white universities, and in many small or moderate-sized cities public schools have been effectively integrated. Yet in many other metropolitan areas the public schools were as segregated in 1980 as in 1954. This segregation will not disappear in the foreseeable future.

Thirty years ago the mention of school segregation most often referred to southern cities in which a minority of black students were isolated into older, run-down schools. Blacks made up a majority of the enrollment in very few, if any, large cities, and it seemed possible to achieve integration by closing the all-black schools in southern cities. Today the situation is very different. Since the early 1970s the extent of racial segregation has been greater in northern cities than in southern ones. In most of the largest cities the majority of students are black or Hispanic; whites make up a small and rapidly decreasing share of the enrollment. If there is to be racial integration of public schools in the near future in the large metropolitan areas, city and suburban school systems will have to be merged. The federal courts are not moving in this direction, and elected officials have seldom endorsed combining largely black city school districts with white suburban ones. Thus racial segregation in elementary and secondary schools will probably persist well into the twenty-first century.

It is easy to explain why racial differences in the occupations of employed workers have declined. For one thing, the educational attainment of blacks has risen, meaning that they are better qualified for prestigious and high-paying jobs. Second, the attitudes of both blacks and whites have changed. Blacks may be less willing to settle for dead-end, low-paying jobs, and white employers may be more willing to promote blacks. Third, the Civil Rights Act of 1964 outlawed racial discrimination in employment. Numerous private employers and governmental agencies have been charged with discriminating against their black employees. Some firms have voluntarily agreed to compensate victims of such unfair treatment and change their hiring practices, while in other situations the courts have imposed penalties or specified stringent new rules for recruitment and promotion (Burstein, 1979; Wallace, 1976).

Almost all large employers do some business with the government or benefit from some governmental program. As such, their hiring and promotion policies must be certified as nondiscriminatory by the Equal Employment Opportunity Commission (EEOC) or by the Department of Health and Human Services. They are required to file detailed information about the race and sex of workers in all their job classifications. If there is a consistent underrepresentation of blacks in the better jobs, it will become apparent to the government and may diminish their employer's chances of obtaining federal contracts. It will also be apparent to black workers, who may file a grievance with EEOC. This system may explain some of the racial convergence in the jobs of blacks and whites.

Although the occupational distribution of blacks has become more similar to that of whites, there has been no such convergence with regard to employment itself. The jobless rate for black men has persistently been double that for white men, and a decreasing proportion of black men participate in the labor force. The social and legal changes that reduced occupational segregation might be expected to reduce the gap in employment and joblessness, but they have not done so.

Several explanations, none of them entirely satisfactory, have been offered for this surprising trend. One view stresses that the skills of workers have improved less rapidly than the requirements for getting a satisfactory job. This leads to a mismatch: workers may think they are qualified for good jobs, but in reality they may lack skills. The national economy has shifted from agriculture to manufacturing and then to services and high technology; thus the need for low-skill workers has declined while openings have developed for trained specialists.

Elijah Anderson (1979) spent time in a Philadelphia ghetto to find out why so many young black men did not work. Most of the men graduated from high school and believed that this qualified them for much better positions than the jobs they could actually get, such as washing cars, delivering packages, or cleaning floors. They knew that men in their community did not move up an occupational ladder: men in their forties or fifties were still working at the same low-prestige, low-pay jobs they had held when they were twenty. Accepting the available work was seen by these young blacks as locking themselves into dead-end careers. Employers, meanwhile, tended to think that these workers, even if certified with a high school diploma, had few skills, would not work diligently, and would steal whenever they had an opportunity. They deliberately reduced wage rates on the assumption that young blacks supplemented their earnings by theft. As an alternative to dead-end participation in the conventional labor force, these young men were lured by the possibility of high incomes from illegal activities. They saw some men in their neighborhoods become at least temporarily rich by marketing women, drugs, or stolen goods. This prospect of wealth was another reason for some to reject the mundane jobs for which they were qualified.

Elliot Liebow (1967) made similar observations about an older group of street-corner men in Washington, D.C. These men lacked skills and realized that employers neither respected nor trusted them. Their own fathers and their peers had failed in the world of work, and they also expected to fail sooner or later. They understood that no matter how competently they worked, employers would pay them as little as possible and lay them off as soon as work slackened. As a result, they stayed out of the labor force as long as they could.

In an earlier era, when a third or more of the labor force worked in agriculture, the situation may have been different. On the one hand, there was a large pool of low-skill jobs that could be filled by people with little education or training. On the other, workers may have had more realistic expectations about employment. Urbanization and industrialization may make it increasingly likely that low-skilled workers will remain unemployed or drop out of the labor force.

Another view is that the expansion of welfare, the development of other benefit programs, and various federal laws discourage men from working. The past two decades have seen a great increase in welfare funding, extensions of unemployment benefits, and the development of new noncash programs such as food stamps and housing subsidies. Martin Anderson reports that in many states the head of a family can receive food stamps, unemployment benefits, and welfare that just about equals the income from a moderate-pay job. "Why should someone work forty hours a week, fifty weeks a year for, say, $8,000 when it would be possible not to work at all for, say, $6,000?" (M. Anderson,1978:47).

Several studies provide empirical support for the hypothesis that the expansion of transfer programs may decrease employment (Butler and Heckman, 1977; Darity and Myers, 1980). Findings from the Seattle and Denver income maintenance experiments suggest that if poor families are guaranteed a modest income the husband and wife will both work fewer hours: about two hours less per week for husbands and five hours for wives (Robins, 1980). These experiments found no racial difference in the impact of guaranteed incomes upon the employment of wives, but black husbands reduced their hours of work by twice as much as white husbands (Robins and West, 1980).

Other federal programs may also encourage exits from the work force. In 1957 the Social Security System initiated a disability benefits program to provide cash income to workers who developed a physical or mental malady that would result in their death or keep them off the job for at least a year. In 1960 there were about six persons receiving disability benefits per thousand employed workers; in 1981 it was twenty-nine beneficiaries per thousand workers. In the same period, the cash payment, in constant dollars, went up by about 50 percent (U.S. Department of Health and Human Services, 1982, tables M-12 and M-39). There is clear evidence that older low-skill male workers have withdrawn from the labor force in response to this expansion of disability benefits. Since blacks tend to have lower earnings potential than whites, the effects have been greater among blacks (Parsons, 1980).

Federal laws intended to improve the welfare of the poor may also limit the employment of black men. Minimum wage laws, for example, may produce higher rates of unemployment or nonparticipation in the labor force. Edward Banfield (1970) contends that during the 1950s and 1960s increases in the minimum wage had no consequences for the employment of highly qualified workers but that rises in unemployment among low-skill groups such as black teenagers closely paralleled increases in the minimum wage.

Walter Williams, in *The State Against Blacks* (1982), argues that eliminating the minimum wage and, perhaps, ending the requirement that blacks and whites be paid the same would benefit blacks by creating job opportunities. His image of both employers and workers differs radically from that of Elijah Anderson and Elliot Liebow. Supposedly, if there were no minimum wage, employers would recruit many currently unemployed black men, discover that they are talented, productive workers, and then advance them to more responsible and higher-paying jobs. Furthermore, even if employed at low wages, Williams contends, these workers would gain valuable on-the-job training.

A third explanation offered for the declining employment of black men is that blacks are residentially concentrated in central cities while jobs are moving to suburban industrial parks or shopping centers. John Kain (1968) observed this trend in the 1960s and predicted that employment opportunities for blacks would get worse as more firms moved out of central cities. This explanation is very plausible, but it assumes that jobs are deconcentrating more rapidly than the black population and that suburban jobs are inaccessible to those who live in central cities. Several investigators have challenged this explanation of the decline in the proportion of black men at work (Masters, 1975) and have found, at best, a weak relationship between the isolation of blacks and their economic status (Jiobu and Marshall, 1971). The suburban black population grew rapidly throughout the 1970s, but the proportion of black men at work continued to decline.

A fourth view contends that employers are now more selective in choosing their black workers. In the past, employers may have assumed that all blacks—regardless of their educations or skills—would end up in those few occupational slots reserved for them. Blacks would not compete for administrative or managerial jobs where they might supervise whites or be public representatives of the firm. Thirty-five years ago, blacks with advanced degrees were hired to plump pillows on sleeping cars or to sort mail in the post office. Today, however, employers may scrutinize the credentials of black applicants very carefully. If they do not treat the blacks they hire the same way they treat similar whites, they may be sued or cited for violating civil rights laws. This situation greatly improves opportunities and pay rates among employed blacks, but it may make it more difficult for some blacks to get that first job.

It is impossible, at present, to certify one of these explanations as the most accurate and reject the three others. It may be that all four factors help to account for the changes of the 1970s. In the future, many people will study census and survey data to determine why black unemployment rates remain so high during both recessions and booms and why an increasing fraction of adult black men are neither working nor looking for jobs.

3

Personal Income and Earnings

Differences between blacks and whites in school enrollment, educational attainment, and occupation decreased in the period from World War II to the 1980s. We might assume that these improvements would equalize the earnings of black and white workers. And in fact there is convincing evidence of a narrowing of the racial gap in earnings, although in 1982, just as in 1960, blacks typically reported smaller incomes and earned less money than whites.

The Incomes of Individuals

Much of the civil rights effort of the past forty years has sought to eliminate differences between the races in earnings and income. Sometimes this has taken the form of demands for equal opportunities in education; in other situations discriminatory employment practices have been attacked. A major breakthrough occurred with the adoption of the Civil Rights Act of 1964. Title VII of that law created the Equal Employment Opportunity Commission and outlawed racial discrimination in hiring, promotions, and pay rates.

It is not easy to portray long-run trends in income or earnings by race, because tabulations about this were sparse before 1960. The available data, however, do suggest that racial differences have gradually contracted. Trends in the income of individuals are shown in Figure 3.1. An individual's income includes money earnings plus cash transfer payments such as Social Security benefits or welfare funds plus any income from rents, royalties, or dividends. The information in Figure 3.1 is restricted to persons aged 15 and over who reported income.

Figure 3.1 indicates that income has risen during the last three decades for men and women of both races. Since these figures are shown in constant dollars, inflation cannot be the cause of the upward trend; people actually have more purchasing power now than in the past. Upon closer scrutiny, several important differences stand out. First, personal incomes went up much more rapidly before the recession of 1974–75 than after. Indeed, for all groups incomes rose between the 1950s and the early 1970s, then reached a plateau, and then declined in the recession of 1981–82. The 1973–75 period is a real turning point: incomes attained their peak at that time but have fallen since then.

Second, rates of increase in personal income were not the same for all groups. Black incomes went up faster than those of whites between the 1950s and the early 1970s. For black men who worked full time for the entire year (that is, 35 or more hours per week for at least 50 weeks), median incomes rose from $7,200 in 1955 to $13,000 in 1973, an increase of 80 percent. During the same interval the incomes of full-time white men increased by only 60 percent.

Third, income trends differ not only by race but also by sex. The incomes of black women moved closer to those of white women throughout this period. In 1982 black women who worked full time had a median total income of $9,300, $1,100 less than white women. Back in 1960 the racial difference was much larger: $2,700.

MEASURING INCOME TRENDS

Any attempt to describe income trends raises several issues. One of these is the question of how best to summarize the income distribution. I have used the term "typical," but it involves some ambiguity. In any year a few people report incomes close to zero, others have moderate incomes, while another few have large incomes, perhaps a million dollars or more. People are certainly not evenly distributed by income; many more make $10,000–$20,000 than $100,000 and over. One way to summarize the income distribution is to add the dollars people receive and then divide by the number of people. This gives the average or *mean* income. This is a valuable number that can be used in many statistical analyses, but it may be influenced by the persons at the upper end of the distribution. A sample that includes

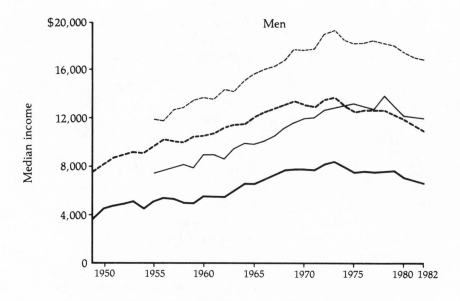

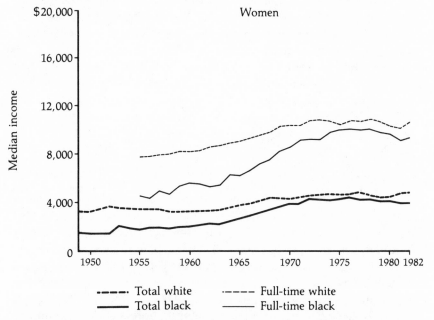

- - - - - Total white ⸻ ⸻ Full-time white
⸻⸻ Total black ⸻⸻ Full-time black

Figure 3.1. Median income (in constant 1979 dollars) of total income recipients, 1949–1982, and of full-time, year-round workers, 1955–1982, by race and sex.

Source: U.S. Bureau of the Census, *Current Population Reports*, ser. P-60, no. 127, table 10; ser. P-60, no. 129, table 67.

several millionaires, even if it is a large sample, will have a high mean income. To give a better indication of the income distribution, *median* income is often used. This is the amount that separates the bottom half of the income distribution from the top half, and thus it is not confounded by the fact that a small number of people receive a large fraction of total income.

The choice of an index to summarize the income distribution affects the conclusions to be drawn from an analysis. For example, white men are much more likely than any other group to be in the highest income category. In 1982, 43 percent of the people who reported any income were white men, but 88 percent of those who had incomes over $50,000 were white men (U.S. Bureau of the Census, 1983b, table 8). The mean income of white men is raised by that small proportion who receive large incomes. As a result, a study using the mean will reveal larger racial and sexual differences in income than a similar study using median income. For men who worked full time in 1982, the racial difference in median income was $4,000; that in mean income, $6,000. Thus the racial gap in purchasing power is shown to be much greater when the measure used is mean income. In this section dealing with personal income, I use median income to avoid giving undue weight to people with very high incomes. In the next section, which is about how much workers earn, a logarithmic transformation of wages is used for the same purpose.

A second basic issue concerns measuring changes in income over time. The term "constant dollars" is used to indicate that we have controlled for inflation and thus that the income levels for a given year may be compared to those for an earlier year in terms of purchasing power. Unless otherwise noted, all the dollar amounts in this book refer to constant dollars with the purchasing power of 1979 dollars. To get estimates of constant dollar amounts, I used the Consumer Price Index, which is calculated monthly by the Bureau of Labor Statistics.

Many have criticized the Consumer Price Index, arguing that it does not measure inflation precisely and that it does not take into account changes in consumers' purchasing patterns. Nevertheless, it is the most widely cited and the best-understood measure, and for these reasons I use it in this book. Some caution is needed in interpreting changes in income over time. But the cost of living undoubtedly changes for blacks in just about the same way it changes for whites, and thus using some other measure of inflation would lead to similar conclusions about the economic status of blacks relative to that of whites.

THE RACIAL INCOME GAP

One of the most challenging questions about racial trends is whether blacks are narrowing the gap that separates them from whites. Different indexes or measures applied to the same data may lead to opposing conclusions. One way to begin to answer this question is to ask if the income of the typical black is getting to be a higher proportion of that of the typical white. The typical black (or white) in this case means someone with the median income for blacks (whites). If there were racial equality in incomes, the median income of blacks would be 100 percent as much as that of whites; that is, the median incomes for the two races would be the same.

White men consistently report higher incomes than any other group. Much of the effort of the Equal Employment Opportunity Commission and the litigation based on Title VII of the Civil Rights Act of 1964 has sought to end those employment practices which ensure that white men are paid more than white women or blacks. For this reason, I will use the income of white men as the benchmark for comparisons in this chapter and in Chapter 4.

The top half of Figure 3.2 shows the median income of black men, black women, and white women as a percentage of the median income of white men. These data refer to full-time, year-round workers. It is clear from the figure that the incomes of blacks have risen more rapidly than those of white men. The median income of black men was 61 percent of that of white men in 1955, rose to 68 percent by 1970, and stood at 71 percent in 1982. Although the incomes of black women are much smaller, they have risen steadily; by 1982 black women's median income was about 56 percent of that of white men. White women show a different pattern: for much of the period since World War II, their incomes have risen less rapidly than those of white men; thus their incomes fell from 65 percent of those of white men in 1955 to a low of 56 percent in 1973. By this measure of personal income, blacks are catching up with white men but white women have been falling further behind for much of the period since World War II.

I have been discussing the incomes of blacks and women relative to those of white men. It is also possible to examine the absolute difference between the median income of a group and that of white men. In Chapter 1, I explained that the incomes of blacks could move

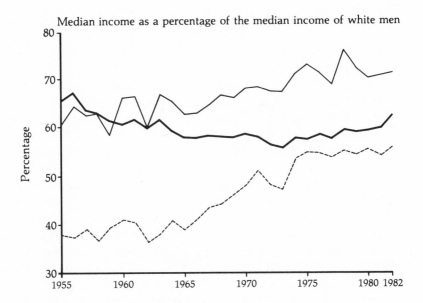

Median income as a percentage of the median income of white men

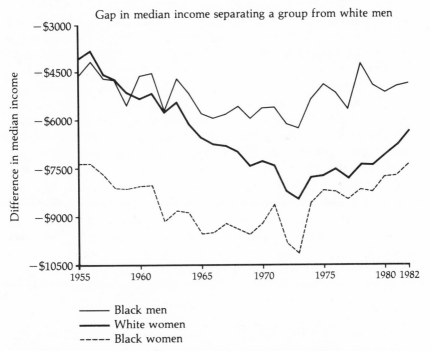

Gap in median income separating a group from white men

——— Black men
━━━ White women
----- Black women

Figure 3.2. Median income of black men, black women, and white women as a percentage of that of white men, and gaps in median income, for full-time, year-round workers, 1955–1982 (constant 1979 dollars).

Source: same as for Figure 3.1.

closer to those of whites in relative terms even while the absolute gap in incomes increased. The absolute difference, when expressed in constant dollars, gives an indication of the difference in purchasing power. The bottom half of Figure 3.2 shows these absolute differences: the median income of white men has been subtracted from the median income of each of the other groups.

Note that for almost twenty years after 1955 differences in income grew larger. Blacks started with much smaller incomes, and thus the income deficit separating them from white men increased even though their incomes were rising at a higher rate than those of white men. A turning point was reached in the 1973–75 recession, when the income advantage of white men was at its maximum. The period since then has not been prosperous for any group; it has been a time of stagnation or decline in personal incomes, and the decreases have been greatest among white men. As a result, women and blacks are narrowing the gap that separates them from white men even though their incomes are not increasing. For example, black men had incomes about $6,300 behind those of white men in 1973 and only $4,800 behind in 1982. Nevertheless, for every group the income difference separating them from white men was greater in 1982 than in 1955.

What should we conclude from this analysis? First, the incomes of blacks have generally risen faster than those of white men and, as a result, the income of blacks as a percentage of that of whites has improved. Most of the gain occurred before the 1973–75 recession. In this sense, racial differences are narrowing and the incomes of blacks are slowly approaching those of white men. Second, the actual differences in incomes increased for much of the period after World War II. In this sense, the economic advantage enjoyed by white men got larger. This has been reversed in the last few years, offering some hope that the incomes of blacks and whites may eventually converge. Third, income trends among women differ by race. Although black women still report low incomes, their incomes have been rising quite rapidly and are now approaching those of white women.

The Earnings of Workers

Many aspects of racial change may appropriately be investigated by looking at earnings rather than incomes. Earnings include only what an individual is paid for working; they exclude welfare payments, rents, royalties, dividends, and alimony. In a labor market with no racial discrimination, black and white workers with similar talents, educations, and hours of work would have similar earnings.

The Bureau of the Census provides the data needed for an investigation of earnings. Censuses and surveys have asked about how much people earned during a year and how long they worked, as well as about their demographic and economic characteristics such as educational attainment, occupation, industry, place of residence, and age. In the following discussion I use data from the Census of 1960, the earliest comprehensive data about the determinants of earnings for a large national sample. For 1970 and 1980 I analyze data gathered in the Current Population Surveys conducted by the Bureau of the Census.

STUDYING RACIAL DIFFERENCES IN EARNINGS

Blacks have traditionally earned less than whites for several reasons. First, blacks have fewer of the skills that are highly rewarded by employers, and they tend to live in areas where wage rates are generally low, particularly in the South. Second, as a variety of recent court cases document, employers have frequently set limits on the occupational achievements of blacks or paid black men and women of both races less than white men performing similar work (Bell, 1973; Wallace, 1976; Burstein, 1979). Third, blacks have traditionally worked fewer hours per year than whites; in 1979, for example, black men who worked averaged about 38 hours per week, while white men who worked averaged about 43 hours per week (see Appendix, Table A.2).

Employers can discriminate by recruiting white workers rather than black or by promoting whites more rapidly than equally qualified blacks or by paying whites more than blacks for similar work. It is not easy to discover the precise extent of racial discrimination by employers or to assess its costs to blacks. One way to study racial discrimination in the housing market is to send out black and white couples matched by characteristics such as income and age to find out if they are offered identical homes or apartments for the same price. It is much more difficult—perhaps impossible—to send out black and white prospective employees to see if they are treated similarly by firms, and it would take many years to find out if they were promoted to higher-paying jobs at similar rates.

Other methods can be used to determine whether similar black and white workers earn similar amounts of money. Statistical models use data about national samples of black and white workers and equate them with regard to characteristics that influence earnings, such as educational attainment, hours of employment, region of residence, and age. The earnings of blacks can then be compared to those of whites.

This type of analysis serves two purposes. First, if black workers earn less than white, it is possible to measure how much of that racial difference is attributable to the fact that blacks have completed fewer years of schooling, are more likely to live in the South, and typically work fewer hours per year than whites. Taking these differences into account yields a more accurate picture of the economic cost of being black. It is also possible to compare this cost in 1960, 1970, and 1980 to determine whether it is growing larger or decreasing.

Second, these models make it possible to describe how earnings are related to factors that influence earnings, such as educational attainment or years of experience. If employers do not discriminate, then blacks and whites who make similar investments in education should have similar earnings, and a year of labor market experience should be equally valuable to workers of both races. These statistical models can reveal, for example, the value of a year of college education for blacks and for whites. If the earnings associated with educational attainment are much greater for whites than for blacks, this fact may indicate the presence of racial discrimination. These models also make it possible to describe how racial differences changed between 1960 and 1980.

Many studies of this type have been conducted in the last twenty years; and a large array of variables have been used to investigate racial differences in economic status.

Without exception, these studies show that the actual earnings of black men are smaller than those of white men, even after blacks and whites are statistically matched with regard to factors that influence earnings. With few exceptions (see Stolzenberg, 1975), these studies have found that the earnings associated with investments in education are lower for blacks than for whites, that labor market experience is much less highly rewarded for blacks, and that in all regions blacks earn less than whites.

The approach I have used to assess differences in earnings assumes that how much a person earns is determined by his or her educational attainment, years of labor market experience, and region of residence. These are the variables that have proved to be most important in previous studies. In this chapter, I report the results of my own study, based on a large and inclusive sample of the population; the study itself is described in the Appendix.

TRENDS IN EARNINGS

The top of Figure 3.3 shows hourly wages for 1959, 1969, and 1979 expressed in constant 1979 dollars.[1] The 1960s were prosperous years, and wage rates went up quite rapidly for each group. Among black men, for example, earnings increased from $3.59 to $5.07 per hour. The 1970s present a different picture: hourly earnings increased for blacks but just about held constant for whites. The typical black worker in 1979 earned just about as much per hour as the typical white worker a decade earlier.

The progress blacks have made may be seen by comparing their wage trends to those of whites. In 1959 white women averaged about 10 cents more per hour than black men. Twenty years later black men earned $1.25 more per hour than white women. Black women had very low average wages in 1959—$2.24 per hour—but by 1980 they earned just about as much per hour as white women. There has been a major change in employment opportunities for black women, which helps to account for the improvement in their earnings. Back in 1959 more than a third of the black women who held jobs worked as domestic servants and another third worked on farms or in service jobs. By 1979 the proportion of black women in these low-wage jobs had been reduced by more than half (U.S. Bureau of Labor Statistics, 1979; 1980).

Blacks are much more likely than whites to be unemployed or out of the labor force. This means that even if there is no racial difference in hourly wages, the annual earnings of blacks will fall below those of whites because they work fewer hours each year. The prosperity of an individual or a family depends much more upon annual earnings than upon hourly wage rates. For this reason, it is important to examine trends in yearly earnings. The bottom of Figure 3.3 shows average annual earnings in constant dollars. The annual earnings may seem rather low because they refer to all people who were employed at any time during a year, not just to those who worked full time.

The trends in annual earnings are similar to those in hourly earnings in some ways but different in others. As with hourly earnings, increases were recorded for all groups in the 1960s and the annual earnings of white men declined a bit in the 1970s. But the annual earnings of both black and white women went up between 1969 and

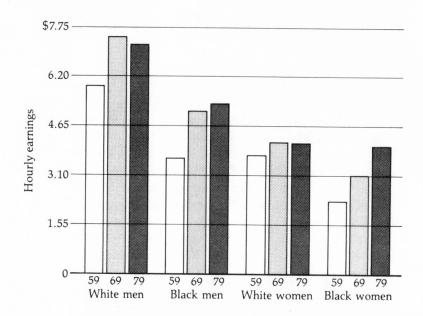

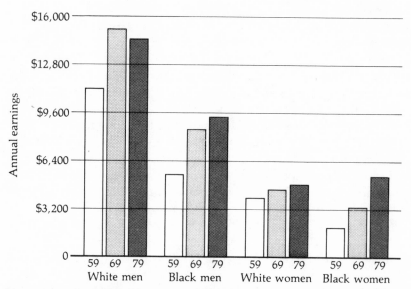

Figure 3.3. Average hourly earnings and annual earnings, by race and sex, 1959, 1969, and 1979 (constant 1979 dollars).

Source: U.S. Bureau of the Census, Public Use Files from the One-in-One-Thousand Sample of the 1960 Census and from the March 1970 and March 1980 Current Population Surveys.

1979. This came about in large part because women worked more hours in 1979 than a decade earlier; during the 1970s the average hours of work increased by about four hours per week for black women and by about two hours per week for white women (see Appendix, Table A.2). By 1980 black women caught up with white women in annual earnings. To do so, they had to put in more hours on the job. Black women earned about 2 percent less per hour than white women, but they worked about three hours more per week.

Both the hourly and the annual earnings of blacks increased during the prosperous 1960s and the not-so-prosperous 1970s. White men experienced a rise in both hourly and annual earnings in the 1960s, but in the 1970s their earnings—both hourly and annual—declined. The hourly earnings of white women hardly changed between 1960 and 1980, but their annual earnings crept ahead, largely because they worked more hours.

EARNINGS AND EDUCATIONAL ATTAINMENT, LABOR MARKET EXPERIENCE, AND REGION

How much will a worker with a given set of characteristics earn, and how are these earnings related to education, experience, and place of residence? It is possible to estimate the dollar value of an additional year of schooling or an additional year of experience, and of the net cost of being a resident of the South. These dollar values differ by race and sex.

I use the phrase *labor market characteristics* to refer to a worker's educational attainment, years of experience in the labor market, and region of residence—the characteristics that influence the worker's earnings. The phrase *rates of return* refers to the net changes in earnings associated with an additional year of education, another year of experience, or the cost of residing in the South. Rates of return express the economic value of each of these labor market characteristics. Individuals presumably have some control over their labor market characteristics, since they may decide to remain in school longer or to move from one region to another. Employers have greater control over rates of return, since they determine how much to pay a person who has a certain educational attainment or amount of experience.

First I will consider the rates of return associated with a year of elementary or secondary education. In 1960 the value (in constant 1979 dollars) of one additional year of education at this level was 35 cents per hour for a white man but only 12 cents for a black man.

Two decades later a year of elementary or secondary schooling was worth 46 cents per hour to a white man and 36 to a black (see upper left of Figure 3.4). Thus the racial difference in the rate of return to pre-college schooling declined. But the sexual difference remains large, especially among whites: in 1980 an additional year of education at this level was worth about twice as much to a white man as to a white woman.[2]

Unfortunately, the Census data do not make it possible to determine the causes of these racial and sexual differences in rates of return associated with educational attainment. Undoubtedly they reflect discriminatory practices on the part of some employers, but they may also reflect racial or sexual differences in the quality of education. They may also be influenced by personal differences among employees. If white women, for example, look for part-time jobs with flexible hours more often than men do, they may not be maximizing the economic value of their own investments in education.

For all groups, college education was more highly rewarded than elementary and secondary education (see upper right of Figure 3.4). Again, however, racial differences declined while sexual differences persisted. In 1960 a year of college education was worth about 15 cents more per hour to a white man than to a black man; by 1980 the advantage for white men was only 7 cents. Black women obtained earnings for their investments in college education equivalent to or better than those of white women throughout this entire period. For white women, meanwhile, the value of an additional year of college was lower in 1980 than in 1960 or 1970: only 38 cents per hour.

A further indication of change is apparent in both top panels of Figure 3.4. In 1960 an additional year of schooling netted a white woman more than a black man, but by 1980 black men received considerably greater returns on their investments in education than did white women.

The value of an additional year of labor market experience (lower left of Figure 3.4) can be succinctly summarized: white men are much more highly rewarded for experience than are black men or women of either race. In 1960 an additional year of experience was worth 15 cents per hour to a white man; by 1980 it was worth 28 cents per hour. Black men are paid roughly half as much for their labor market experience as white men. Labor market experience has very little, if any, financial payoff for women. The earnings associated with years of experience were not significantly different from zero for black women in any year.

There is considerable debate about these findings and how to interpret them. One perspective contends that employers generally prefer men—especially white men—for the highest-paying jobs and consider women sporadic workers who will leave the labor force to have children or to care for their families. Therefore, employers may be acting rationally if they provide men with more on-the-job training than women, promote them more often, and advance their salaries more rapidly than those of women. An investigation using data from the Michigan Panel Study of Income Dynamics found that white males spent more than twice as much time in on-the-job programs as did women or blacks (Corcoran and Duncan, 1979).

Another perspective stresses the measurement of labor market experience. This measure equals the number of years that elapsed after a person completed his or her formal training. White men spend most of this time working, as do many black men, although because blacks face a much higher unemployment rate they accrue less actual experience than white men do. However, many of the women who were employed when these surveys were conducted had spent several years out of the labor force, frequently because of family responsibilities.

Several investigators have studied the earnings of women with uninterrupted careers or have tried to use more accurate measures of women's actual employment experiences. Some data of this type are available, but they do not cover the entire span considered in this analysis, and the samples include relatively few blacks. Larry Suter and Herman Miller (1973), for example, found that women who had worked continuously throughout their careers earned much more in a given year than those who had dropped into and out of the labor force, implying that labor market experience actually is rewarded for women. Jacob Mincer and Solomon Polachek (1974) argued that using appropriate measures of real work experience and interruptions reveals that women are paid in a fashion quite similar to men (see also Polachek, 1975). Replications of this investigation (Sandell and Shapiro, 1978) and other studies (Corcoran and Duncan, 1979; Rytina, 1982) dispute this finding and generally report that women are paid less than men for their actual labor force experience but that the sexual differences are smaller when appropriate measures of actual years on the job are used (see also Mallan, 1982; U.S. Bureau of the Census, 1982c, tables 1 and 2).

The lower right panel of Figure 3.4 shows that it is costly, in terms of hourly earnings, to live in the South regardless of race, but that

One year of elementary or secondary education

One year of labor market experience

☐ White men
■ Black men
▨ White women
▨ Black women

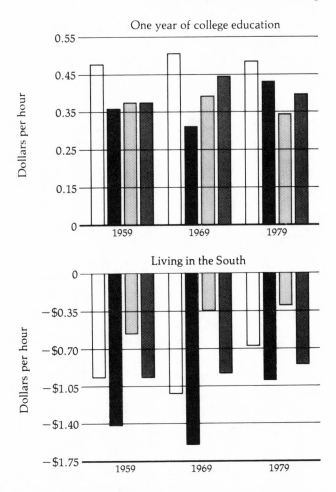

Figure 3.4. Estimated dollar value (in constant 1979 dollars) of one year of elementary or secondary education, one year of college education, one year of labor market experience, and residence in the South, by race and sex, 1959, 1969, and 1979.

Source: same as for Figure 3.3.

the cost is exceptionally high for blacks. This indicates that the wages of blacks and whites are less alike in the South than in other regions. In 1980 a white man in the North or West earned 68 cents more per hour than a white man in the South with a similar educational attainment and labor market experience, but a black man in the North or West earned a dollar more per hour than his counterpart in the South. The net cost of residing in the South, in terms of earnings, was also much greater for black women than for white women. Wage rates went up more rapidly in the South than in other regions in the 1970s, and as a result the net cost of residing in the South declined.

THE RELATIVE EARNINGS OF BLACKS AND WOMEN

Between 1960 and 1980 the earnings of blacks rose more rapidly than those of whites, and there is good reason to believe that racial discrimination in pay rates declined. White women, however, fared rather poorly during this period, although there is some evidence that their earnings went up a bit more rapidly than those of white men in the 1970s.

These conclusions are based upon the investigation of the factors that influence earnings among people aged 25–64. Once again I compare the earnings of each group to those of the most prosperous group, white men. I begin in Figure 3.5 by showing the actual annual earnings of each group as a percentage of those of white men. (Recall that trends in annual earnings reflect both hourly earnings and hours of work.)

In 1959 black men had annual earnings just about half as great as those of white men, and black women averaged only 19 percent as much as white men. Twenty years later the earnings of black men had risen to almost two-thirds those of white men, and black women earned 37 percent as much. So in annual earnings blacks are gradually catching up with whites. Throughout the period, the actual earnings of white women remained at about one-third those of white men.

I have mentioned several reasons why blacks and women earn less than white men: blacks often spend fewer years attending school than whites and are more likely to live in the South where wages are low; blacks and women typically work fewer hours each year than white men; and employers may treat white men more favorably. It is possible to estimate the importance of each of these reasons by creating a hypothetical situation. Suppose blacks and white women had the same labor force characteristics as white men but were paid for these

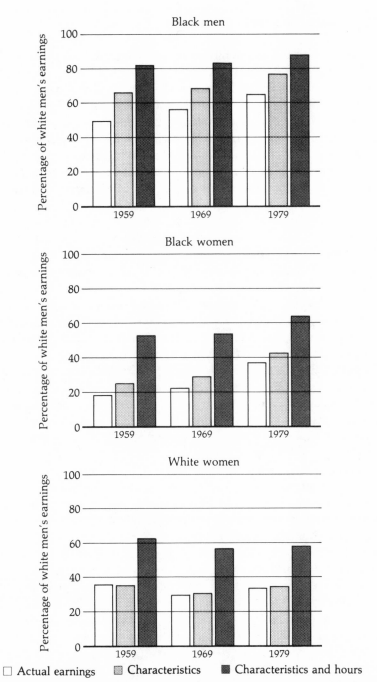

Figure 3.5. Actual and hypothetical annual earnings of black men, black women, and white women as a percentage of the actual annual earnings of white men, 1959, 1969, and 1979.

Source: same as for Figure 3.3.

characteristics at their own rates of return. Further, suppose they not only had the same labor force characteristics as white men but also worked the same number of hours per year as white men—but were paid at their own rates of return. Would they earn as much as white men? The answer is no: their earnings would come closer to those of white men, but the racial and sexual differences in earnings would by no means disappear. This hypothetical exercise is interesting because the remaining difference between the earnings of white men and those of the other groups is one way to measure discrimination in employment.

Figure 3.5 presents three vertical bars for each year. The first bar shows the ratio of the actual annual earnings of a group to those of white men. The second bar indicates the ratio of earnings under the assumption that a group has the educational attainment, years of labor market experience, and regional distribution of white men but its own rates of return. The third bar indicates the earnings ratio under the assumption that blacks and women also work as many hours during the year as white men but have their own rates of return.

Consider the assumption about labor force characteristics. As indicated in the top panel of the figure, in 1959 black men, on average, actually earned 49 percent as much as white men. If they had had the educational attainment, years of labor market experience, and regional distribution of white men but their own rates of pay for these characteristics, they would have earned 65 percent as much as white men.

In 1979 black men's earnings were still far below those of white men. This did not come about solely because they stayed in school fewer years or lived in the South. If they had had the same labor market characteristics as white men in 1979, they would have earned only three-quarters as much.

The findings are similar for black women. If they had had the educational attainment, years of experience, and regional distribution of white men, they would have earned considerably more than they actually earned. Their earnings, however, would still have lagged far behind those of white men because—as indicated in Figure 3.4—a year of education is still worth less to a black woman that it is to a white man.

White women are different. Their educational attainments are similar to those of white men. Indeed, white women drop out of high school less frequently than white men, so they complete more years of elementary and secondary schooling than white men. Also, their regional distribution is identical to that of white men. If white women had the labor market characteristics of white men but their own rates of return, their hypothetical earnings would be just about the same as their actual earnings: that is, about one-third of the earnings of white men.

One of the major reasons why the annual earnings of blacks and women lag behind those of white men is the difference in hours worked. Blacks experience much more unemployment than white men, and women of both races typically put in fewer hours on the job than men. The earnings of blacks and women would increase substantially if they not only had the characteristics of white men but also worked as many hours. If they matched white men in labor force characteristics and hours worked but were paid at their own rates of return, black men would have earned 88 percent as much as white men in 1979, black women 64 percent as much, and white women 58 percent as much.

Hypothetical earnings are used to investigate and illustrate racial and sexual differences. They are certainly not specific predictions of what blacks and women would earn if they had the labor market characteristics of white men and worked as long. If there were a great increase in the labor supply because blacks and women worked more hours, there would be greater competition for jobs and wage rates might decline. If blacks had the educational attainment of white men, there would be a greater supply of highly trained personnel and this too might lower wages.

DISCRIMINATION IN PAY RATES

The hypothetical earnings calculation for a black man in 1979 indicates that if he had the characteristics of the typical white male worker and spent as many hours on the job, he would earn only 88 percent as much as the white man. Does this differential of 12 percent measure racial discrimination in pay rates? In 1959 the hypothetical earnings of black men fell 19 percent behind the actual earnings of white men. Should we conclude that racial discrimination in pay rates declined in this interval but was not eliminated?

There are many ways to measure discrimination. The approach used here may not present evidence about unfair pay practices that would be convincing to a judge or a jury in a lawsuit, but it does provide very useful information about discrimination in the labor market. (For a description of this and other techniques for estimating discrimination, see Conway and Roberts, 1983.) Since the discrepancy between the hypothetical earnings of a group and the actual earnings of white men comes about because of differences in pay rates, it offers an assessment of discrimination. This difference has been called the cost of being a Negro (Siegel, 1965; Smith and Welch, 1977) or the cost of racial discrimination in the labor market (Duncan, 1969; Featherman and Hauser, 1978; Thurow, 1969). If black men and women had the same rates of return as white men, their hypothetical earnings would equal the actual earnings of white men. In such a circumstance, it would be extremely difficult to believe that employers persistently discriminated against blacks or women in setting wage rates.

Considerable caution is needed in interpreting the differences between the hypothetical earnings of a group and the actual earnings of white men. These estimates of discrimination depend upon the specific model used, and thus different analyses will derive different estimates. As Featherman and Hauser (1978:348) state, "discrimination measured in this way may be confounded with effects of omitted variables such as cultural or ability differences between the races." Including additional variables, using different demographic characteristics, or altering the statistical treatment of the variables could change the hypothetical earnings figures and the estimates of the amount of discrimination. A large number of cross-sectional studies have used additional variables, including test scores to measure intellectual ability, health characteristics, measures of the quality of education, duration of work with a given employer, as well as measures of attitudes. The inclusion of such variables leads to results similar to those presented here. Without exception, investigators find the hypothetical earnings of blacks and women to be less than the actual earnings of white men.

The difference between the hypothetical earnings of blacks and the actual earnings of white men does not measure the complete cost of racial discrimination. The hypothetical figure is calculated on the assumption that blacks spend as many years in school as white men and work as many hours. Some of the racial difference in educational attainment and hours of employment may come about because of the unimpeded choices of blacks—but some of the difference may be the outcome of past or present racial discrimination. The lower educational attainment of blacks may result from discrimination in school systems; the lower hours of work of blacks may be caused by discriminatory practices on the part of employers such that blacks are "last hired, first fired."

Four conclusions flow from this analysis of earnings trends and discrimination among workers aged 25–64. First, the actual earnings of blacks and women rose more rapidly than those of white men during the 1960s and 1970s. As a result of these changes, the earnings of blacks moved closer to those of white men. Second, the low earnings of blacks and white women do not come about solely because they have different educational attainments or years of experience, live in different regions, or work fewer hours than white men. Blacks and white women are paid less for their labor market characteristics than are white men. Third, there is good reason to believe that racial discrimination in pay rates declined after 1960, although it was not eliminated. The hypothetical earnings of blacks are closer to the actual earnings of white men in 1979 than in 1959. Fourth, the pattern of change in earnings is different for white women. The earnings of white women declined in comparison with those of white men during the 1960s and rose only a bit more rapidly than those of white men in the 1970s. Evidently the factors that influence pay rates and discrimination among blacks are different from those which affect white women.

WHY HAVE EARNINGS RISEN?

For men and women of both races, annual earnings (in constant dollars) were greater in 1979 than in 1959. Three reasons for this can be identified. First, there have been changes in labor market characteristics; employees typically had greater educational attainments in 1979. Second, all groups reported an increase in the average number of hours worked. Third, the rates of return associated with labor market characteristics changed; for example, as Figure 3.4 illustrates, a year of college was more valuable to a black worker in 1979 than in 1959.

It is possible to estimate how much each of these three factors contributed to the increase in earnings, that is, how much earnings would have risen if the only change had been in hours of employment or in labor market characteristics or in rates of return. These estimates are shown in Figure 3.6. There is no clear-cut way to separate the changes in earnings, because the three factors changed concurrently. For example, at the same time hours of employment went up, rates

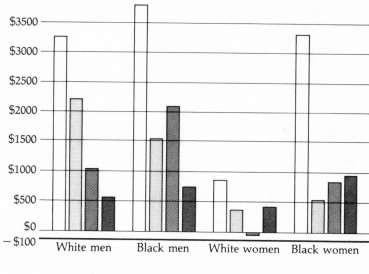

□ Total change
▨ Change related to labor market characteristics
▦ Change related to rates of return
■ Change related to hours of work

Figure 3.6. Change in annual earnings and components of change, 1959–1979 (constant 1979 dollars).
Source: same as for Figure 3.3

of return also increased. This means that there are interaction effects. These are not presented in Figure 3.6; as a result, the three separate components in the figure do not add up to the total change.

The figure reveals that the earnings of blacks rose more than those of whites and that the reasons for change differ by race. Among whites a primary reason for higher earnings was the change in labor market characteristics: white men and women had greater educational attainments in 1979 than in 1959. Increasing the hours of employment also augmented the earnings of white women.

Among blacks changing labor market characteristics—the rise in education and the movement away from the South—played a role, but changes in rates of return were more important. This finding is consistent with the view that racial discrimination in pay rates declined. Back in 1959 blacks were paid much less for their investments in education than were whites, and the net cost of residing in the

South was greater for blacks. This changed during the 1960s and the 1970s as rates of return increased more rapidly among blacks than among whites.

The rates of return for white women actually went down slightly in this period. That is, a white woman with a given set of characteristics in 1979 earned somewhat *less* than her counterpart with identical characteristics in 1959. Recall from Figure 3.4 that for white women the returns associated with educational attainment increased after 1959 but those for years of labor market experience declined. Once again, the trends for white women differ from those for blacks of either sex.

The information about total change in Figure 3.6 indicates that the earnings of men increased by a larger amount than those of women. For both races, the sexual gap in earnings grew larger. This means that women are falling further behind men in purchasing power. In 1960 the typical employed black woman earned $3,800 less than the typical employed black man; by 1980 the difference was $4,500. Among whites the sexual gap in earnings increased from $4,500 in 1960 to $10,700 in 1980.

Conclusions

Despite several recessions, the period since the end of World War II has been a generally prosperous one for men and women of both races. There are racial differences in the rates of gain, and the evidence suggests that blacks are gradually catching up with whites. From the 1950s through the early 1970s, the personal incomes of blacks rose more rapidly than those of whites, and in the past decade incomes have decreased a bit more among whites than among blacks. Despite gains for blacks, racial differences remain quite large. In 1982 the median personal income for black men was $6,600; that for white men, $11,100. The income gap is much smaller among women: in 1982 black women had average incomes just a couple of hundred dollars below those of white women.

To investigate whether blacks and women obtain the same pay as white men for their labor market characteristics, I considered the earnings of all persons aged 25–64 who were employed—even those who worked only part time—in 1959, 1969, or 1979. The average hourly wages of all groups went up in the 1960s, but in the 1970s the wages of whites just about stagnated while those of blacks continued to rise. As a result, the earnings of blacks moved closer to those of whites. In 1959 white men averaged about $5.85 per hour and black men $3.59, for a racial difference of $2.26. Twenty years later white men earned $7.20 per hour and black men $5.32, a difference of $1.88. Black women just about caught up with white women in hourly pay rates, although women of both races continue to earn much less than men.

To estimate the costs to women and blacks of discrimination in the labor market, I assumed that black men and women of both races had the labor market characteristics of white men but their own rates of return for their labor market characteristics. I calculated a hypothetical earnings figure for each group; the difference between a group's hypothetical earnings and the actual earnings of white men offers one assessment of wage discrimination against that group.

Considerable progress has been made, but substantial racial differences still exist. In 1959 a black man with the characteristics and hours of work of the typical white man would have earned 19 percent less than the white man. In 1979 the black man would have earned 12 percent less. The comparable figures for black women were 47 percent less than white men in 1959 and 36 percent less in 1979. This improvement occurred primarily because the rates of return of blacks moved closer to those of whites, suggesting a lessening of discrimination in the labor market. Nevertheless, blacks still earn less than white men with similar qualifications.

Black men work fewer hours per year, on average, than white men do. If much of this difference in employment is caused by racial discrimination, then a study focusing on hourly, rather than annual, earnings will give a more accurate estimate of the cost of being black. Black men with the same labor force characteristics as white men earned 65 percent as much per hour in 1959 and 76 percent as much twenty years later. Thus, focusing on hourly wages leads to a much larger estimate of the cost of being black but also shows a dimunition in racial discrimination in pay rates during the 1960s and 1970s.

Data that would make it possible to estimate the effects of racial discrimination in pay rates on hourly earnings are generally not available for years before 1960. If they were, they would probably show that the earnings of blacks have been catching up with those of whites since the Depression and that the cost of being black has been falling. It is certain that after 1960 the earnings of blacks went up more rapidly than those of whites and that racial discrimination in pay rates declined. It is also certain that the gains made by blacks were not restricted to the 1960s, when the civil rights movement peaked and the national economy grew rapidly. Blacks made substantial gains in the 1970s, a decade in which there were few new civil rights bills and few civil disturbances and in which the economy grew rather lethargically. If the trends of the 1970s persist, racial differences in earnings will continue to decline.

4

Who Benefited?

Many observers believe that the gains of the 1960s and 1970s were not dispersed throughout the black community. Rather, they contend that certain groups of blacks—such as the highly educated, the young, or those working for governmental agencies—made unusually large gains while others experienced little improvement.

Richard Freeman, for example, argued that there had been "a dramatic collapse in traditional discriminatory patterns in the market for highly qualified black Americans" (1976:xx). William Wilson asserted that "the more talented and highly educated blacks are experiencing unprecedented job opportunities in the corporate and government sectors" and contrasted them with poorly trained blacks, who "find themselves locked in the low wage sector where there is little opportunity for advancement" (1978:121). Nathan Glazer reviewed affirmative action programs in employment and concluded: "It seems clear that the main impact of preferential hiring is on the better qualified—the professional and technical . . . Undoubtedly, some of the benefit reaches down, but the lion's share must inevitably go to the better qualified portion of the black population" (1975:73).

To determine whether these writers are correct that a substantial fraction of the black population did not benefit from the economic improvements described in Chapter 3, I will once again focus on employed persons aged 25–64 in 1959, 1969, or 1979. I will consider workers classified by educational attainment, by broad occupational categories, by sector of employment, and by region.

Educational Attainment

To test whether the greatest economic gains were made by highly educated blacks, I classified individuals by race, sex, and educational attainment. For each of five educational categories, I used an approach similar to that of the previous chapter. The hourly earnings of a worker in a specific educational category were seen as depending upon his or her years of labor market experience and region of residence.[1]

I addressed several questions about racial differences in earnings for the different educational groups. Do blacks earn much less than whites who have the same amount of education? Does the size of the racial difference vary by educational level? Have differences decreased over time? Are Freeman, Wilson, and Glazer accurate in stating that racial differences have about disappeared among the college-educated but remain large for those with only a few years of schooling? Do employed blacks at a given educational level earn as much as whites with the same characteristics (years of labor market experience and region of residence)? If blacks not only have the characteristics of whites but also work as many hours, do their annual earnings equal those of whites?

The format that will be used to present results throughout this chapter is illustrated in Figure 4.1, using imaginary data. Suppose blacks at a selected educational level reported annual earnings that are 60 percent of those of similarly educated whites. This is plotted in Figure 4.1 as a light gray bar. Then suppose that instead of their own characteristics those blacks had the regional distribution and years of labor force experience of similarly educated whites—but were paid for these characteristics at their own rates of return.[2] In such a circumstance, their hypothetical earnings might be 70 percent as large as the earnings of white men. This is plotted as a dark gray bar. Finally, if blacks not only had the same characteristics as whites but also worked as many hours during the year as whites—but still retained their own wage rates—they would hypothetically earn 80 percent as much as whites. This is shown as an outline extension of the dark gray bar.

In this imaginary example, blacks actually earned only six dollars for every ten dollars earned by whites, so the first bar is at the 60 percent mark. The second bar can be interpreted as a measure of racial discrimination. If you believe that the main reason blacks work fewer hours per year than whites is that employers discriminate against blacks, then you may conclude—from the 70 percent height of the

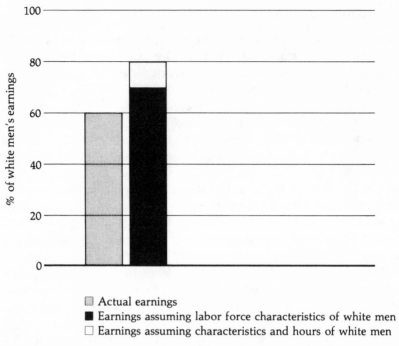

Figure 4.1. **Example of figures appearing in this chapter. Actual and hypothetical earnings of blacks as a percentage of those of white men.**

dark gray bar—that racial discrimination costs blacks 30 percent of the earnings of whites. That is, if blacks in this educational category had the characteristics of white workers but their own wage rates, they would still earn only 70 percent as much as whites. If you think that most of the racial difference in hours of employment comes about because blacks *choose* to work fewer hours than whites, you will conclude that racial discrimination costs blacks 20 percent of what whites earn. That is, if blacks at this educational level had the characteristics of whites and chose to work as many hours during the year, they would earn 80 percent as much as whites.

BLACK MEN

As reported in the previous chapter, the earnings of black men rose more rapidly than those of white men between 1960 and 1980. Figure

4.2 shows that this occurred at all educational levels. (Data for persons with one to three years of college are not shown in the figure.) In 1959 black men with only an elementary school education earned 58 percent as much as similarly educated white men; in 1979 they earned 69 percent as much. For men who completed college, black earnings increased over this period from 63 percent to 76 percent of white earnings. The improvements were greatest at high educational levels, but economic gains were certainly not restricted to blacks with extensive educations.

Recall that absolute differences are not the same as relative differences. Relative to white men, the most successful black men were those with a college education in 1979, who earned 76 percent as much as similarly educated white men. However, the absolute racial gap in earnings increased with educational attainment. In 1979 black men at the bottom of the educational distribution averaged earnings of $2,800 less than white men; among men who completed four or more years of college, blacks earned an average of $4,800 less than whites.

This phenomenon is a persistent one. It was found by Paul Siegel and Lester Thurow, two of the first to analyze demographic data to investigate racial differences in earnings. Siegel (1965) found that in 1960 the dollar cost of discrimination was almost five times as great for black male college graduates as for black men who failed to complete elementary school. Using a different model, Thurow (1969) reported that in 1960, taking into account years of labor market experience, a black man with eight years of education earned $1,400 less than a similarly educated white man, and a black man with a college education earned $3,600 less than his white counterpart. If black men invest in education, their earnings certainly rise, but the gap in purchasing power, that is, the dollar gap in earnings, separating them from similarly educated white men also increases.

Reductions in apparent racial discrimination in pay rates were largest for black men who stayed in school for at least twelve years. Consider men who finished high school but did not go on to college. In 1959 a black man who had the characteristics of the typical white high school graduate but was paid at the rates actually observed among blacks would have earned 59 percent as much as the comparable white. If he also worked as many hours as the typical white high school graduate, he would have earned 75 percent as much, implying that discrimination cost him an amount equal to 25 percent of the earnings of white men. Twenty years later, black men were in

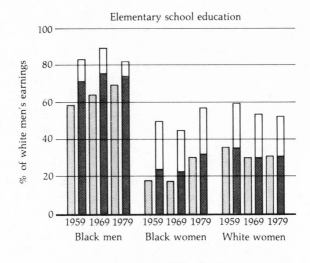

Elementary school education

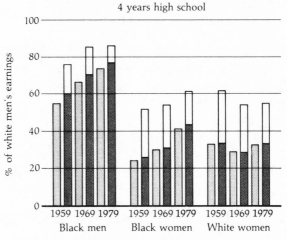

4 years high school

☐ Actual earnings
■ Earnings assuming labor force characteristics
    of white men
☐ Earnings assuming characteristics and hours
    of white men

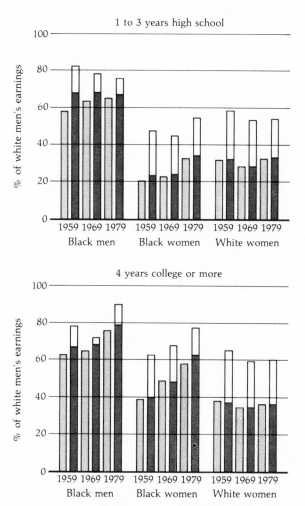

Figure 4.2. Actual and hypothetical earnings as a percentage of those of white men, 1959, 1969, and 1979, by educational attainment.

Source: U.S. Bureau of the Census, *Census of Population: 1960*, Public Use Sample; Current Population Survey, March 1970, Public Use File; Current Population Survey, March 1980, Public Use File.

a much more favorable position relative to whites, suggesting that discrimination had decreased. A black high school graduate with the characteristics and hours of work of the typical white graduate but his own rates of return would have earned 86 percent as much as the white man. Similar gains were recorded for black men who attended college, but the hypothetical earnings of blacks who did not finish high school did no more than keep pace with the earnings of white men. This implies that black men who finish high school face less discrimination in wage rates than they did twenty years ago but that there has been little change for those who drop out earlier.

The evidence is definite: the actual earnings of black men in every educational category rose more rapidly than those of white men, and the cost of being black declined for men who had a high school education or more. However, black men—even those with college degrees—have not reached wage parity with whites. Among college-educated men in 1979, a black man with the characteristics and hours of work of the average white college graduate could expect to earn only 90 percent as much as the white man. His earnings would fall almost $2,000 below the $19,700 earned by college-educated white men.

BLACK WOMEN

The actual earnings of black women increased more rapidly than those of white men at every educational level. The gains, however, were greatest among those who attended college. Black women with college educations earned 38 percent as much as college-educated white men in 1959 and 58 percent twenty years later. Among people with only an elementary school education, the earnings of black women rose more modestly relative to those of white men, from 18 to 31 percent.

There is also evidence that discrimination against black women declined during these two decades. In 1959, for those with one to three years of college, a black woman with characteristics and hours of work of the typical white man would have earned 47 percent as much as the white man. In 1979 she would have earned 64 percent as much.

Unlike the situation among black men, discrimination in wage rates declined for black women who had less than a high school education. For example, among those with only elementary school training, a black woman who had the characteristics of the typical white man and worked as many hours earned 50 percent as much as the white man in 1959 but 58 percent as much in 1979. For black women, the gains in earnings and declines in wage discrimination occurred at all educational levels.

WHITE WOMEN

Changes in earnings were very different among white women. Between 1959 and 1979 the actual earnings of white women did not gain on those of white men. At all educational levels and for the entire twenty-year span, white women reported earnings roughly 35 percent as great as those of white men.

The labor force characteristics of white women—their regional distribution and their ages—are very similar to those of white men. This means that when hypothetical earnings are calculated for white women on the assumption that they have the characteristics of white men but their own wage rates and hours of employment, the estimated earnings are similar to their actual earnings. However, white women work for fewer hours than white men. If they worked as many hours as white men, they would earn just about 60 percent as much as the men. This confirms, for whites, the frequently reported generalization that women earn 59 cents for every dollar earned by men. The generalization is accurate whether you are talking about college graduates or women who never completed high school. It has also been true at least since 1959. If a white woman attends college, she is likely to increase her earnings, but those extra years spent in school will not reduce the gap separating her earnings from those of a similarly educated white man.

Racial differences in the earnings of women have declined sharply, and a projection of recent trends implies that at all educational levels black women will soon attain economic parity with white women. In 1979 black women with less than a high school education still earned less than similarly educated white women, but for those with a high school education or some college the annual earnings of black women exceeded those of white women. One reason for this is the greater labor force activity of black women: in 1979 black women with a college education worked about nine hours more per week than similarly educated white women. After such differences are taken into account, the hourly wages of college-educated black women are higher than those of white women. Black women are better able than white women to translate their years of experience into earnings, undoubtedly reflecting a racial difference in the career patterns of women who finish college. Unlike the situation among men, black women who invest in education can expect to earn at least as much as comparable white women.

Differences within Occupations

Examining the earnings of black and white men in various occupations, Richard Freeman (1976) observed that startling changes occurred in the 1960s. By 1969 black architects earned 97 percent as much as white architects. The figure was 96 percent for electronic technicians, 91 percent for elementary school teachers, and 89 percent for pharmacists. Freeman's analysis implied that a continuation of the trends of the 1960s would soon lead to a racial parity in earnings, at least in prestigious jobs.

To determine whether these economic gains were widespread or limited to a few fields, I next examine annual earnings by occupation. Several difficulties limit this analysis. Survey data gathered in 1970 and 1980 include only a few thousand blacks, too few to break down into specific occupations such as pharmacist, lawyer, or welder. The Census of 1980 obtained detailed occupational data from a one-in-five sample of blacks, but jobs were classified in a new way, so occupational categories are not comparable for 1970 and 1980 (U.S. Bureau of the Census, 1981e; Priebe, 1980). Instead of specific occupations, I use four broad categories: professionals and managers, clerical and sales workers, operatives and laborers, and service workers.

Professional and managerial workers report the highest earnings, followed by those with clerical or sales jobs. Operatives and laborers include machine operators, many assembly-line workers, and all industrial laborers. Service workers are the lowest-paid group. This is a heterogeneous collection of jobs, including food service workers, launderers, and domestic servants as well as those in protective service such as firemen and police officers. By 1980 only 2 percent of black workers held farm jobs, so agricultural employment is excluded (U.S. Bureau of Labor Statistics, 1981).

Within each occupational category, I compare the actual annual earnings of black men, black women, and white women to those of white men. Then I determine how much these groups would earn if they had the characteristics of the typical white man but were paid at their own rates of return.[3] Finally, I calculate how much they would earn in the year if they not only had the characteristics of the typical white man but also worked as many hours. The results are shown in Figure 4.3.

Although an employer can discriminate against blacks by making it very difficult for them to get into managerial jobs, I do not look at those practices which may reserve the best jobs for white men and shunt blacks and women into low-paid occupations. (For analyses of racial factors in occupational achievement, see Duncan, 1969; Blau and Duncan, 1967; Featherman and Hauser, 1978.) Those blacks who obtain the top jobs in a firm may face another type of discrimination; the employer may pay them less than he pays similarly qualified whites. This analysis concerns only this second type of discrimination—wage discrimination within occupational categories.

BLACK MEN

The actual earnings of black men rose more rapidly than those of white men between 1959 and 1979 in each of the occupational categories. A black man with a professional or managerial job earned 55 percent as much as the typical white man in 1959, 65 percent as much in 1979. An improvement of similar magnitude was recorded at every occupational level. The movement of blacks away from the South and the rapid upgrading of the educational attainment of blacks help to explain these gains in relative earnings.

Black men in all occupational categories apparently benefited from decreases in discrimination. If a black man and a white man had the same characteristics and worked the same number of hours, their earnings were more alike in 1979 than in 1959. This occurred because the rates of return for educational attainment and labor market experience for blacks became more like those for whites. Among clerical and sales workers, for example, a black man who had the characteristics of the typical white man earned 75 percent as much as the white man in 1959, 89 percent as much in 1979. This improvement was clearly not restricted to the more prestigious occupations; in all categories the cost of being black declined during both the 1960s and the 1970s.

WOMEN

The actual earnings of black women lag far behind those of white men, but there are suggestions of improvement. In most occupational categories the earnings of black women moved closer to those of white

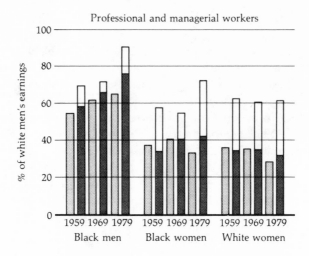

Professional and managerial workers

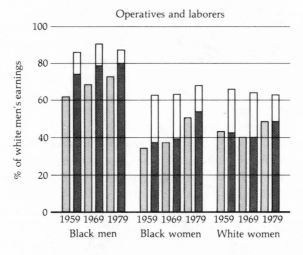

Operatives and laborers

▨ Actual earnings
■ Earnings assuming labor force characteristics
   of white men
☐ Earnings assuming characteristics and hours
   of white men

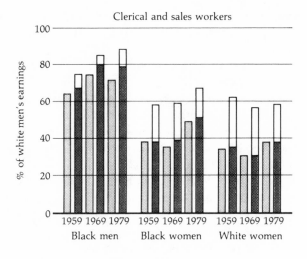

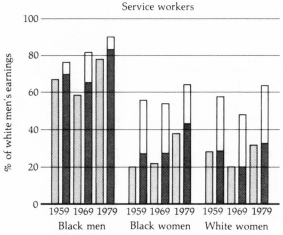

Figure 4.3. Actual and hypothetical earnings as a percentage of those of white men, 1959, 1969, and 1979, by occupation.

Source: same as for Figure 4.2.

men between 1959 and 1979. An exception is the professional and managerial category, where the discrepancy in earnings grew larger in the 1970s.

There is evidence that discrimination against black women declined. The hypothetical earnings of black women moved closer to the actual earnings of white men, a change that occurred because the rates of return associated with education and experience became more alike for the two groups. This process was not restricted to a few occupational categories; for black women, wage discrimination apparently decreased at all occupational levels.

White women show a different pattern from blacks of either sex. Once again, in all occupational categories and over the entire twenty-year period, a white woman who had the characteristics of the typical white man and worked just as many hours during the year could expect to earn about 60 percent as much as the white man. Racial differences in earnings have decreased at all occupational levels, but there has been no change in the sex difference among whites.

In 1960 black women who had white-collar jobs earned more money than white women with such jobs; in both 1970 and 1980 black women had an earnings advantage over white women in every occupational category. A major reason for this is that black women worked more hours per year than white women. However, the statistical models suggest that by 1980 black women were also somewhat more successful than white women in converting their educational attainment into earnings. Among professional and managerial women in that year, for example, an extra year of college added 61 cents to the hourly earnings of a black woman but only 51 cents to those of a white woman. Black men had no such advantage: a year of college was worth 69 cents per hour to a man of either race.

Title VII of the Civil Rights Act of 1964 called for equal employment opportunities and made it illegal to discriminate on the basis of race with regard to either employment or compensation. Any policy that would restrict opportunities for minorities or segregate them on the job was proscribed. It is impossible to measure the full impact of this law, but it is certain that the earnings of blacks in all major occupational categories, not just in the most prestigious ones, moved closer to those of whites. Detailed tabulations from the Census of 1980 may reveal that blacks have attained earnings equality with whites in some specific occupations, as Freeman's investigation implied. Substantial racial differences in earnings persist, however, and although discrimination has declined, it has not been eliminated. In any of the broad occupational classes in 1979, a hypothetical black man who had the education, labor market experience, and hours of employment of the typical white man earned only 90 percent as much as the white man.

Differences within Industrial Sectors

Several writers have observed that employment opportunities and earnings have improved for blacks because many more of them now work for the government. During the 1960s the number of blacks who held jobs rose by about 800,000. Almost 90 percent of that gain resulted from more employment in the government sector. For whites, only one-third of the increase in total employment was due to more government jobs (Wilson, 1978; U.S. Bureau of the Census, 1963c, table 22; 1973b, table 44). The availability of more positions in local, state, and federal governments meant that middle-class blacks could move into a much broader array of high-paying and secure white-collar jobs. The black man with a college degree was no longer restricted to the pulpit or the classroom.

Two quite different explanations have been advanced for the rise in government employment. Michael Brown and Steven Erie (1981) believe that the antipoverty programs of the 1960s were designed to provide minority workers with occupational skills, supposedly to enable them to move into better jobs in the private sector. By the mid-1970s, however, the approach of antipoverty programs shifted from training to income maintenance, and they did little more than supply the poor with cash or with in-kind benefits such as food stamps, school lunches, and housing allowances. Brown and Erie argue that blacks are greatly overrepresented among both the recipients and the administrators of these transfer programs. In their view, most of the gains in government employment for middle-class blacks came about because social welfare programs expanded. An unforeseen consequence of the War on Poverty, they contend, is a system of welfare colonialism in which middle-class blacks, as government employees, run programs for impoverished and dependent blacks.

Richard Freeman (1976) presents a different perspective, arguing that the political activities of blacks changed fundamentally in the 1960s. The Voting Rights Act of 1965 permitted blacks to cast ballots in southern states where they had not voted since Reconstruction. They rapidly became a decisive force. In the North, as blacks recognized the impact of their votes, new coalitions emerged, especially in large cities and industrial states, and the influence of blacks on elections increased. The number of blacks elected to public office increased fourfold between 1968 and 1980: from 1,125 to 4,890 (U.S. Bureau of the Census, 1973c, table 78; 1981f, table 821). As Glazer and Moynihan (1970) observe, in the realm of ethnic politics, blacks differentiate themselves from other groups. Having experienced much higher rates of unemployment, they have traditionally made a specific demand on their elected representatives: more jobs. Thus, one result of greater political power for blacks was an increase in their employment in the public sector. Freeman's investigation of the southern states demonstrated that as blacks voted in greater numbers their representation on government payrolls increased.

Many analysts believe that the labor market is not homogeneous but rather divided into distinct sectors. Sociologists and economists have devoted much effort to describing the "balkanization" (Kerr, 1954) of the labor market. One approach, dual labor market theory, suggests that jobs may be divided into two fundamental types (Gordon, 1972; Hodson and Kaufman, 1982). Jobs in the primary labor market offer high pay, security, chances for advancement, and many fringe benefits. Jobs in the secondary market offer low pay, often do not last long, and frequently provide no fringe benefits.

Presumably, workers classify themselves or are classified by employers as most appropriate either for jobs in the primary sector or for jobs in the secondary sector. Once classified, a person tends to remain in that type of work. Employers will hire persons for the primary jobs only if they think the workers possess the requisite skills, have good work habits, and will remain employed for a long period of time. White men who have career goals and head stable families are strong candidates for these primary jobs. Women who expect to quit in order to raise families, students who wish to work irregularly so they can attend class, and people with sporadic employment histories end up in secondary jobs.

Peter Doeringer and Michael Piore believe that blacks are overrepresented in these poorer jobs:

> Leisure time in low-income neighborhoods is frequently dominated by street-corner life, a life style widely prevalent among low-income people in general and in the black ghettos in particular. For the individual attached to the street, status and position in the world are defined by his group. His life has reality only in a group context; divorced from the group,

he is lonely and lost. The goal of group life is constant excitement . . .

The secondary labor market is attuned to street life in a way which primary employment is not. Its limited demands upon the individual permit continued participation on the street; when work schedules interfere with group activity, the individual simply skips work. Petty thefts and work disputes become stories of bravado. The piece-work payment system, found in some secondary jobs, permits the worker to choose his own work pace and, by adjusting compensation to productivity, helps to ensure that poor work habits do not unduly penalize the employer. Primary employment, in contrast, requires the individual to abandon street life and to conform to an ethical code which is not recognized on the street. (1971:175–176)

While these analysts classify jobs and their occupants, others focus on the industrial structure of the nation's economy. They also see the labor market as divided into distinct sectors, and they believe that the sectors are not equally advantageous to workers. Most often, these investigators distinguish core industries, which offer good jobs, from peripheral industries, which offer poorer jobs.

Entrenched in durable manufacturing, the construction trades and, to a lesser extent, the extraction industries; the firms in the core economy are noted for high productivity, high profits, intensive utilization of capital, high incidence of monopoly elements, and a high degree of unionization. What follows normally from such characteristics are high wages . . . Concentrated in agricultural, nondurable manufacturing, retail trade, and sub-professional services; the peripheral industries are noted for their small firm size, labor intensity, low profits, low productivity, intensive market competition, lack of unionization and low wages. (Bluestone et al., 1973: 28–29).

Union rules, skill requirements, geography, and discrimination may restrict access to jobs in the core industries. The less skilled, the less protected, the less educated, and the less lucky find jobs in the periphery. Not just earnings but also the pattern of careers differs between the two sectors (Beck, Horan, and Tolbert, 1978; Wallace and Kalleberg, 1979). Workers who enter core industries can expect regular wage increases and promotions. If they are treated unfairly, management or the unions will have formal grievance procedures. Workers who go into jobs in peripheral industries may be laid off at any time and will have almost no opportunities to advance. If they complain, they will be fired. Minimum wage laws and federal regulations to protect workers generally apply to core industries but provide exemptions for some employers in peripheral industries.

All of the investigators who present this view of the labor market recognize that there are good jobs and bad ones and that various barriers inhibit the free movement into good jobs. Good jobs lead to better jobs and thus to higher returns for labor market experience or for investments in education. Bad jobs lead nowhere in particular unless to other bad jobs and to unemployment. Minorities and women tend to occupy the least rewarding jobs, while white men are over-represented in the secure and high-paying jobs (Bonacich, 1976). The good jobs, which the dual labor market analyst would call jobs in the primary labor market, are most often found in the core industries; the bad jobs, or secondary labor market jobs, are frequently in peripheral industries.

THE DISTRIBUTION OF WORKERS AND WAGES BY INDUSTRIAL SECTOR

In order to determine whether blacks are underrepresented in the industrial sectors with the better jobs and overrepresented in the peripheral sector, I will once again describe black and white men and women aged 25–64 who were included in the 1960 census or the 1970 or 1980 survey. I will subdivide the economy into three productive sectors: core industries, peripheral industries, and government (Featherman and Hauser, 1978).

The government sector encompasses those working for federal, state, or local agencies, including persons employed at hospitals, universities, or power plants operated by governmental bodies. The occupations in this sector range from medical doctor to day laborer. For the nongovernment sectors, I use a scheme advocated by Elwood Beck and his associates to classify workers by industry. Core industries include most durable goods manufacturers and the utilities, transportation, communication, wholesale trade, and mining industries. Peripheral industries include farming, most nondurable manufacturing such as food processing and the needlework trades, retail sales, personal services, and entertainment industries (Beck, Horan, and Tolbert, 1978). Individuals are classified by the type of job they held in 1960, 1970, or 1980, but their reported earnings are for the previous year.[4]

Are white men especially likely to have jobs in core industries, where the best jobs are? Figure 4.4 shows the proportion of each group working in the three industrial sectors. White men are, indeed, well represented in core employment. When the 1980 survey was conducted, almost six out of ten white men held such jobs. For black men the proportion was somewhat lower: just over half had such jobs. Women are certainly underrepresented in core employment: in 1980 only 41 percent of the white women and 35 percent of the black were working in this sector. Men—and particularly white men—have quite an advantage with regard to core employment.

Between 1959 and 1979 employment in peripheral industries declined as fewer people raised farm products and as the number of women in domestic service plummeted. Throughout the period, however, white men were underrepresented—relative to blacks or women—in these industries. Government employment increased for all groups, but the rate of increase was unusually high for black women—the same group for whom decreases in peripheral employment and increases in core employment were most dramatic.

Figure 4.4 shows that from 1960 to 1980 the employment distribution of blacks and women became more like that of white men. Race and sex differences declined, especially for black women, who moved from doing housework to working in government offices. Some of the institutional barriers or discrimination that once made it difficult for blacks and women to get work in manufacturing, utilities, or construction industries may have disappeared during this twenty-year period.

Another question of interest is how wages differ by industrial sector. Is it true that workers in core industries earn more than those in the peripheral sector? Figure 4.5 shows the average hourly wage rates (in constant 1979 dollars) for 1959 and 1979 in the three sectors. Hourly wages, rather than annual earnings, are examined because the number of hours worked in a typical year differs greatly from one sector to another.

Wages are indeed low in the peripheral sector. In 1979 white men with such jobs earned $5.45 per hour, or $2.50 less than those working in core industries. Black women in peripheral industries in 1979 averaged just a bit more than the minimum wage of $2.90 per hour, but many of these women worked in agriculture or as domestic servants and therefore were not covered by the minimum-wage law. People

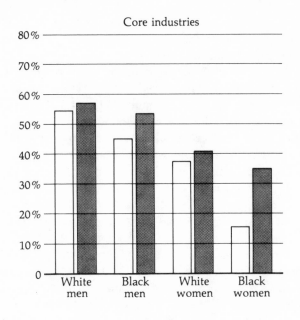

Core industries

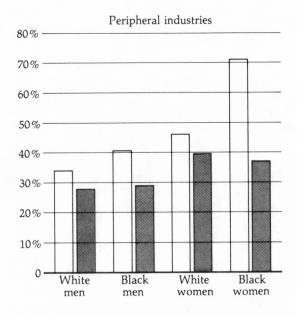

Peripheral industries

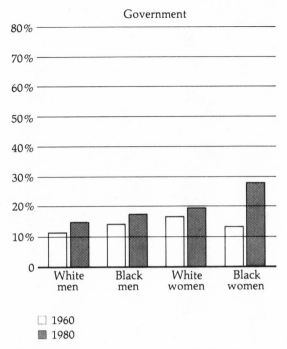

Figure 4.4. **Distribution of workers by industrial sectors, by race and sex, 1960 and 1980.**

Source: same as for Figure 4.2.

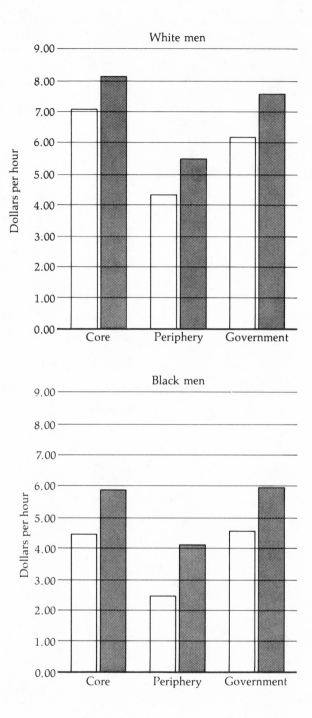

White men

Dollars per hour

| 9.00 | 8.00 | 7.00 | 6.00 | 5.00 | 4.00 | 3.00 | 2.00 | 1.00 | 0.00 |

Core   Periphery   Government

Black men

Dollars per hour

| 9.00 | 8.00 | 7.00 | 6.00 | 5.00 | 4.00 | 3.00 | 2.00 | 1.00 | 0.00 |

Core   Periphery   Government

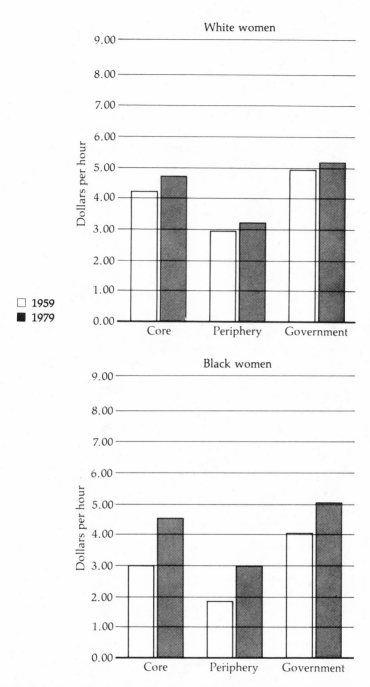

Figure 4.5. Hourly earnings by industrial sector, 1959 and 1979 (constant 1979 dollars).

Source: same as for Figure 4.2.

in peripheral industries not only report the lowest hourly wages but also tend to work the fewest hours per year, so they are at a double disadvantage.

The belief that wage rates are highest in core industries is accurate only for white men. In 1959 a white man working in one of those industries averaged almost a dollar more per hour than a white man working for the government; twenty years later the advantage was about 60 cents an hour. For all the other groups, wages were just a bit higher in the government than in the core industries. For instance, black women working for the government averaged about 52 cents more per hour than those in core industries.

WAGE GAINS WITHIN INDUSTRIAL SECTORS

Blacks have historically earned less than similarly qualified whites. One might expect that racial differences in wages would decline at different rates in the different sectors of the economy. For example, the increasing voting power of blacks might lead to the greatest declines in racial differences in the government sector. Figure 4.6 presents information about earnings for the period 1959–1979 for the three industrial sectors.[5] The format is the one that was introduced in Figure 4.1: for each year, the light gray bar represents the actual annual earnings of a group (in constant 1979 dollars) compared to those of white men; the darker gray bar measures what the group's earnings would be if they had the same characteristics as white men but their own rates of return; and the outlined extension of the second bar shows what members of the group would earn if they not only had the characteristics of white men but also worked as many hours.

For black men, actual earnings rose more rapidly than those of white men in each industrial sector: black men in core industries earned 64 percent as much as white men in 1979 compared to just 51 percent twenty years earlier. This is evidence of both a substantial racial gain and a large remaining racial difference. The smallest improvement was in the government sector, but throughout the period this was the sector in which the earnings of black men were closest to those of white men. A black man drawing a government pay check earned 73 percent as much as a white man in 1979, compared to 71 percent in 1959.

In 1961 President Kennedy issued Executive Order #10925, which decreed that private firms that sold to the federal government must not only hire and promote without regard to race but also adopt affirmative action plans. Presumably, this prompted firms in the core industries to pay equally educated or equally experienced blacks and whites the same wages (Smith and Welch, 1977; Welch, 1973; Burstein, 1979). Figure 4.6 indicates that in the government and in core industries black men who had the same characteristics and hours of work as white men had earnings that were closer to those of white men in 1979 than in 1959. Such changes suggest a substantial reduction in wage discrimination. But the same change occurred in peripheral industries, where firms are small in size and presumably less affected by affirmative action requirements since they seldom have federal contracts. Indeed, if you believe black men work fewer hours per year than white men largely out of choice rather than because employers discriminate, you will conclude that by 1979 there was little wage discrimination against black men in the peripheral sector. A black man who had the characteristics and hours of work of the typical white man earned 95 percent as much as the white man.

WOMEN

Once again, black and white women show very different earnings trends. The actual earnings of black women rose more rapidly than those of white men, although black women continue to earn much less than white men. The gap is most extreme in the peripheral industries, where in 1979 the earnings of black women were, on average, only 28 percent of those of white men. Black women's hypothetical earnings, computed by assuming they had the characteristics of white men but their own rates of return, also moved closer to the earnings of white men, indicating a decrease in wage discrimination.

Few changes were recorded among white women. Their earnings did increase, but no faster than those of white men; as a result, sex differences in earnings among whites remained just about constant. Throughout the twenty-year period, in both core and peripheral industries, a white woman who had as much education and experience as the typical white man and worked as many hours earned roughly 60 percent as much as the white man. White women in the government did slightly better.

By 1979 black women reached earnings parity with white women in all three industrial sectors. Figure 4.5 shows that the hourly earnings of black women still lag behind those of white women, although differences are now small. But, as pointed out earlier, black women

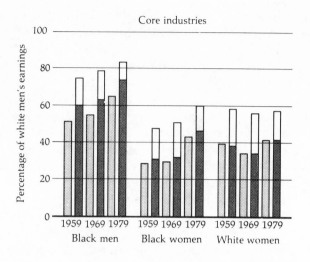

Core industries

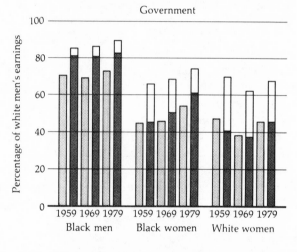

Government

▨ Actual earnings

■ Earnings assuming labor force characteristics
of white men

☐ Earnings assuming characteristics and hours
of white men

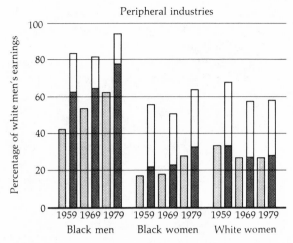

Figure 4.6. Actual and hypothetical earnings as a percentage of those of white men, 1959, 1969, and 1979, by industrial sector.
Source: same as for Figure 4.2.

work more hours than white women. In the government sector in 1979, for instance, black women averaged six more hours per week on the job than white women.

Perhaps the government is more of an equal opportunity employer than private firms. Consider just employees with two years of college who have been in the labor force for a decade, work full time, and live in southern cities. Their annual earnings in 1979 fell below those of similar white men in the three sectors as follows:

	Core industries	Peripheral industries	Government sector
Black men	−16%	−13%	−14%
Black women	−37	−35	−27
White women	−33	−31	−25

All three groups come closer to white men in earnings in government jobs than in the core industries. Women of both races also come closer in government than in the peripheral industries. It may be that the civil service regulations of federal and local governments allow managers little discretion to vary salary by race or sex and thus keep wage discrimination relatively low.

This is not a declaration that there are no discriminatory pay practices in federal or local government. Even in the government, a black or a woman can expect to earn less than a white man with similar qualifications. Patricia Taylor (1979) analyzed civil service data on the earnings of civilian federal employees in 1977. After taking into account many factors that influence earnings, such as occupation, place of residence, age, and years of federal employment, she found that white men earned considerably more than black men or women of either race.

At the beginning of this section I mentioned analysts who argue that economic improvements among blacks have come about largely because of government employment and others who contend that segmentation in the labor market reserves many of the better jobs for white men while isolating blacks and women in dead-end jobs. I have found only limited support for these views. It is true that, compared to white men, blacks and white women are underrepresented in core industries where wages are high and overrepresented in peripheral industries where wages are low. But over time, patterns of representation have changed as blacks and white women have moved into the core industrial sector.

Blacks and women are also quite well represented in government employment. Between 1960 and 1980 government employment increased more rapidly than private-sector employment; the proportion of all workers holding government jobs rose from 12 to 17 percent (U.S. Bureau of the Census, 1963a, table 206; 1982d, table P-3). This shift augmented the earnings of blacks, but it is easy to overestimate its consequences. In 1980 only one black worker in five was employed by a federal, state, or local agency.

During this twenty-year period the earnings of blacks moved closer to those of whites in all industrial sectors. This change in earnings is much more important than the shift into government employment in accounting for the rising earnings of blacks. In 1959 black men earned 50 percent as much as white men; in 1979 they earned 65 percent as much. Approximately one and a half points of that fifteen-point gain may be attributed to the changing industrial distribution of black men; that is, the shift from peripheral industries to the government or to core industries. Approximately twelve points of the gain are attributable to higher earnings of black men within each of the sectors. For black women, changes in industrial distribution played a larger role. In 1959 black women's earnings averaged 21 percent of those of white men; in 1979, 40 percent. Of that nineteen-point improvement, eight points are attributable to the shift away from the peripheral industries and into the government and the core industries. But for both men and women, the major reason for higher earnings among blacks is the upgrading of wages, not the shifting distribution of workers.

Regional Differences

At the national level, the earnings of blacks rose more rapidly than those of whites and racial discrimination in wage rates declined. Did this occur in all regions or only in certain parts of the country? The status of blacks compared to that of whites has historically been least favorable in the South, and surveys report that southern whites hold the most conservative racial attitudes (Taylor, Sheatsley, and Greeley, 1978). On the one hand, southern blacks might make the smallest gains, since white opposition to black progress may be greatest in that region. On the other hand, blacks in the South might make large gains since they were so far behind at the beginning.

Freeman (1976), examining trends in income, was impressed both by the rapid contraction of racial differences in the South and by the large gap that still existed. Michael Reich (1981) also noted unusually large gains in income for blacks in the South and found only meager evidence that the incomes of blacks went up any faster than those of whites in the North and West. The overall improvement for blacks, he argued, came about largely because blacks migrated away from the South and because southern blacks moved toward income parity with whites.

To investigate regional trends, I classified individuals by their place of residence. Figure 4.7 shows the hourly earnings in each region for 1959 and 1979. For all groups and in both years, it was costly to live in the South. In 1979 white men in the South earned eighty cents per hour less than men in the North Central region, which was next lowest. The regional gaps were particularly large for blacks. In 1959 black men outside the South earned two dollars more per hour than those in the South, a difference that helps to explain why so many blacks moved away from the region.

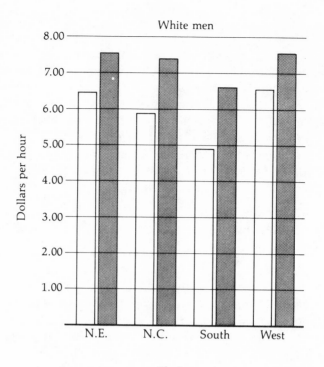

White men

Dollars per hour

8.00
7.00
6.00
5.00
4.00
3.00
2.00
1.00

N.E.　　N.C.　　South　　West

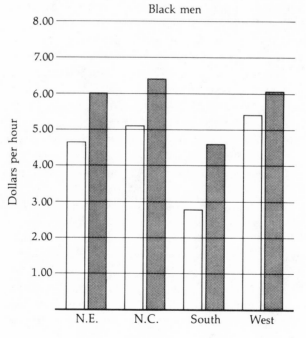

Black men

Dollars per hour

8.00
7.00
6.00
5.00
4.00
3.00
2.00
1.00

N.E.　　N.C.　　South　　West

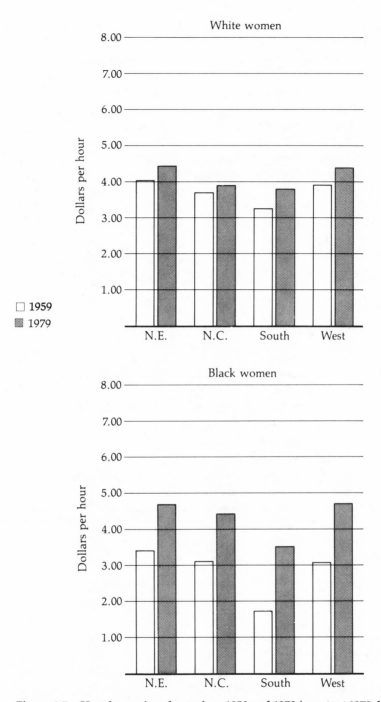

Figure 4.7. Hourly earnings by region, 1959 and 1979 (constant 1979 dollars).
Source: same as for Figure 4.2.

In the two decades after 1959, wages went up faster in the South than elsewhere. Regional differences in earnings decreased as a result, but the South remains the region with the lowest wages.[6] Persistent racial differences are also evident among men: by 1979 there was only one region—the North Central—in which black men earned as much per hour as white men had twenty years earlier.

Using the approach introduced earlier in this chapter, Figure 4.8 compares the actual annual earnings of black men, black women, and white women in 1959, 1969, and 1979 to those of white men. Next it indicates how much the members of each group would earn if they had the educational attainment and labor force experience of the typical white man but their own rates of return, and finally how annual earnings would compare if they not only had the characteristics of white men but also worked the same hours.

BLACK MEN

The earnings of black men increased more rapidly than those of white men in all regions, but the gains were greatest in the South. Between 1959 and 1979 in the South, the earnings of black men rose from 47 percent to 64 percent of those of white men. Despite this improvement, black men—relative to white—are still least prosperous in the South and most successful in the North Central region.

Apparent racial discrimination in earnings decreased in all regions, but the timing of change differed by area. In the South, the amount black men would earn if they had the characteristics of white men but their own rates of return moved closer to the actual earnings of white men, suggesting that the net cost of being black was declining in both decades. Improvement was also recorded in both decades in the North Central area, but in the West and Northeast black men gained far more in the 1960s than in the 1970s.

WOMEN

The actual earnings of black women rose faster than those of white men in both decades and in all four regions. And yet in spite of improvement, black women in all parts of the nation still earn only a small fraction of what white men earn. In 1979 black women were most prosperous in the West, but even there they averaged only 46 percent as much as white men; in the South they earned just one-third as much. The hypothetical earnings of black women, assuming they had the education, years of experience, and hours of employment of white men but their own rates of return, indicate decreases in apparent wage discrimination. Unlike the situation for black men, improvements were recorded for black women in both decades and in every region.

Once again, there was little change in the relative earnings of white women. In all three survey years and in all regions, they earned about one-third as much as white men. Their hypothetical earnings, assuming they had the characteristics of white men and worked as many hours but had their own rates of return, were about six dollars for every ten dollars earned by a white man. This also was true in every region. Nowhere in the country did the apparent cost of being a woman decline among whites.

During the 1960s black women attained earnings parity with white women in every region outside the South, primarily because they worked more hours than white women. In 1970 their hourly earnings lagged behind those of whites, but by 1980 black women everywhere but in the South earned more per hour than white women (see Figure 4.7). The analysis suggests that neither black nor white women were highly rewarded for years of experience but that black women had a higher rate of return for educational attainment than did white women.

I began this section by asking whether racial gains occurred in all regions and whether improvements for blacks came about largely because they migrated out of the low-wage South. Undoubtedly, the shifting residences of blacks played a role in raising their earnings: the proportion of blacks living in the South fell from 57 percent in 1960 to 50 percent twenty years later. But geographic change was not the major reason for their improved economic status. The earnings of black men rose from 50 percent of those of white men in 1959 to 65 percent in 1979, and only about three points of that fifteen-point gain may be attributed to changes in regional distribution. In all regions, the earnings of blacks went up faster than those of white men and the apparent cost of racial discrimination dropped. Factors such as the push for civil rights, the changing attitudes of whites, the Civil Rights Act of 1964, the Equal Employment Opportunity Commission, and numerous court decisions had effects throughout the nation and were much more important than changing geography in accounting for the higher earnings of blacks.

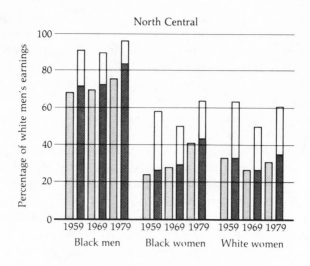

North Central

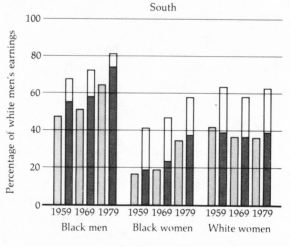

South

☐ Actual earnings
■ Earnings assuming labor force characteristics
   of white men
☐ Earnings assuming characteristics and hours
   of white men

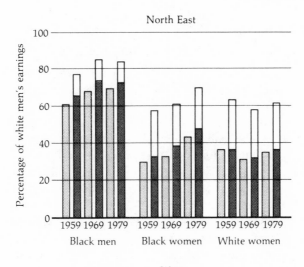

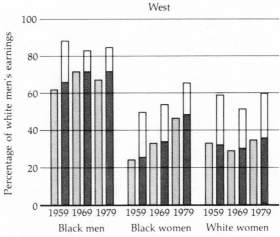

Figure 4.8. Actual and hypothetical earnings as a percentage of those of white men, 1959, 1969, and 1979, by region of residence.

Source: same as for Figure 4.2.

Earnings and Age

The earnings of blacks became more like those of whites during the 1960s and 1970s. Did this happen for all age groups, or did the improvement occur primarily because young blacks entering the labor force earned just as much as their white counterparts?

There are two possible kinds of change in racial earnings patterns: period changes and cohort changes. Suppose an employer, either intentionally or out of a lack of awareness, permitted discriminatory job assignments and pay practices. In the early 1960s he might have hired college-educated black men to unload boxcars, and perhaps his black and white employees who actually did similar work had very different job titles and wage rates. With the emergence of the civil rights movement, the adoption of new federal laws, and the threat of costly litigation, the employer became aware of those discriminatory policies which had led to much higher wages for whites. Perhaps he issued an order that inequitable racial differences be immediately eliminated. Perhaps the firm examined the educational attainment, years of experience, and job qualifications of all workers and found that many blacks should be reclassified and have their pay raised while many whites should be given less prestigious jobs and smaller salaries. If the firm carried out such adjustments all at once, racial differences in earnings would decline for workers of all ages in that one year. This is called a period effect, because racial differences decrease in a specific period for all age groups.

Many firms probably found it difficult or impossible to rectify all of the differences at once. Seniority provisions, union regulations, and many other practices may have sorted black and white workers into different job classifications and different pay scales. Changing all this immediately might trigger strikes, cause many resignations, and lead to immense problems for management. Rather than changing the wages of long-term employees, the employers may have decided to treat *new* workers equitably. Under such a policy, younger black and white workers would earn similar wages but the white advantage among older workers would not diminish. This type of change is called a cohort pattern, because racial differences decline from one entering cohort of workers to the next but not for all age groups simultaneously. Racial parity in earnings will be attained much more slowly if change occurs on a cohort basis than if it occurs on a period basis.

Many investigators believe that racial changes in earnings occur chiefly on a cohort basis. That is, young blacks and whites who enter the labor market are paid more equitably than those who started working before the Civil Rights Act called for equal pay. James Smith and Finis Welch (1977) argue that this is the case and that a major reason for the higher earnings of young blacks is the improved quality of black education. Edward Lazear (1979) agrees about the cohort change but offers a different explanation. He contends that the Civil Rights Act of 1964 and the efforts of the Equal Employment Opportunity Commission led employers to pay the same wages to entering blacks and whites, but that firms would provide more on-the-job training to white men and continue with other policies that advanced the wages of whites beyond those of their black peers. Because of this, he argues that the wage gains for blacks recorded in the late 1960s and early 1970s were illusory.

PERIOD CHANGE

To determine whether period change or cohort change is a better explanation of the improvements in black earnings, I first examine period changes in earnings from 1960 to 1970 and from 1970 to 1980. Persons employed in 1959, 1969, or 1979 were classified by age.[7] As before, I begin by comparing the actual earnings of black men, black women, and white women to those of white men, then calculate hypothetical relative earnings on the assumption that these groups have the characteristics of white men but their own rates of return, and finally assume they also work as many hours as white men but keep their own rates of return. The results are presented in Figure 4.9.

Black men. The actual earnings of black men show improvement in both decades. Black men aged 25–34 earned 50 percent as much as their white age-mates in 1959, 56 percent as much in 1969, and 71 percent as much in 1979. The actual earnings of men aged 35–44 show a similar pattern of improvement in both intervals. For the two older groups, however, relative earnings went up in the 1960s but not in the 1970s. The 1960s were years of improvement for all black men, but in the 1970s the gains were much larger for men under 45 than for older men.

Estimating how much black men would earn if they had the educational attainment, regional distribution, and hours of employment of white men but their own rates of return, and comparing this amount to the earnings of white men, gives an estimate of the cost of being black. This analysis yields evidence against the period explanation of

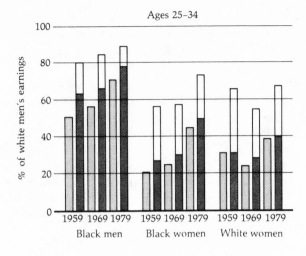

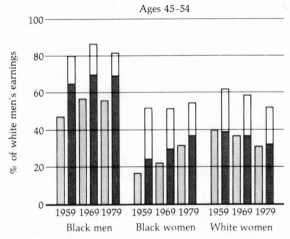

☐ Actual earnings
■ Earnings assuming labor force characteristics
   of white men
☐ Earnings assuming characteristics and hours
   of white men

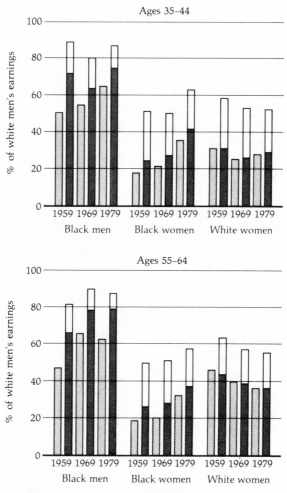

Figure 4.9. Actual and hypothetical earnings as a percentage of those of white men, 1959, 1969, and 1979, by age.

Source: same as for Figure 4.2.

decreasing discrimination. Because the racial earnings gap narrowed in both decades for men aged 25–34 but not for older men, I conclude that discrimination declined on a cohort basis rather than on a period basis.

Women. The evidence from the earnings of black women also suggests that the cohort explanation is better than the period one. The actual earnings of black women increased more rapidly than those of white men in every age group, even though a substantial difference remains. The hypothetical earnings of black women also rose more rapidly than the actual earnings of white men for the younger age groups, demonstrating a lessening of discrimination. The reduction in discrimination was much smaller at the older ages.

White women, again, fared rather poorly. At the older ages, their wages fell further behind those of white men and the apparent cost of sex discrimination in earnings went up. This fact is difficult to reconcile with the social and legal changes that occurred during this period. I stressed in Chapter 3 that a difficulty in the analysis of women's earnings is that there are no adequate measures of actual years of employment or of seniority with one employer. It could be that a sizable proportion of white women who were 45 and over in 1960 had worked for their entire lives and were career-oriented and that by 1980 this age range included many white women who had returned to the labor force after raising a family. The average employment experience of older white women may be lower than it was in the past.

COHORT CHANGE

If racial changes in earnings occur on a cohort basis, then blacks who start out earning less than whites should remain behind whites for the rest of their careers. In such a situation, it will take a very long time to eliminate racial differences. Once a young group of blacks reaches earnings equality with white men—and Figure 4.9 shows that this has not yet happened—we will have to wait until they come to the end of their working lives for there to be parity at all ages.

The data in Figure 4.9 can be rearranged to show the relative earnings of birth cohorts, that is, people born within ten-year intervals. Presumably, the members of a birth cohort enter the work force at about the same time; thus it is possible to describe changes in the earnings of the same group of individuals as they grow older. The first panel in Figure 4.10, for example, shows earnings trends for people who were born in the period 1905–1914. They were at ages 45–54 in 1960 and 55–64 in 1970. The same birth cohorts in the surveys of 1960, 1970, and 1980 may not necessarily contain the same people. Some who worked in 1960 retired or died before the next census, and a few individuals in these birth cohorts began their occupational careers in the 1960s.[8] There are no data on what these people earned when they were 25–34 or 35–44 in 1940 or 1950.

If the cohort explanation of racial change is correct, the heights of the bars in Figure 4.10 should remain the same as birth cohorts move from one decade to the next. If black men 25–34 in 1960 earned 50 percent as much as white men, they should also have earned 50 percent as much at ages 45–54 in 1980.

Black men. The actual earnings of black men went up faster than those of white men for every birth cohort and in both decades. In other words, there was a "period" change during both the 1960s and 1970s; the earnings of black men in all birth cohorts moved closer to those of white men as they got older. This was brought about by such things as the shifting regional distribution of blacks and the movement away from low-wage employment in peripheral industries. It cannot be attributed to changes in educational attainment, because most people complete school by age 25, the minimum age for inclusion in this sample.

The story is more complicated for discrimination in wage rates. Here the evidence supports the view that discrimination was primarily reduced on a cohort basis. Consider black men born between 1925 and 1934. If they had had the characteristics of white men and worked as many hours but had their own rates of return, at ages 25–34 they would have earned 80 percent as much as white men. At ages 35–44 and 45–54, their hypothetical earnings were still 80 percent of those of their white age-mates. The actual earnings of black men went up a little faster than those of white men for these cohorts, but the cost of being black remained pretty much the same.

Women. Similar conclusions apply to the earnings of black women. As birth cohorts aged, their actual earnings rose more rapidly than those of white men, but the apparent cost of wage discrimination to each cohort remained just about constant.

The earnings of white women showed little improvement relative to those of white men. The cost of sex discrimination among whites actually increased with age. This does not mean that the earnings of

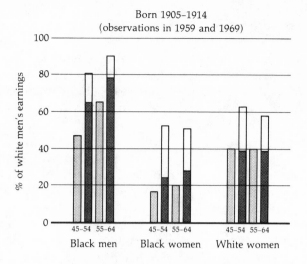

Born 1905–1914
(observations in 1959 and 1969)

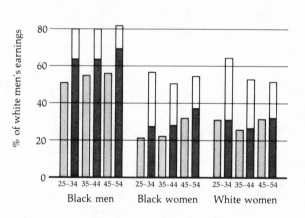

Born 1925–1934
(observations in 1959, 1969, and 1979)

Actual earnings

Earnings assuming labor force characteristics
of white men

Earnings assuming characteristics and hours
of white men

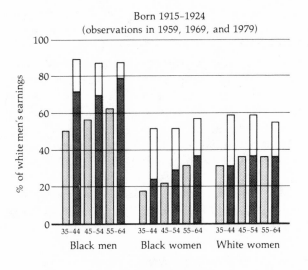

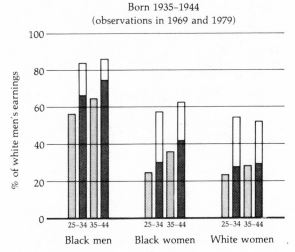

Figure 4.10. Actual and hypothetical earnings as a percentage of those of white men, 1959, 1969, and 1979, for birth cohorts.
Source: same as for Figure 4.2.

white women will necessarily always lag far below those of white men; there is some evidence of a very small change on a cohort basis. In 1980 white women 25–34 had actual earnings about 39 percent as much as white men, and sex discrimination apparently cost them an amount equal to 33 percent of the earnings of white men (these data are not shown in Figure 4.10). Twenty years earlier, young white women earned only 31 percent as much as white men and sex discrimination cost them an amount equal to 35 percent the earnings of white men. Perhaps future cohorts of white women who enter the labor force will report earnings closer to those of their white male age-mates.

Figure 4.10 indicates that the earnings of blacks definitely do not fall further behind those of whites as they get older. Lazear (1979) argued that the improvement in the earnings of blacks was temporary because civil rights laws forced employers to pay young blacks and young whites identically; he expected a widening racial gap as cohorts aged. If this were the case, the actual earnings of blacks relative to those of whites would decrease as cohorts got older. In fact, exactly the opposite occurs.

It is impossible to accept exclusively either the period explanation or the cohort explanation of racial change. With regard to the actual earnings of blacks, the period explanation seems more appropriate: the earnings of black men and black women rose more rapidly than those of white men for most age groups during both the 1960s and 1970s. These findings are consistent with those of other studies in reporting that as birth cohorts grow older the earnings of blacks and whites become more similar (Haworth, Gwartney, and Haworth, 1975; Freeman, 1976).

The apparent cost of racial discrimination in wage rates shows a different pattern, one that is more consistent with the cohort explanation. The cost of being black, once you have entered the labor market, does not decline very much as you grow older. Once a racial—or sexual—difference in earnings is established, it persists—perhaps because of seniority provisions and the many other techniques used to sort individuals into different types of jobs.

For policy reasons, it is extremely important to know how racial changes in earnings occur. The Civil Rights Act of 1964 and the lawsuits that followed were designed to eliminate inequitable practices that kept the earnings of blacks or women below those of similarly qualified white men. The evidence in this section suggests that only a little progress was made in eliminating such practices among workers who were well into their job careers in the mid-1960s. Racial differences have been reduced largely because blacks and whites who have entered the labor force recently have more similar earnings than do those who started working two, three, or four decades ago (Duncan and Hoffman, 1983). This implies that the approach to a racial or sexual parity in earnings will be a slow one. It will be particularly slow because there are still racial and sexual gaps in the earnings of young workers. In 1980, among those 25–34 who had the labor force characteristics and hours of employment of white men, black men earned 90 percent as much as white men, and women of both races earned about 70 percent as much. New and different strategies will be required if racial and sexual differences in earnings are to be eliminated quickly and for all age groups.

Have Any Blacks Caught Up in Earnings?

The absence of racial difference is often newsworthy, because it is taken as evidence that our society is truly color-blind. For example, Moynihan (1972) believed that the income of black husband-wife families outside the South in which both spouses worked was approaching that of similar white families. He took this as evidence of declining discrimination. Freeman (1976) drew a similar conclusion from his finding that in some specific occupational categories black workers made as much as whites.

It is one thing to find that small groups of elite blacks such as Oscar winners, star athletes, or doctors of nuclear physics earn as much as similar whites. We would have greater confidence that discrimination is declining if we found that large groups of blacks earn as much as whites. This chapter reported that recent economic gains were greater for highly educated blacks than for others and that improvements were quite large among young blacks. To test whether the highly educated blacks who have joined the labor force since the civil rights revolution earn as much as whites, I compared the actual hourly earnings of blacks and whites who were 25–34 in 1960, 1970, or 1980. Table 4.1 gives the information for four educational levels.

The earnings of highly educated young black men have not yet reached parity with those of similar whites, but they are clearly moving in that direction. Back in 1960 college-educated young blacks earned 74 percent as much per hour as similar white men; in 1980 they earned

Table 4.1. Hourly earnings of blacks as a percentage of those of whites, for men and women classified by education, persons aged 25–34 in 1960, 1970, or 1980.

	1960	1970	1980
Men			
Two years high school	68%	78%	77%
Four years high school	65	73	82
Two years college	70	76	89
Four years college	74	79	96
All educational levels	63	71	81
Women			
Two years high school	70%	99%	99%
Four years high school	70	104	104
Two years college	81	113	105
Four years college	93	122	105
All educational levels	66	88	98

Source: same as for Figure 4.2.

Note: Data gathered in 1960, 1970, and 1980 refer to earnings in the previous year. Estimates of hourly wages were developed for the model that regressed log of hourly wages on years of elementary and secondary schooling, years of college, and region of residence.

96 percent as much. In other words, a black man who finishes college can now expect to earn almost as much per hour as a white man. Moving down the educational scale, the actual earnings of young blacks fall further behind those of similar whites. Black women, by contrast, reached earnings parity with white women during the 1960s. For more than a decade young black women who have finished high school have had hourly earnings at least as high as those of similarly educated white women.

Conclusions

In this chapter I determined which blacks benefited most from the economic changes of the 1960s and 1970s. Earnings for almost every group of blacks rose more than earnings for comparable whites. To be sure, the improvements in earnings were greater for those with at least a high school education and for the young, but in fact the earnings of blacks improved compared to those of whites at all occupational levels, in all sectors of the economy, and in all regions. It is a distortion to claim the benefits went only to highly skilled or young blacks.

The apparent cost of racial discrimination in wage rates also decreased throughout the nation and in all sectors of the economy. The analysis of birth cohorts, however, suggests that if black workers begin their occupational careers earning less than similarly qualified white workers they may continue to earn less throughout their careers. Racial differentials in wages are reduced by paying new black and white workers similar amounts more than by altering the wages of people who are well along in their careers.

Almost without exception, gains in earnings and reductions in apparent wage discrimination have been greater among black women than among black men. Sexual differences in earnings, however, have not changed in the same way as racial differences. For almost all groups of white workers, the actual earnings of women have done no more than keep pace with the earnings of men, and the apparent cost of sex discrimination in wage rates among whites did not decline between 1960 and 1980.

PROGRESS OF BLACK WOMEN

In the past, black women faced the double problem of racial and sexual discrimination. Apparently this is no longer the case. Black women have nearly caught up with white women in school enrollment and educational attainment, and the change in the occupational distribution of black women has been more substantial than that of white women. By 1980 black women had hourly earnings just a bit below those of white women. The earnings models show that black women earned at least as much as white women with similar labor market characteristics, implying the absence of racial discrimination in the wage rates of women. Since black women typically work more hours per year than white women, their annual earnings now are higher.

Is it possible that racial discrimination in this society has declined while sexual discrimination, at least in the area of wage rates, has not changed? Or is there something unique about black women that explains why their earnings have risen rapidly? It is possible to pinpoint three factors that may explain the changing economic status of black women. First, black women are much more likely than white women to be the chief breadwinners in their families. In 1980, for example,

10 percent of the white women aged 25–64 but 33 percent of the black headed their own families (U.S. Bureau of the Census, 1981d, table 2). Economic necessity may lead black women to obtain those specific types of education which are highly rewarded by employers. The need to support their families may also make black women more likely to maximize their earnings even if to do so they must work in the middle of the night, in remote locations, or at unattractive but high-paying jobs.

Second, there may be an advantage to being a black woman in the contemporary labor market. The Equal Employment Opportunity Commission must certify that firms with federal contracts comply with guidelines about the representation of women and minorities on their staffs. After being accused of discrimination, many large employers and governmental agencies have been ordered by courts to hire minorities and women or have signed consent decrees to avoid further litigation. The appointment or promotion of a black woman simultaneously moves an employer toward two goals. This may increase the demand for black women and should decrease discrimination.

Finally, it is possible that attitudes toward blacks have changed more rapidly in our society than attitudes toward women. Burstein (1979) looked at responses over a thirty-year period to questions such as these:

> "Do you think Negroes should have as good a chance as white people to get any kind of job or do you think that white people should have the first chance at any kind of job?"

> "Do you approve of paying women the same salaries as men if they are doing the same work?"

> "Do you approve of a married woman earning money in business or industry if she has a husband capable of supporting her?"

By the late 1970s most people endorsed equal treatment for both blacks and women, but the pace of change over time was faster where racial equality was the issue. If an employer pays a white woman less than a white man who performs similar work, he may not be aware of the discrepancy. He may erroneously assume that they are doing different work, perhaps because he has assigned them different job titles. However, paying a black woman less than a white man who does similar work may be recognized as possible racial discrimination. The white woman could accuse her employer of sexual discrimination, but the black woman could charge both sexual and racial discrimination. Since passage of the Civil Rights Act of 1964, employers may have become more sensitive to racial discrimination than to sexual discrimination.

5

The Welfare of Families and Individuals

The information about earnings presented in the previous chapters clearly demonstrates economic gains for all groups of black workers during the 1960s and the 1970s. Two frequently cited indicators of the economic status of blacks are the ratio of black to white family income and the proportion of blacks falling below the poverty line. For both black and white families, earnings are the major source of income, constituting about 80 percent of total income (U.S. Bureau of the Census, 1981c, tables 2 and 38). Thus the convergence in the earnings of black and white workers might be expected to bring the incomes of black families closer to those of white families. Furthermore, poverty might be expected to decrease more among blacks than among whites. But the actual changes in family income and poverty are not consistent with these expectations. The economic welfare of black families, compared to that of white families, did improve in the 1960s but did not in the 1970s, even though the wages of black workers continued to rise more rapidly than those of whites.

The top half of Figure 5.1 traces the median income of black families as a proportion of that of white families—that is, the ratio of the median income of black families to that of white families—from 1950 to 1982. If the ratio of black to white median family income increases, most people assume that blacks are making economic progress and that racial differences are declining. If this ratio gets smaller, most people assume that the economic status of blacks is deteriorating.

Because of the increasing relative earnings of blacks, one might expect a linear trend toward a higher ratio of black to white family income. The data certainly do not fulfill that expectation. One might also expect that in times of high economic growth the ratio of black

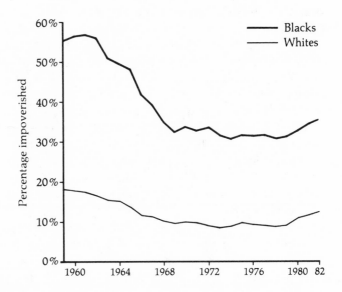

Figure 5.1. Ratio of black to white median family income, 1950–1982, and proportion impoverished, 1959–1982.

Source: U.S. Bureau of the Census, *Current Population Reports*, ser. P-60, nos. 97, 124, 125, 127, and 140. (Data for years before 1967 refer to whites and nonwhites.)

to white family income would rise. This also has not happened.[1] Instead, during the 1950s the ratio of median family incomes improved very little. Between 1959 and 1970 the economic status of black families improved, as the ratio rose from 52 to 61 percent. Trends in the 1970s were very different, however. After the 1973–75 recession, the ratio of black to white median family income gradually decreased. In 1982, black families had average incomes about 55 percent of those of whites. This implies that the economic status of black families, compared to white, was just about the same in the early 1980s as in the early 1960s.

I have repeatedly stressed that it is important to consider both the relative standing of blacks and the absolute gap that separates them from whites. The absolute racial difference in family income assesses the difference in purchasing power. This measure reveals even less evidence of gains for blacks. If the median incomes of black and white families increase at about the same rate, the absolute racial gap in income will get wider, because white families start out with larger incomes. This happened during the 1950s: the racial difference in purchasing power (measured in constant 1979 dollars) grew from $4,700 to $6,800. Even during the prosperous 1960s, when the income of black families rose more rapidly than that of whites, the racial gap increased, reaching $7,400 in 1970. This gap continued to widen during the 1970s. In 1982 the typical black family had a median income $8,300 below that of whites (U.S. Bureau of the Census, 1983b, tables 2 and 3). This finding contrasts with the declining racial gap in the earnings of employed workers.

The bottom half of Figure 5.1 reports the proportion of black and white individuals who were impoverished. Since 1959 the Bureau of the Census has estimated the extent of poverty by comparing a family's or household's income before taxes to a minimum financial requirement—the poverty line. This requirement depends upon a family's size and place of residence and is adjusted annually for inflation. Money income from all sources including welfare benefits is considered, but other types of income such as food stamps, subsidized housing, or school lunches are excluded. In 1982 a family of four fell below the poverty line if its income was less than $9,900 (U.S. Bureau of the Census, 1983b).

During the 1960s, poverty was substantially reduced among both blacks and whites. The proportion of blacks who were poor declined from 55 percent in 1959 to 32 percent in 1969. There was little change during the 1970s; throughout that decade about one-third of the black population was impoverished. Poverty began to increase at the end of the 1970s, and in 1982 36 percent of blacks fell below the poverty line. Because of population growth, the actual number of poor blacks rose substantially, from 7.5 million in 1970 to 9.7 million in 1982 (U.S. Bureau of the Census, 1983b, table 15). Among whites, the rate of poverty was just about constant at 9 percent throughout the 1970s, but increased to 12 percent in 1982.

There appears to be a mystery here. In the 1970s earnings rose considerably faster for black workers than for white workers, but black families did not improve their income status relative to white families, and the number of blacks in poverty increased. One major reason for this is that the living arrangements of adults and children changed. Among both races, the households with the highest incomes and lowest rates of poverty are those which include a husband-wife family. Families headed by women typically report low incomes, and the majority of blacks in female-headed families are below the poverty line (U.S. Bureau of the Census, 1983b, table 15). If there had been no change in the family living arrangements of blacks between 1970 and 1980, economic gains for black families in the 1970s would have been much more like those of the 1960s, and the changes in family income would have been similar to those of white workers.

The ratio of black to white family income is the most widely used statistic describing the economic welfare of blacks. It is important to consider the dramatic changes that are occurring in family living arrangements, because they have a great impact upon family income. Later in this chapter I will suggest that per capita income is a more revealing measure than family income, since it reflects how many people share the monies a family receives. Quite important in the 1970s was the decline in family size, which raised per capita income among both races.

Changing Living Arrangements

If a man earns a large salary and supports his family or if a couple both earn salaries and support their children, quite likely they will be prosperous. If, however, a woman has to provide for herself and her children without benefit of a husband's paycheck, her financial situation will likely be precarious. She may not be able to work many hours, and, as indicated in the previous chapters, even if she works as long as a man does she will earn less.

Four major trends over the period since 1960 have had important implications for family income and poverty. First, people have tended to marry at later ages and the proportion of marriages ended by divorce has increased rapidly. As a result, the typical adult now spends more years as a single person before marriage and many live as separated or divorced persons after their marriage ends. Second, a larger fraction of women head their own families rather than living in husband-wife families or with other relatives. Additionally, the characteristics of families headed by women have changed, and they are now much more likely to include young children (Rawlings, 1980; Bianchi and Farley, 1979). Third, an increasing proportion of children are born to unmarried women: in 1980 it was about one birth in six in the United States (U.S. National Center for Health Statistics, 1982, table 15). Finally, the proportion of children who live with both of their parents has declined, and there has been a corresponding rise in the proportion of children who live with their mother but not with their father. These trends are evident in both the black and the white communities. However, the pace of change has been much greater among blacks, especially during the 1970s, and this has had a substantial effect upon the relative income levels of black families.

MARITAL STATUS

Because of advances in the age at which people marry and rises in divorce, a decreasing proportion of adults are wives or husbands at any given time. The decennial census and the Current Population Surveys provide information about marital status. Individuals aged 15 and over are classified as either single, currently married, widowed, or divorced. The currently married group is classified into two categories: married-spouse-present and married-spouse-absent. Some couples in the latter group may be living apart for employment reasons or because of military service, but in most cases the separation is a prelude to the termination of the marriage.

The marital status of the adult population for years between 1950 and 1982 is shown in Figure 5.2. These data have been standardized for age, so the changes shown do not come about because of shifts in age composition. Three major differences in marital status distinguish the races. First, blacks now typically delay getting married to an older age than whites. In recent decades age at first marriage has gone up much more for blacks than for whites: in 1950, 32 percent of white and 31 percent of nonwhite women aged 20–24 were not yet married; in 1982 the corresponding figures were 55 percent for white

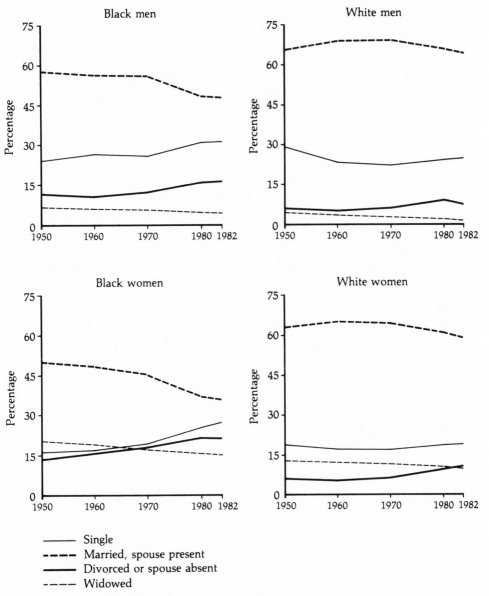

Figure 5.2. Marital status of persons aged 15 and over, by race and sex, 1950–1982 (data standardized for age).

Source: U.S. Bureau of the Census, *Census of Population: 1950*, PC(1), table 104; *Census of Population: 1960*, PC(1)-1D, table 176; *Current Population Reports*, ser. P-20, nos. 212 and 365. (Data for 1959 and 1960 refer to whites and nonwhites.)

women and 72 percent for black women (U.S. Bureau of the Census, 1953, table 102; 1983c, table 1).

Second, blacks who marry experience higher rates of marital dissolution than whites. Although death rates for all groups are quite low at the young adult ages, those for blacks are about one and one-half to two times as high as those for whites, implying that a higher proportion of black marriages are terminated by death (U.S. National Center for Health Statistics, 1980, table V–1). At current rates, if a couple marries when both are 25 and the wife survives to age 50, the chances that her husband will die in the intervening period are 8 in 100 for whites and 17 in 100 for nonwhites.

The rate of marital dissolution by discord—divorce, separation or desertion—is also roughly twice as great for nonwhites as for whites. For example, in the 1965 and 1970 National Fertility Surveys, about 5 percent of the white couples and 10 percent of the nonwhite couples who had a fifth wedding anniversary ended their marriage before their tenth anniversary (Thornton, 1978). Within the first fifteen years of marriage, about half of the first marriages of blacks were dissolved, compared to about one-fourth of those of whites (McCarthy, 1978). The higher rate of marital dissolution for blacks does not reflect a racial difference in economic status or in age at first marriage; the same differential of about two to one was evident at all educational levels and among women who married at various ages.

Third, black and white married couples differ in what they typically do after they separate. Whites are much more likely than blacks to obtain a divorce. In the 1973 National Survey of Family Growth, about nine out of ten white couples who separated obtained a divorce within five years, but only half that proportion of black couples did so (McCarthy, 1978). This difference has implications for remarriage after the first marriage ends. In data gathered in the National Fertility Survey, two-thirds of the white women but only one-third of the nonwhite women whose first marriage ended by discord or death remarried by the time of the survey (Thornton, 1977). Again, this appears to be a racial difference rather than one attributable to economic standing or age at marriage. At all educational levels, for all ages at marriage, and regardless of the number of children, whites were about twice as likely as nonwhites to remarry.

The outcome of these trends in age at marriage, marital stability, and remarriage is illustrated in Figure 5.2. The proportion who have never married, that is, who are single, has risen throughout this period for blacks. It has also increased among whites during the 1970s.

This increase, which reflects the tendency of young people to defer their first marriage, has been much greater among blacks.

Racial differences in the proportion of adults who are married and live with their spouses are now large. In 1950 half of the nation's nonwhite women lived with husbands, but by 1982 this proportion had fallen to 36 percent. For black men the change was from 58 percent living with a wife to 48 percent. We sometimes think that the overwhelming majority of adults are married and live with their spouses. But now only a *minority* of adult blacks are in this situation: just over a third of black women are married and living with a husband. Among whites, meanwhile, the proportion who were married with a spouse present rose a bit between 1950 and 1970 and declined thereafter. Throughout the three decades it was much higher for whites than for blacks.

The proportion who were divorced or married but not living with their spouses shows a corresponding trend in the opposite direction. By 1982 one black woman in five was either divorced or separated. There has been a similar trend toward more marital disruption among whites, but the proportion who were divorced or separated is half as great for whites as for blacks.

Figure 5.2 also reveals that changes in marital status were more substantial in the 1970s than in the previous two decades. For example, the proportion of black women who were single went up about three percentage points between 1950 and 1970 but then rose six points in the following decade as the age at first marriage increased sharply. Similarly, the shift away from living as a wife was much greater after 1970 than earlier. Changes in marital status among whites were also more substantial after 1970 than before (Cherlin, 1981).

BIRTHS BY MARITAL STATUS OF THE MOTHER

There has been a major change in childbearing in the United States in the last three decades: a growing proportion of children are born to women who are not married. At the end of World War II about one birth in twenty-five was to an unmarried woman; by 1980 it was one birth in six (Grove and Hetzel, 1968; U.S. National Center for Health Statistics, 1982, table 15). The trends differ by race, and since the mid-1970s more than half of the nation's black births have been to unmarried women.

Figure 5.3 shows trends in the proportion of total births occurring to unmarried women. The data about legitimacy status may not be

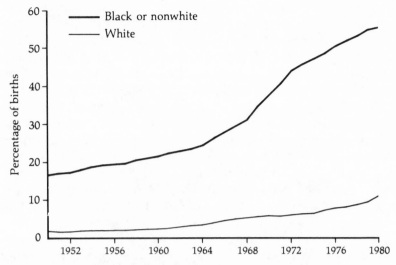

Figure 5.3. Percentage of total births delivered to unmarried women, by race, 1950–1980.

Source: U.S. National Center for Health Statistics, *Vital Statistics of the United States: 1977*, vol. I, table 1–31; *Monthly Vital Statistics Report*, vol. 29, no. 1, supplement; vol. 30, no. 6, supplement 2. (Data for years before 1969 refer to whites and nonwhites.)

of high quality and should be viewed with caution; only forty-one states and the District of Columbia currently ascertain the marital status of mothers. On the basis of data from reporting states, national estimates are developed of births to married and unmarried women. Few studies have investigated the accuracy of reporting or whether there are racial differences in the extent to which legitimacy status is misreported (Clague and Ventura, 1968).

The available figures suggest a large racial difference in the proportion of total births occurring to unmarried women but show a similar trend over time. The percentage illegitimate among whites was just under 2 percent in 1950, 6 percent in the late 1960s, and 10 percent a decade later. Among blacks (data for years before 1969 refer to nonwhites) the proportion of births that were to unmarried women went from 17 percent in 1950 to about 32 percent in the late 1960s and to 55 percent in 1980.

Figure 5.3 might give the impression that unmarried women are bearing children at a much higher rate than ever before. Actually, the rate at which unmarried black women had children declined during the 1970s. The rise in the proportion of births illegitimate came about for many reasons. One important cause is the deferral of marriage. If the birth rates of both unmarried and married women remain the same over time but women put off getting married, the proportion of births illegitimate will go up, because the typical woman will have many more years in which to have an illegitimate child and fewer years to bear a legitimate child.

Another reason for the increase in the proportion of children born to unmarried women has to do with premarital pregnancy. A substantial fraction of both black and white women are pregnant when they first marry—but fewer pregnancies lead to quick marriage today. Through the mid-1960s, the proportion of premarital pregnancies resulting in births that led to marriage before the baby was born was 80 percent for white women and just under 50 percent for black women. After 1970, however, the frequency with which premarital pregnancies led to marriage dropped sharply. In the late 1970s under 70 percent of the white and under 33 percent of the black premarital pregnancies were followed by a quick marriage (U.S. Bureau of the Census, 1978c, table 16).

THE LIVING ARRANGEMENTS OF CHILDREN

A growing proportion of marriages are dissolved by divorce and an increasing proportion of children are born to unmarried women. As a result, children are now less likely to live in a household with both their parents and more likely to live with their mother only.

Data from the decennial censuses and from the annual surveys of population provide information about the living arrangements of children under age 18. Figure 5.4 shows the proportion of children living with both their parents—either natural or adoptive parents—the proportion living with their mother but not their father, and the proportion living with neither parent. These data have been standardized for age of children to take changes in age distribution into account.

Observe, first, that among both races the proportion living with both parents has declined since 1960 while the percentage living with their mother only has increased. For both races, the proportion in the latter status just about doubled in the two decades after 1960, with most of the increase coming in the 1970s. The proportions were much

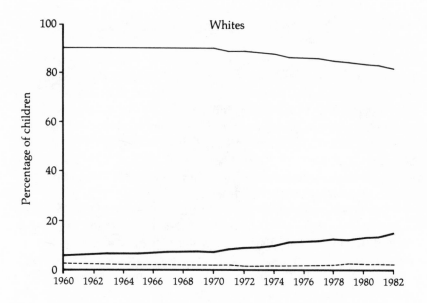

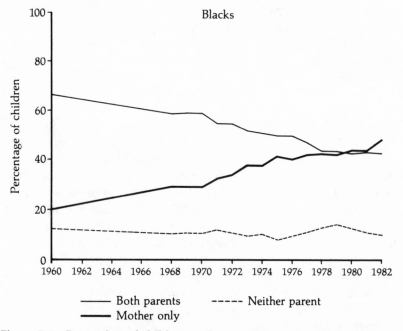

———— Both parents   ----- Neither parent
———— Mother only

Figure 5.4. Proportion of children under age 18 in various living arrangements, by race, 1960–1982.

Source: U.S. Bureau of the Census, *Census of Population: 1960*, PC(2)-4B, tables 1, 2, and 19; *Current Population Reports*, ser. P-20, nos. 187, 198, 212, 225, 242, 255, 271, 287, 306, 323, 338, 349, 365, and 372. (Data for 1960 refer to whites and nonwhites. Data for 1961–1967 are estimates.)

higher among blacks, however: by 1982 there were more black children living with their mother only (47 percent) than living with both parents (42 percent) (U.S. Bureau of the Census, 1983c, table 3).

Second, there is a very large and increasing racial difference in the living arrangements of children. Throughout the period the proportion of children living in traditional households with two parents was much greater for whites than for blacks. In 1960, 90 percent of the white and 66 percent of the black children lived with both parents—a racial difference of twenty-four points. By 1982 it was 81 percent of the white children and 42 percent of the black—a difference of thirty-nine points.

The proportion of children living with their father but not their mother (not shown in the figure) changed very little in this interval: it was about 1 percent of the white and 2 percent of the black children. Similarly, there was only a modest change in the proportion who live with neither parent. There is, however, a substantial racial difference in this indicator of family stability. About 2 percent of the white but 12 percent of the black children live in households that include neither their mother nor their father.

Racial differences in the living arrangements of children come about for two primary reasons. First, a much higher proportion of black than white children are born to single women. By 1982 about one black child in five was living with a mother who had never married; among whites, about 2 percent of the children under age 18 were living with a mother who had never married (U.S. Bureau of the Census, 1983c, tables 4 and 5). Second, because of racial differences in rates of remarriage, black children who experience marital disruption are much more likely than similar white children to remain living with their mother only. Using data from the 1973 Family Growth Survey, Larry Bumpass and Ronald Rindfuss found that after a marriage ended the mothers of almost two-thirds of the white children remarried within five years and the mothers of 85 percent remarried within ten years. Thus the mother-only family is a temporary one for whites. But for black children, the mothers of only 18 percent remarried within five years, and the mothers of only one-third remarried within ten years. The majority of black children who experience marital disruption never return to a two-parent family (Bumpass and Rindfuss, 1979).

The traditional stereotype of family life in the United States held that young adults marry in their early twenties, have children after they marry, maintain their own homes, and raise their children in these homes. Presumably, the husband is the major breadwinner and provides for the economic security of this stable family. Such a description may have characterized American families in the past, but the changes summarized in this chapter unambiguously indicate a shift away from such a family system (Cherlin, 1981). Many people now put off marriage until their mid or late twenties. Current rates suggest that more than half of the marriages occurring in the 1970s will end in divorce (Preston and McDonald, 1979; Weed, 1980). A growing proportion of women conceive and bear their children outside of marriage. Increasingly, children are raised in households that include their mother but not their father.

All these shifts away from the traditional family system have been greater among blacks than among whites. As a result, blacks and whites are becoming increasingly different with regard to all aspects of their family living arrangements.

Family Income

In the 1970s the earnings of black workers rose faster than those of whites but the ratio of black to white family income fell. I have described changes in the living arrangements of children and adults in order to account for this discrepancy between trends in earnings and trends in family income. A measure such as average family income reflects both income levels and types of families. Families that include a husband-wife couple, for example, report much higher incomes than families headed by women. Because of changes in fertility and living arrangements, the share of all families headed by women, rather than by married couples, has gone up sharply. Among blacks 21 percent of the families were headed by a woman in 1960; 41 percent in 1982. Among whites the corresponding change was from 8 to 12 percent (U.S. Bureau of the Census, 1963d, table 4; 1983d, table 1).

Before examining income trends for specific types of families, I need to be specific about what a family is and how income is measured.

DEFINING A FAMILY

The Bureau of the Census defines a family as two or more individuals who share a housing unit and are related by blood, marriage, or adoption (U.S. Bureau of the Census, 1983d). A family is called a

husband-wife family if both partners of the married couple live together in the housing unit. Families headed by a female contain a
woman who is living with one or more relatives but not with her
husband. The overwhelming majority of these families headed by
women—89 percent among blacks and 87 percent among whites in
1982—include a woman who lives with her children, but a few of
them consist of two sisters or an aunt and her niece (U.S. Bureau of
the Census, 1983d, table 3).

In addition to husband-wife and female-headed families, there are
a small number of families headed by a man who lives with relatives
but not with a wife. This may be a father living with his children or
two or more brothers sharing an apartment. In 1982 about 3 percent
of all white families and 5 percent of all black families had "other
male" heads (U.S. Bureau of the Census, 1983d, table 1). Because
these types of families are rare, data are not shown for them in this
chapter.

Not everyone, of course, lives in a family. Some people live in
barracks, dormitories, prisons, or other group quarters; others live
alone or with nonrelatives. Nevertheless, economic trends among
families do describe the welfare of the bulk of the population: 87
percent of the black population and 91 percent of the white lived in
families in 1982 (U.S. Bureau of the Census, 1983d, tables 1 and 24).

MEASURING INCOME

Every March, as part of the Current Population Survey, the Bureau
of the Census asks the residents of some 65,000 sample households
detailed questions about their income during the previous year. This
survey defines as income all wages and salaries; any after-expense
income from a business enterprise or a farm; monetary transfer payments such as Social Security checks, welfare assistance, unemployment compensation, and veteran's benefits; and interest, royalties,
dividends, child support payments, alimony, and annuities. Only
persons aged 15 and over are asked about their income, so income
obtained by those under 15 does not appear in the data.

Several kinds of receipts are not counted in the income statistics;
they probably affect people at opposite ends of the income scale.
Capital gains from the sale of securities or property are not included.
Neither are noncash transfer payments such as food stamps, rent
supplements, or subsidized school lunches.

Users of these data must be concerned about their accuracy and completeness. Since census data are confidential and cannot be used to initiate tax investigation, respondents have no motive to misreport their income. But some individuals refuse to provide any data about their income and others give only partial information. About 4 percent of the people contacted in the March 1980 survey answered none of the income questions, and 27 percent answered some but not all the questions (U.S. Bureau of the Census, 1981g:212). Income figures are imputed to these respondents using information about their characteristics such as their place of residence, educational attainment, and occupation. This probably does not bias our knowledge of general trends, but it must overestimate the cash income of some families and underestimate that of others.

There is also a tendency to underreport income, perhaps because certain sources are easily forgotten. A number of studies have compared the amounts of income counted by the Census Bureau to independent estimates. For instance, the Social Security system provides estimates of total wages, and the Internal Revenue Service can estimate self-employment income from businesses and farms. The most important sources of income are, apparently, quite accurately reported. Estimates of wage and salary income and Social Security benefits obtained by the Census Bureau are at least 95 percent as large as the independent estimates of the same sources. For welfare benefits, retirement income from private pension plans, and unemployment compensation, the Census Bureau's estimates are only 75 to 80 percent as high as the independent estimates. Other types of income, including interest payments, dividends, and workman's compensation, are even less accurately reported.

Wages and salaries account for about four-fifths of all income in the United States. Since they are reported quite completely, we can estimate that about 90 percent of the cash income people receive is reported in these surveys. Census Bureau surveys make no distinction between legal and illegal income, so receipts from drug sales, prostitution, and criminal activities should be included, although it is impossible to know if such income is reported.

I will analyze the most complete and detailed income statistics available. They probably give a faithful picture of the pattern of income levels, but they may underestimate total income by as much as 10 percent. The amounts I will discuss include welfare payments and unemployment compensation, but are not adjusted for tax payments. That is, I am dealing with monetary income before taxes.

CHANGES IN FAMILY INCOME

During the 1960s and the early 1970s, the income (in constant dollars) of both black and white families rose. There were, however, substantial differences by race, by type of family, and by decade. In brief, the income of husband-wife families increased much more rapidly than that of female-headed families, and gains were greater in the 1960s than in the 1970s. Figure 5.5 shows trends in the median incomes of black and white families of different types for the period 1959–1981.

A useful way to summarize a decade's economic trends is in terms

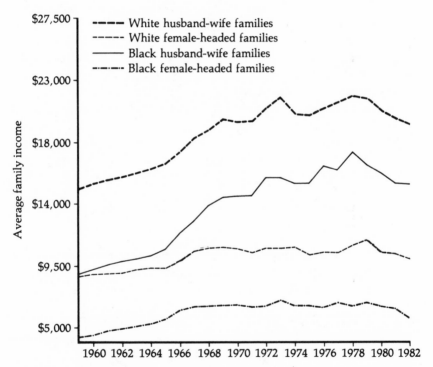

Figure 5.5.   **Median income of families, by race and family type, 1959–1982 (constant 1979 dollars).**

Source: U.S. Bureau of the Census, *Census of Population: 1960*, PC(1)-1D, table 224; *Current Population Reports*, ser. P-20, nos. 155, 168, and 175; ser. P-60, nos. 47, 51, 53, 59, 66, 75, 80, 85, 90, 97, 101, 105, 114, 118, 123, 129, and 140. (Data for 1959 refer to whites and nonwhites. Data for 1960-1963 are estimates.)

of the average annual rate of increase in income. I calculated rates of change in family income for two periods: 1959–1969 and 1969–1979. The results of these calculations are shown in Figure 5.6. Again, these annual rates involve constant-dollar amounts, so we can be certain that a positive growth rate means that families have greater purchasing power.

The information in Figures 5.5 and 5.6 leads to several conclusions about family income. First, at all dates, income levels were greatest in white husband-wife families and lowest in families headed by black women. Second, for both races incomes increased quite persistently from 1959 through the 1973–75 recession, but there have been few improvements in the income of total black families or total white

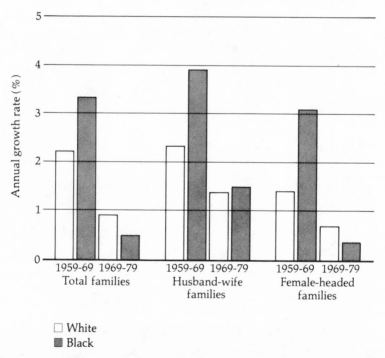

☐ White
▨ Black

Figure 5.6. Average annual growth rate of total family income, by race and family type, 1959–1969 and 1969–1979 (constant 1979 dollars).
Source: same as for Figure 5.5; also U.S. Bureau of the Census, *Census of Population: 1960,* PC(2)-4B, table 4B; *Current Population Reports,* ser. P-20, nos. 218 and 356. (Data for 1959 refer to whites and nonwhites. Data for 1960–1963 are estimates.)

families since then. Indeed, there has been a decline in income since the late 1970s, and in the early 1980s families had purchasing power equivalent to that of comparable families about fifteen years earlier. Third, among both races income levels increased at a much higher rate in husband-wife families than in female-headed families. In fact, income levels continued to go up in both black and white husband-wife families after the 1973–75 recession.

At the beginning of this chapter I observed that median income increased more rapidly for white families than for black in the 1970s, a reversal of the trend of the 1960s. Figures 5.5 and 5.6 reveal that the story is a complicated one. Figure 5.6 indicates the average annual growth rate of total family income and the incomes of both husband-wife and female-headed families for the periods 1959–1969 and 1969–1979. During the 1960s the incomes of both types of black families rose more rapidly than those of comparable white families. Thus it is not surprising that the income of total black families went up more than that of total white families: 4.2 percent per year for blacks, 2.8 percent for whites. In the 1970s the income of black husband-wife families increased faster than that of white husband-wife families. Families headed by black women also experienced a rise in income, albeit at about the same rate as similar white families. This means their purchasing power was greater at the end of the 1970s than at the beginning. For total black families, however, median incomes were smaller in 1979 than a decade earlier. This came about because an increasing proportion of all black families are the low-income families headed by women. If there had not been such a major shift in family composition among blacks in the 1970s, the income of total black families would have at least kept up with that of total white families. Changes in family living arrangements had the effect of substantially reducing all the indicators of economic welfare that are based on total families.

PER CAPITA INCOME

Although the ratio of black to white median income for total families is often cited to describe the status of blacks, the measure is a complicated one, and, as the previous section illustrates, changes over time are strongly influenced by the choices people make about their families. This measure also fails to take into account changes in family size.

An income of $18,000 provides much more financial security if it is shared by three persons than if it is divided among six or seven. Black families are typically larger than white families. Thus a comparison of family income is misleading unless it takes into account differences in family size. In 1980, for example, the total incomes of black families were 64 percent of those of white families, but on a per capita basis they were only 56 percent of those of whites. Focusing on total family income overstates the prosperity of black families; even if black families achieve total incomes equal to those of white families, their economic status will remain below that of whites because their families are larger. For these reasons, I will examine a more realistic indicator of financial welfare—per capita income. Figure 5.7 shows trends in per capita income and Figure 5.8 shows average annual rates of change in per capita income.

Trends in per capita income are quite different from those for median family income. Both total family income and per capita income went up more rapidly in the 1960s than in the 1970s, but the change from one decade to the next was much smaller for per capita income. As noted earlier, there were few gains in median income after the 1973–75 recession. But clear improvements are evident when per capita income is the yardstick of economic prosperity: on this measure, families were improving their financial status in both decades. The gains in the 1970s occurred primarily because the number of persons sharing income declined. During the 1960s there were almost no changes in family size, but the effects of falling fertility rates and new living arrangements became evident in the next decade. During the 1970s the size of the average black family decreased from 4.3 to 3.7 persons; among whites the change was from 3.5 to 3.2 persons (U.S. Bureau of the Census, 1971, table 1; 1981h, table 1).

The information about specific types of families reveals that per capita purchasing power rose at a fairly substantial rate in the 1970s except for families headed by white women. Taking changes in family size into account, black families—both those with a married couple and those headed by a woman—continued to gain on similar white families during the 1970s just as in the previous decade. The decrease in family size was an important factor helping to improve income levels in the 1970s. Since family size declined more among blacks, their per capita income rose more rapidly.

Families headed by white women had an unusually low rate of income growth in both decades. While a complete explanation of this is beyond the scope of this book, Chapter 3 indicated that the earnings of white women rose slowly compared to those of black women or

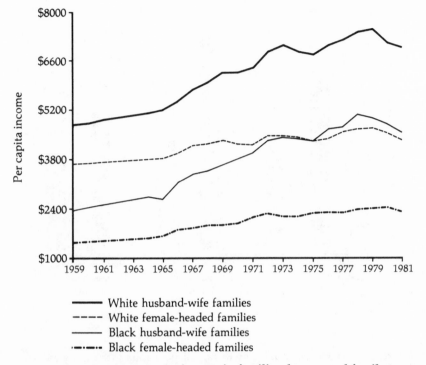

Figure 5.7. **Average per capita income in families, by race and family type, 1959–1981 (constant 1979 dollars).**
Source: same as for Figure 5.5; also U.S. Bureau of the Census, *Census of Population: 1960,* PC(2)-4B, table 48; *Current Population Reports,* ser. P-20, nos. 139, 153, 164, 173, 191, 200, 218, 223, 246, 258, 276, 291, 311, 326, 340, 352, and 366. (Data for 1959 refer to whites and nonwhites. Data for 1960-1963 are estimates.)

men of either race. Among women who headed their own families, the earnings of blacks increased about 60 percent between 1959 and 1975 while those of whites went up only 15 percent (Bianchi, 1980). Furthermore, the size of families headed by white women declined much less than that of families headed by black women.

The trends in per capita income indicate clear economic gains in the 1960s and 1970s for both races. Furthermore, per capita income has gone up more rapidly in black than in white families: between 1959 and 1979 this measure of real purchasing power rose 85 percent for blacks, 50 percent for whites.

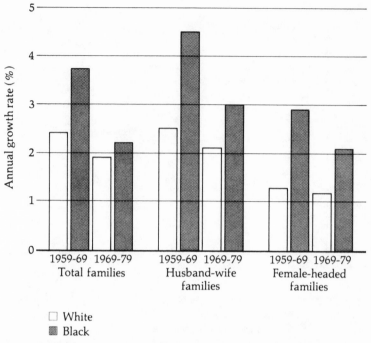

Figure 5.8. Average annual growth rate of per capita income, by race and family type, 1959–1969 and 1969–1979 (constant 1979 dollars).
Source: same as for Figure 5.6

A variety of factors influence per capita income. Wages, for instance, have risen. But there has been a shift away from the type of family with the highest incomes—husband-wife families—toward the type with the lowest incomes—families headed by women. At the same time, family size has decreased, leading to higher per capita income.

I measured the separate effects of these different reasons for a change in income. For the periods 1959–1969 and 1969–1979, and for both races, I determined how much of the change in per capita income was caused by higher income per family, the changing distribution of families by type, and changes in family size. Figure 5.9 indicates how much per capita income would have increased or decreased if only each specific factor had changed. (The components do not sum

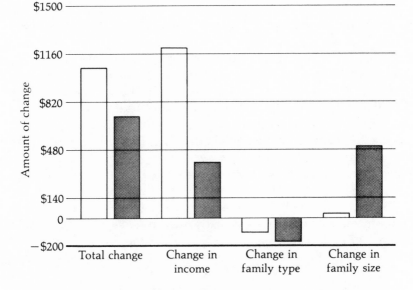

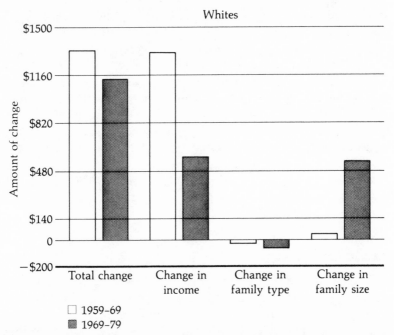

Figure 5.9. Total change in per capita income and components of change attributable to changes in income, changes in the distribution of families by type, and changes in family size, 1959–1969 and 1969–1979.

Source: same as for Figure 5.7.

to the total change because I do not present information about inter-action effects.)

Although the rate of increase in per capita income was greater for blacks than for whites in both decades, the actual change in income was greater for whites. In the 1960s per capita income went up about $1,400 for whites, $1,000 for blacks; in the 1970s it rose by $1,100 for whites, $800 for blacks. For both races, the improvements in per capita income were greater in the 1960s than in the 1970s. In the 1960s, most of the gain for both races came about because of higher incomes. The wages of men and women increased and the labor force participation of women went up, leading to higher incomes for families.

The picture for the 1970s is strikingly different. The continued growth in the income of families, particularly husband-wife families, explains about half of the increase in per capita income for both races. But declines in family size also played an important role; indeed, among both races this factor was more important than the rise in the amounts of money families received. One of the chief ways families maintained or increased their economic well-being during the 1970s was by re-ducing fertility. The changing distribution of families by type had the opposite effect, limiting the growth of per capita income. This factor was also most important in the 1970s. The rise in the proportion of families headed by women had especially great consequences among blacks. The proportion of blacks living in husband-wife families fell from 57 percent in 1970 to 50 percent in 1980, while the propor-tion in families headed by women rose from 28 to 35 percent (U.S. Bureau of the Census, 1971, table 1; 1981h, tables 1 and 3; 1982b, table 3). Had these changes not occurred, per capita income for blacks living in families would have gone up by $884 rather than by $714.

Income Inequality

One of the confusions in analyzing racial trends is that some measures clearly suggest that blacks are making progress while other measures are equally clear in indicating that the status of blacks is getting worse. Looking at family income trends from one perspective implies there have been continuing improvements in the economic status of blacks, but a second look from another perspective implies that blacks are falling further behind whites.

Let us begin with the more optimistic data. If the income of black families goes up more rapidly than that of whites, average black income becomes a larger and larger proportion of white income. This has been happening. Figure 5.10 shows per capita income in black families as a percentage of per capita income in white families. Data are reported for total families, husband-wife families, and families headed by women.

Using the ratio of black to white per capita income as a measure yields convincing evidence that blacks are catching up with whites. In 1959 the per capita income of all black families was 47 percent that of white families; in 1970, 54 percent; and in 1980, 56 percent. Per capita income levels rose especially rapidly in black husband-wife families, so that by 1980 their per capita income was two-thirds that of similar white families. The smallest gains were recorded for families headed by women, but even in this group there is some evidence that blacks are gaining on similar whites. Per capita income in black female-headed families was only 40 percent of that of white families in 1959, 51 percent in 1969, and 53 percent in 1980. Much more progress was made in narrowing the gap in the 1960s than in the 1970s, but all of these indicators imply an improvement in the economic status of blacks relative to that of whites.

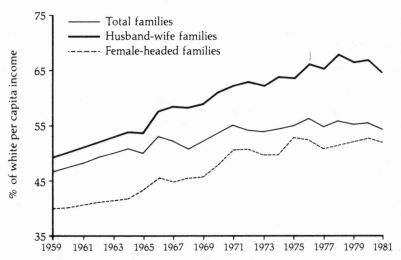

Figure 5.10. Per capita income of black families as a percentage of that of white families, by family type, 1959–1981.
Source: same as for Figure 5.7.

PER CAPITA PURCHASING POWER

I concluded in Chapter 3 that in some cases, even though the earnings of black workers went up faster than those of white workers, the actual racial gap in earnings grew wider. This was because the smaller growth rate of whites was applied to a much larger base amount. A similar pattern is evident for income. Both total family income and per capita income have grown at a higher rate among blacks (see Figures 5.6 and 5.8), yet the racial difference in per capita income was larger when President Reagan took office than when President Eisenhower completed his term. In terms of purchasing power, blacks not only are failing to catch up with whites, they are falling further behind.

Information about racial differences in purchasing power is shown in Figure 5.11. The per capita income figures for each type of family are compared to those for white husband-wife families—the most prosperous group. For all black families, per capita income was $2,500 less than that of white husband-wife families (in constant 1979 dollars) in 1959, $3,000 less in 1970, and $3,300 less by 1980. Stated differently,

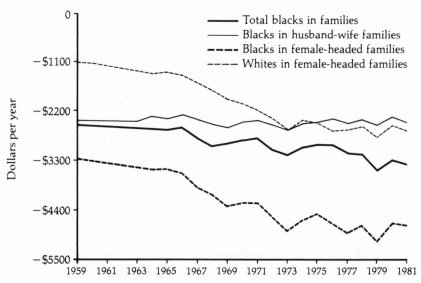

Figure 5.11. Gap in per capita income separating specified types of families from white husband-wife families, 1959–1981 (constant 1979 dollars).
Source: same as for Figure 5.7.

in 1959 these white families had about seven dollars more to spend on every family member each day than did black families. Despite economic progress and many obvious racial gains, the advantage for whites twenty years later was about ten dollars each day for every member of the family.

Although the per capita income of black husband-wife families grew faster than that of similar white families, the racial gap in per capita purchasing power for these families remained about the same: both in 1959 and in 1980, white husband-wife families had about $2,500 more to spend per person than did black husband-wife families.

One type of income discrepancy increased dramatically: the purchasing power of families headed by women fell further behind that of husband-wife families (Bianchi and Farley, 1979). Families headed by black women are in an especially disadvantageous position. In 1980, these families had about $15 less per person to spend each day than did white husband-wife families.

An identical trend is evident for white families headed by women. Their per capita fell from $1,100 behind that of white husband-wife families at the start of this period to $2,700 behind at the end. Families headed by women are becoming less well off in comparison with husband-wife families within both the black and white communities. This disparity will probably continue to grow, because per capita income increased more rapidly in husband-wife families in both decades and for both races.

This chapter presents a possibly bewildering array of measures of the economic status of black families. An analyst who believes conditions are getting either much better or much worse can find a widely accepted index to prove the point. Let me stress several conclusions about the status of blacks.

First, all measures indicate that improvements were greater before the 1973–75 recession than after. Furthermore, the most recent recession may be another turning point; most indicators of welfare trends turned down in the period 1979–1982.

Second, comparing the median income of all black families to that of all white families gives a misleading picture of trends because of the shift away from the traditional husband-wife family. The change in family composition was greater among blacks than among whites and greater after 1970 than before.

Third, for assessing the welfare of families, it is most appropriate to examine trends in the per capita income of the specific types of families. For twenty years after 1959, per capita income rose for both blacks and whites in both husband-wife and female-headed families. Economic conditions were improving, and the standard of living, at least in monetary terms, got better. The rates of gain—for both husband-wife and female-headed families—were greater for blacks than for whites. This is an indication of racial progress; a continuation of this trend will inevitably lead to a black-white convergence. A major reason for the rise in per capita income in the 1970s was the decline in family size.

Fourth, as stressed in Chapter 1, the analysis of racial trends is often confounded by the issue of whether relative or absolute gains of blacks are most important. When actual racial differences in per capita purchasing power are examined, there is little evidence that the gap separating blacks from whites narrowed, since the gap in purchasing power remained just about constant: about $2,400 per capita each year for those in husband-wife families and $2,200 for those in female-headed families (see Figures 5.7 and 5.11). Per capita income went up faster in black families than in white families, but the racial difference in purchasing power stayed the same.

Poverty

As noted earlier in this chapter, poverty decreased during the 1960s, and the improvements were greater among blacks than among whites, but during the 1970s there was little change in the proportion of the population who fell below the poverty line. Before examining trends in racial differences in poverty, I will explain how poverty is measured.

Each year the Bureau of the Census uses data from its March survey to compute a family's or a person's total cash income. If this pretax amount falls beneath the poverty line, the family or individual is classified as impoverished. Thus, the extent of officially recognized poverty depends upon what is counted as income and what is designated as the poverty line. In 1955 the Department of Agriculture found that families typically spent about one-third of their income for food. In 1961 that agency developed several nutritionally adequate diets and determined the minimum it would cost to purchase this food. This amount was then multiplied by three to determine the poverty line. The amount allowed for food varied by size and type of family. The 1961 poverty lines were made appropriate for other years by adjusting the dollar amounts by the annual Consumer Price

Index. Thus the same basic poverty levels have been used for more than twenty years.[2] In 1982 an urban family of two parents and two children was considered impoverished if its cash income was less than $9,862 (in current dollars) (U.S. Bureau of the Census, 1983b, table A-1).

There are several basic criticisms of this way of defining poverty. First, some critics contend that the poverty lines are unrealistically low for people living in many areas of the country. They believe that a family of four might be able to get by on $9,900 in Dothan, Alabama, but would find it impossible to survive on such a meager amount in New York or San Francisco. Because of this criticism, the Census Bureau regularly publishes estimates of how many people have incomes below 125 percent of the poverty line. This identifies the nearly poor: people or families whose incomes are just above the poverty line.

A second criticism concerns the way cash income is counted for purposes of determining poverty. Benefits from welfare payments, unemployment compensation, alimony, and child support should be reported by people contacted in the March Surveys. However, there is reason to believe that total income is underreported by as much as 10 percent, because sources other than wages tend to be forgotten or only partially reported. The income enumeration omits capital gains and does not take assets into account. This suggests that if more complete income data were gathered, rates of poverty might be lower. But it is also true that the income statistics are not adjusted for tax payments. All the poor pay sales taxes, and many undoubtedly pay income and property taxes. If the poverty population were estimated on the basis of after-tax income it would be larger (U.S. Bureau of the Census, 1983e).

Third, the income statistics omit all nonmoney transfer benefits, be they perquisites obtained by corporate executives or food stamps obtained by the poor. These are particularly important for estimating poverty because federal welfare programs that provide food, shelter, and medical benefits for the low-income population expanded rapidly—more than 5 percent annually—during the 1970s (Smeeding, 1982). This contrasts to a growth rate of less than 1 percent per year for wage and salary income (U.S. Bureau of the Census, 1981f, tables 709 and 765). In other words, benefits for the poor in the 1970s were increasing at a rate five times that of wages and salaries. The benefits obtained through these non-cash transfer programs are not reflected in the present poverty statistics. After looking at trends in poverty using the traditional statistics that deal with before-tax cash income only, I will briefly discuss the implications of the various benefit programs.

Figure 5.12 shows trends for the period since 1959 (the first year for which statistics are available) in the poverty rate—that is, the proportion below the poverty line—for the total population and for people in families headed by a man or by a woman. Several findings stand out. First, there were, and still are, very high levels of poverty in the black community. In the late 1950s more than half of the black population lived in poverty. The poverty rate for blacks fell to a minimum of 30 percent in 1974 and then climbed back to 36 percent in 1982.

Second, there are very large and persistent racial differences in poverty. At all dates, the poverty rate has been just about three times as high among blacks as among whites.

Third, changes in the poverty rate occurred in a parallel manner for both races. For the total population of blacks or whites, there were few reductions in poverty before 1963. Poverty decreased quite sharply during the next decade, reaching a minimum among whites in 1973 and among blacks in 1974. Between the mid-1970s and the end of that decade, the poverty rate changed very little, but since 1979 it has risen for both races. The rate of poverty in 1982 was just about what it was in 1967.

Fourth, at all times and for both blacks and whites, poverty rates were lowest for families headed by men. (Almost all such families include a married couple.) They were much higher for families headed by women. In 1982, for example, 59 percent of the families headed by black women fell below the poverty line, compared to 19 percent of black husband-wife families.

Blacks made gains in educational attainment and in earnings, and those blacks who held jobs moved into better occupations in the 1970s. We might ask why this did not lead to reductions in poverty in the 1970s similar to those which occurred in the 1960s. One factor to examine is the overall rate of economic growth. During the 1960s, the GNP increased by about 4 percent each year, but in the next decade the rate was about 3 percent. The poverty rate is linked to economic

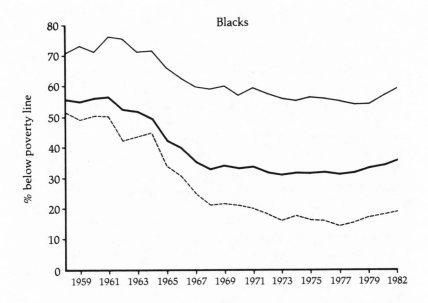

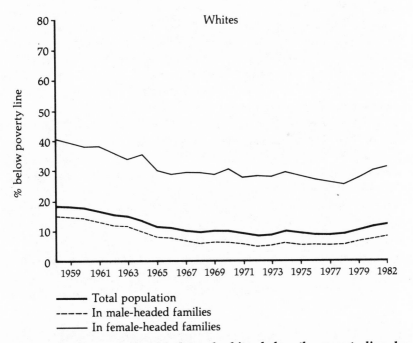

Figure 5.12. **Proportion of blacks and whites below the poverty line, by type of living arrangement, 1959–1982.**

Source: U.S. Bureau of the Census, *Current Population Reports,* ser. P-60, no. 127, table 18. (Data for blacks for years 1960–1966 are estimates.)

expansion, but the relationship is not a particularly strong one. Since 1966 a real increase of one percent in the GNP has had the effect of lowering the proportion of blacks in poverty by about one-third of one percent and the proportion of whites by about one-quarter of one percent.[3] A closer look at the economic data suggests that poverty fell rapidly during the late 1960s regardless of economic change. In the 1970s poverty and economic growth were not strongly linked, although the proportion and number of the poor went up among both races during the recession of 1973-75 and the one at the end of the decade. Thus, economic differences between the 1960s and 1970s account for some of the persistence of poverty but not all of it. This analysis also suggests that high rates of economic growth would produce only moderate declines in poverty.

It is clear that changing living arrangements help to explain persistence of high rates of poverty in the 1970s. In that decade the poverty rate for the total black population changed little, but for each specific type of living arrangement the rate went down just as it had in the 1960s, reaching a mininum in 1978 or 1979. For families headed by men, the poverty rate fell from 21 percent to a low of 13 percent. Even in families headed by black women, poverty declined before the recession at the end of the 1970s. If there had not been a shift away from husband-wife families in the 1970s, declines in poverty in that decade would have been more like those of the previous decade.

Changes in poverty for 1979-1982 differ from those of earlier periods. There were times in the past when the poverty rate went up from one year to the next, but never before were increases recorded for three consecutive years. Furthermore, poverty has increased since 1979 for all types of living arrangements, including white husband-wife families. Economic changes in the early 1980s appear to be substantially different from those of the previous two decades and seem to have wiped out gains made during the previous ten years among both races. But we will need data from additional years to determine whether there has been a turning point in the long-run trend toward less poverty or just a temporary setback resulting from this recession.

THE CHANGING COMPOSITION OF THE POOR POPULATION

The total number of people in poverty fell in the 1960s by about 25 percent among blacks and 40 percent among whites. For both races the number below the poverty line was lowest just before the 1973–75 recession. Since then, the impoverished population has risen, and there were just about as many poor people in 1982 as in the mid-1960s. This trend does not, however, describe all types of living arrangements. For blacks the number of children and adults living in husband-wife families who were below the poverty line continued to decrease throughout the 1970s. This occurred partly because there are now fewer people living in such families and partly because the poverty rate for such families decreased. The number of children and adults in female-headed families who were poor rose during the 1970s for both blacks and whites.

One important consequence of the changing living arrangements has been the "feminization" of poverty. That is, a growing proportion of the poor live in families headed by women or are women who live by themselves. This can be seen in Figure 5.13, which shows the composition of impoverished population. For both races the proportion of the poor who lived in families headed by men decreased throughout this period. This decrease was matched by a corresponding rise in the proportion of the poor who lived in families headed by women. In 1959 two-thirds of the impoverished blacks were members of husband-wife families and about one-fourth were in families headed by women. By 1980 the situation had reversed: about 60 percent lived in families headed by women and one-fourth lived in husband-wife families. Solving the problem of black poverty must now involve either raising the income levels of families headed by women or shifting people into husband-wife families, whose poverty rates are much lower.

There has been a similar but less dramatic feminization of poverty among whites: shifts in marital status and living arrangements in the 1970s were smaller for whites than for blacks. The proportion of the white poor living in families headed by women went up from 15 to 24 percent in the period covered in Figure 5.13.

Figure 5.13 also shows that the proportion of the poor who are unrelated individuals increased throughout this period. Unrelated individuals are persons who live alone or with nonrelatives; most of them are 55 or older and live by themselves (U.S. Bureau of the Census, 1982f, table 22). Poverty rates for unrelated individuals decreased in both the 1960s and 1970s, undoubtedly because of improved Social Security benefits, the expansion of Social Security coverage, and the growth of private pension plans. Despite these obvious economic gains, about 38 percent of the older blacks and 12 percent of the older whites fell below the poverty line in 1982 (U.S. Bureau of the Census, 1983b, table 15).

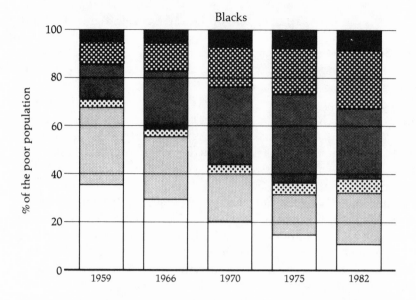

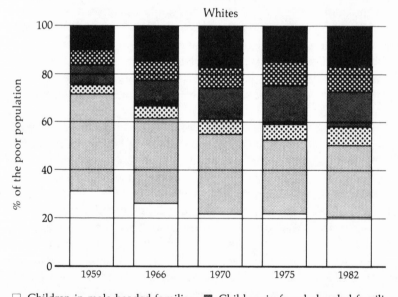

☐ Children in male-headed families   ■ Children in female-headed families
▨ Adults in male-headed families   ⊠ Adults in female-headed families
⊡ Male individuals   ■ Female individuals

Figure 5.13. Composition of the impoverished population, by race, 1959–1982.

Source: U.S. Bureau of the Census, *Current Population Reports*, ser. P-60, no. 140, table 15.

POVERTY IN THE 1970S

This description of poverty relies upon the monetary income people reported, including welfare benefits. The poverty rate fell sharply in the 1960s but declined very little in the 1970s, and throughout this period the poverty rate among blacks was just about three times what it was among whites. But, as mentioned earlier, the income data may be somewhat misleading because they do not take into account non-monetary government benefits such as food stamps and medical aid programs.

In the late 1960s and early 1970s, Congress debated various programs that would have reduced or eliminated poverty by providing cash supplements to low-income families. The best-known of these was the negative income tax. None of these policies was enacted, but Congress shortly thereafter greatly increased the appropriations that provide in-kind—that is, noncash—benefits to the needy. These include food stamps, school lunches, and subsidized housing. There was also a great increase in the Medicaid program, which provides medical care to needy or disabled families, and the Medicare program, which insures the medical expenses of the elderly. All these programs except Medicare are "means tested"; that is, families must have small cash incomes and few assets to obtain benefits.

A very high proportion of the poor and near-poor households are aided by these government programs. Since 1979 the Census Bureau has asked respondents in the March income survey whether they benefited from any of the most common programs. Table 5.1 classifies households by their cash income levels and shows the proportion of blacks and whites who got support from each program or were covered by Medicaid at any point during 1981. Those who fell below the poverty line are designated as poor, while "near-poor" refers to those who had cash incomes between the poverty line and 125 percent of that amount.

These in-kind benefits assist a high proportion of the nation's black households. Overall, 46 percent of all black households were covered by at least one of the four programs at some time during 1981. Half of all black households that included a child aged 5–18 benefited from school lunch programs, and more than one-quarter of the black households received food stamps. More than four out of five poor black households and three out of five near-poor black households were aided by one of these programs. The rates were considerably lower among whites, but half of the poor and one-third of the near-poor

Table 5.1. Proportion of households receiving non-cash benefits in 1981, by race and poverty status.

	Black households				White households			
	Total households	Poor	Near poor	Not poor	Total households	Poor	Near poor	Not poor
Number of households (in thousands)	8,961	2,974	753	5,234	72,845	8,410	4,018	60,417
Proportion receiving:								
At least one means-tested benefit	46%	81%	59%	24%	14%	50%	33%	7%
Food stamps	28	64	29	8	6	33	14	2
School lunches	50	81	61	28	15	53	44	8
Public or subsidized housing	12	22	16	6	2	10	7	1
Medicaid	28	58	37	10	8	33	16	4

Source: U.S. Bureau of the Census, *Current Population Reports*, ser. P-60, no. 135, table 1.

white households received some benefit, most often lunches for their school-aged children. Thus by 1981 a high proportion of the nation's poor and near-poor were having their cash incomes supplemented by benefit programs that had been developed or expanded during the previous decade.

At first glance, it may seem odd that so many households above the poverty line got means-tested benefits. This comes about because of the requirements for participation in various programs. If a family suffers from unemployment for the first six months of a year, it might be eligible during that period for all of the programs mentioned in Table 5.1. However, if the family head obtains a high-paying job during the last six months of the year, she may earn enough to bring the family far above the poverty line for the entire year. Poverty statistics are based on annual cash income, while eligibility for program benefits may depend upon income during shorter periods.

Because the majority of impoverished households in the United States now obtain noncash benefits, the data about poverty developed from monetary information substantially overestimate the extent of deprivation. A more accurate estimate of poverty will result if the cash value of in-kind transfer payments is included. The Bureau of the Census made such estimates using data gathered in the March 1980 survey.

There are numerous difficulties in doing this. If a family receives food stamps or the children eat subsidized lunches at school, how do we adjust the family's cash income? Should we use the estimated market value of the benefits, the cost to the government, or the amount of cash the family would take in lieu of the benefits? If a poor person receives $40,000 of medical care, should you credit her income with that amount, by the market cost of equivalent health insurance premiums, or by some other amount? (Smeeding, 1982)

One strategy focuses upon the food and housing programs and estimates the market value of these benefits. The incomes of those who receive such benefits may be adjusted upward to reflect the financial gains they obtain from the programs. This is one of several approaches, and it places no monetary value upon medical care. The following table shows estimates from the March 1980 survey of the proportion impoverished based upon monetary income with and without adjusting for the estimated market value of in-kind food and housing programs.

	Blacks		Whites	
	Money income	Money plus food and housing	Money income	Money plus food and housing
Poor	30%	24%	9%	7%
Near poor	9	12	4	5
Not poor	61	64	87	88

Three conclusions can be drawn from this table. First, attributing monetary value to in-kind benefits substantially reduces the estimated extent of poverty. The change in the estimated proportion below the poverty line in 1979 was from 30 to 24 percent for blacks and from 9 to 7 percent for whites. The adjustment for noncash benefits increases the proportion who are near poor or well above the poverty line. Second, because more blacks than whites benefit from these programs, adjusting for the value of the programs makes a bigger change in the proportion impoverished for blacks than for whites. This suggests that comparing only monetary income overstates the deprivation of blacks relative to whites. Third, the inclusion of in-kind benefits does not eliminate either poverty or the racial gap. Even taking such assistance programs into account, about one black in four and one white in fourteen were impoverished in 1979: the poverty rate of blacks was still more than three times that of whites.

I have stressed that the most widely used poverty statistics, which imply that few gains were made during the 1970s, omit in-kind benefits, which expanded rapidly in that decade. Government spending (in constant dollars) for food stamps rose by a factor of four, for school lunches by a factor of three, and expenditures for public housing just about doubled in this decade (Smeeding, 1982). Perhaps if these benefit programs were taken into account poverty would be shown to have decreased as much in the 1970s and in the 1960s.

The first survey asking about participation in such programs was conducted in 1979, almost a decade after the programs became widespread. Thus I am unable to trace time trends. But I can determine possible reductions in poverty in the 1970s by assuming that all of the in-kind benefits went into effect during the 1970s. This is an unrealistic assumption, since in fact the federal government supplied some food stamps, school lunches, and public housing in 1970.[4] However, this assumption does permit the estimation of reductions in poverty during the 1970s, both using information about monetary income alone and using data that include in-kind benefits.

Type of estimate	% below poverty line	
	Black	White
Money only, 1959	55%	18%
Money only, 1970	34	10
Change, 1959–1970	−21	−8
Money only, 1979	31	9
Change, 1970–1979	−3	−1
Money + food and housing, 1979	24	7
Change, 1970–1979	−10	−3

A focus on money income alone seriously underestimates the reduction in poverty that occurred in the 1970s. Looking only at money income leads to the conclusion that between 1970 and 1979 the proportion impoverished fell only 3 percent among blacks and 1 percent among whites. But assuming that all the in-kind transfer programs went into effect during the 1970s and including their value in the calculation of poverty yields reductions three times as large: 10 percent among blacks and 3 percent among whites. (I have not estimated the monetary impact of the most expensive in-kind programs, Medicaid and Medicare, which have more than doubled their expenditures since the late 1960s. Adding their value to the calculations would produce even more impressive reductions in poverty in the 1970s).

Conclusions

The 1960s and 1970s were decades of economic expansion, and among both blacks and whites incomes increased while poverty declined. But the 1960s were more prosperous than the 1970s, and reductions in poverty in the latter decade were brought about not so much by increases in cash income as by the expansion of in-kind transfer programs: food stamps, school lunches, and subsidized housing. Gains were recorded for all types of families but were much larger for husband-wife families than for those headed by women. Per capita income (in constant dollars) doubled in black husband-wife families between 1959 and 1979 but went up only 65 percent in families headed by black women. The corresponding increases for whites were 60 percent for husband-wife families and 30 percent for those headed by women.

In looking at these economic trends, one is struck both by the tremendous progress that has been made and by the very substantial racial differences that persist. When federal agencies first estimated poverty, 55 percent of the black population fell below the poverty line. This declined to 30 percent in 1979 and may have been as low as 24 percent including in-kind payments. Nevertheless, the proportion of the population that is poor is still at least three times as high for blacks as for whites. A very clear indication both of the nation's efforts to improve standards of living and of the persistence of poverty is the tremendous expansion of federal programs that emerged during the War on Poverty. By the early 1980s more than one-quarter of the black population was covered by Medicaid or benefited from food stamps and just about half of the black households with young children received federally subsidized school lunches. Presumably, if there were not so much persistent poverty among blacks, rates of participation would be much lower, similar to what they are among whites.

CHANGES IN LIVING ARRANGEMENTS

The family is still society's major mechanism for redistributing money from those who earn to those who are dependent. Any discussion of recent changes in income and poverty must take family living arrangements into account. Husband-wife families not only have the highest incomes but also report the greatest increases in prosperity. Poverty was once common among husband-wife families but has been greatly reduced, partly because it is increasingly common for both spouses to have cash incomes. By 1982 the wife was at work in 60 percent of the black and half of the white husband-wife families (U.S. Bureau of the Census, 1983b, table 1). Those who live in families headed by women, by contrast, have low incomes and are often poor. Compared to the situation for husband-wife families, only limited progress has been made in eliminating poverty in female-headed families (see Figure 5.12).

Increasingly, women bear children before they marry. Although the majority of women eventually marry, many of them also go through separation and divorce. Following this disruption, most children stay with their mother rather than their father, so the woman becomes a family head with the obligation of supporting herself and her children.

In 1982, 96 percent of the black and 89 percent of the white children under 18 who lived with only one parent were with their mother (U.S. Bureau of the Census, 1983c, table 5). Family headship is a temporary status for many white women, because they eventually remarry, but black women frequently remain heads of their families for long periods. One implication of this is that black children who fall below the poverty line stay there much longer than white children. Using longitudinal data from approximately five thousand families collected in the Michigan Panel Study of Income Dynamics (Morgan et al., 1974), Martha Hill (1983) traced the economic status of children from 1969 to 1978. Seventy percent of the black children, compared to 21 percent of the white, fell below the poverty line at some year in the interval. Among those falling into poverty, black children stayed poor an average of five years, white children only 2.6 years.

The changing composition of black families kept the poverty rate high in the 1970s and helps to explain why, in a time of racial progress, the income of black families did not catch up with that of whites. Back in 1965, when Moynihan wrote his controversial report *The Negro Family in the United States: The Case for National Action* (U.S. Department of Labor, 1965), he called for the expansion of economic opportunities for blacks, especially for black men. Supposedly, if these men were not the victims of racial discrimination they would get better educations, obtain prestigious jobs, earn more money, and maintain traditional husband-wife families.

Although the gains are not universal, many of the changes Moynihan recommended have occurred. Black men now face fewer barriers if they wish to get an advanced education. The occupational distribution has been upgraded, and the gap in earnings between black and white men has narrowed as racial discrimination declined. However, all measures of family living arrangements suggest that there is much less family stability among blacks now than when Moynihan offered his views. More births occur outside of marriage, a much higher proportion of black women head their own families, and a much lower proportion of black children live with both parents.

Two factors may account for this decrease in family stability. First, there is a long-term shift away from the traditional family system: more people are delaying their first marriage, dissolving marriages that they find unsatisfactory, and raising children outside traditional families. The trend in this direction is unambiguous, and the pattern of the period immediately after World War II—early marriage, high fertility, and almost universal marriage—was a deviation from a trend that began in the nineteenth century (Cherlin, 1981; Masnick and Bane, 1980). This shift away from traditional living arrangements may explain much of the change among blacks. There may be a racial difference in the pace of change; some of the data in this chapter suggest that whites may be catching up with blacks in terms of out-of-wedlock births, delayed marriages, female family headship, and children living with their mother only. As Victor Fuchs (1983) notes, the conjugal family is of declining importance in American society.

Second, Moynihan and most other writers assume that economic success and financial security lead to family stability. This may be erroneous. Perhaps, if they have the resources, a growing proportion of adults will choose to live in something other than a husband-wife family. They may be able to experiment with a variety of relationships while they are young, thereby delaying their marriage, and if their first marriage is not satisfying they may be able to terminate the relationship, live by themselves, and then later select a new spouse or lover or choose an entirely different lifestyle. If there is economic security, some men and women may decide to bear and raise children even if they do not want to live as a spouse.

Although it is difficult to determine which is cause and which is effect, the economic improvements of recent decades—including more employment for women and the expansion of welfare—may help account for changes in family living arrangements. Government spending for health, education, and income security programs, including those which support families where no husband is present, have expanded in recent decades. The number of persons, for example, benefiting from Aid to Families with Dependent Children grew from 3.1 million in 1960 to 11.1 million in 1980—a rise of 261 percent while the total population grew only 26 percent. The monthly benefit per recipient, in constant dollars, rose by 28 percent. In recent years about 44 percent of the recipients of this program have been black (U.S. Bureau of the Census, 1981f, tables 559 and 564).

One outcome of the greater employment of women and the expansion of welfare may be a rise in family headship by women and an improvement in the economic status of such families. Income levels in these families lag far behind those of husband-wife families, but there have been gains. In 1959 per capita income in families headed by black women was just $1,300 (in constant 1979 dollars); by 1981 this rose to $2,300. For families headed by white women the change was from $3,300 to $4,400 (U.S. Bureau of the Census, 1963a, table 224; 1963d, table 4; 1983a, table 8; Bianchi, 1981).

The income maintenance experiments also imply that higher incomes or guaranteed incomes may be associated with less—not more—family stability. Using data gathered in Seattle and Denver, Hannan, Tuma, and Groeneveld (1978) analyzed family stability. They believed that guaranteed incomes would have different consequences for different couples. Some marriages, they reasoned, were on the verge of dissolution because of financial crisis. Assuring them an income would prevent this type of instability. Other couples, they believed, remained together primarily because they could not afford to live apart or to care for children on their own. For these couples, a guaranteed income would encourage marital separation. The investigators found that the latter effect greatly outweighed the former: couples with guaranteed incomes had significantly higher rates of marital dissolution than couples in the control group who lacked such a guarantee. Within two years, 23 percent of the black couples with an assured income compared to 15 percent of those in the control group separated or divorced; among whites the proportions were 17 percent for those with a guaranteed income and 10 percent for those without it (Groeneveld, Tuma, and Hannan, 1980). Although the income maintenance experiments differ in many important ways from federal welfare programs, they demonstrate that guaranteeing a modest amount of income to families near the poverty line may increase the divorce rate.

It is difficult to predict with confidence what may happen to family living arrangements in the future. An extrapolation of long-run and recent trends suggests that a higher proportion of births will occur to women who are not married, that a growing proportion of marriages will end in divorce, and that an increasing proportion of women will head their own families rather than live with a husband (Masnick and Bane, 1980).

The rise in family headship by women has slowed the growth of family income and exacerbated poverty rates, but another change in family structure—the decline in fertility—has had exactly the opposite effect. Couples are having fewer children, so that husband-wife families have fewer members and if the marriage is terminated the mother will have fewer children to support. Declining fertility played an important role in raising per capita income between 1960 and 1980. If fertility rates continue to fall, they will contribute to further growth of per capita income and decreases in poverty.

6

Class Differences
in the Black Community

In recent years, a number of observers have argued that the black community is becoming polarized by economic status or social class. This perspective can be traced back at least to 1965, when Daniel Patrick Moynihan asserted, "There is considerable evidence that the Negro community is, in fact, dividing between a stable middle class group that is steadily growing stronger and more successful and an increasingly disorganized and disadvantaged lower class group" (U.S. Department of Labor, 1965:5–6). Shortly thereafter, Andrew Brimmer noted that "A particularly distressing trend is evident in the distribution of income in the Negro community: the middle and upper income groups are getting richer, while the lowest income group is getting poorer" (Brimmer, 1966:267).

Three assertions about social change precede the conclusion that the black community is becoming polarized by social class. The first is that at least some segments of the black population now compete successfully with whites and obtain economic rewards similar to those of whites. Richard Freeman, in *Black Elite* (1976), observed that during the 1960s and 1970s the ratios of black to white incomes rose substantially, major corporations hired black professionals for the first time, blacks entered many fields that had traditionally been closed to them, and the income differential that had separated young black and white college graduates disappeared. William Wilson (1978:151) seconded this view: "talented and educated blacks are experiencing unprecedented job opportunities in the growing government and corporate sectors, opportunities that are at least comparable to those of whites with equivalent qualifications."

The second assertion is that, despite general racial progress, many blacks did not participate in the prosperity of the last decade. For a component of the black population, economic conditions may have worsened. Vernon Jordan, writing in a recent annual report of the National Urban League (1980), notes that during the 1970s the proportion of blacks impoverished remained just about constant; the unemployment rate, especially among young blacks, increased; and the ratio of black to white family income declined. Nathan Glazer (1975:71–72) argued that unemployment rates for blacks in central cities rose even during periods of prosperity, and described a "tangle of pathology in the ghetto." In Glazer's view, neither rapid economic growth nor affirmative action would benefit those unskilled and impoverished blacks who are locked into their unfortunate circumstances. Several ethnographic accounts such as Carol Stack's *All Our Kin* (1975), Elijah Anderson's *A Place on the Corner* (1978), Elliot Liebow's *Tally's Corner* (1967), and Ulf Hannerz' *Soulside* (1969), vividly portray the plight of poor blacks who reside in ghettos and have few opportunities for advancement.

The third assertion is that racial prejudice and discrimination have declined or have even been eliminated in the United States. Numerous national studies of the racial attitudes of whites demonstrate that antiblack prejudice has fallen sharply throughout the entire country and in all social classes (Hyman and Sheatsley, 1964; Taylor, Sheatsley and Greeley, 1978; Converse et al., 1980). Issues that once provoked great resistance from whites, such as sitting next to blacks on buses or permitting blacks to vote, are no longer included on attitudinal surveys because they are no longer controversial. The abilities of blacks, their own skills, and their own diligence are now seen as much more important than the attitudes of whites in determining the success or failure of blacks.

These three assumptions about changes in race relations in the United States have led analysts such as Moynihan and Wilson to conclude that the black commuity is becoming polarized by social class. Sar Levitan, William Johnston, and Robert Taggart (1975:185) summarize this view:

> One interpretation of these divergent developments is that blacks are increasingly divided into two groups—those who have succeeded and those who have been left behind. There seems to be a large group of blacks whose problems are becoming more severe and more intractable, an "underclass," locked in a vicious cycle of poverty or a "secondary labor market." Persons in this class share the characteristics of low income, poor health, unstable families, ghetto living arrangements, and dependence

on welfare . . . Rising welfare, crime and family deterioration are taken as evidence that this underclass has grown . . . At the other end of the spectrum, it is argued, stands the emerging black middle or upper class. Persons with higher incomes and education and white collar or craft jobs are approaching equality with whites and are presumed to share positive attitudes, a work orientation, a saving ethic and a desire for upward mobility.

It is much easier to use the term "class" than to define it or precisely measure it. As ordinarily used, it refers to a combination of social and economic achievements such that people of the same class have roughly similar positions in the labor market and can afford similar life styles. The most frequently used indicators of social class are educational attainment, occupational achievement, income, and assets.

In descriptions of lower-class persons that contrast them to those in the upper classes, many other indicators are mentioned. Presumably, within the lower classes there is a frequent dependence upon welfare, petty crime is common, work habits are irregular, unemployment rates are high, and family life is disorganized. These characteristics are closely related to the assumption that lower-class individuals do not have the skills or educational attainment to achieve very much in terms of occupation or earnings (Cottingham, 1982).

The major aim of this chapter is to investigate whether lower-class blacks are falling further behind successful blacks. To a lesser extent, I will investigate whether the status of lower-class blacks is getting worse compared to that of lower-class whites and whether upper-class blacks have really caught up with upper-class whites. I will consider demographic indicators of class status: educational attainment, occupational achievement, family income, and employment. Then, to provide additional evidence to test the polarization hypothesis, I will look briefly at some subjective information about social class from recent surveys that have asked national samples of the population, "What is your social class?"

Educational Attainment

Educational attainment is esteemed in itself; it is also related to occupational achievement and earnings, since high-paying jobs require more education than low-paying jobs. To begin examining the idea that polarization is increasing, I will look at changes in the distribution of educational attainment among black and white men aged 25 and over in the period since 1959. First I will consider the gap between those toward the top and those toward the bottom of the distribution of educational attainment. To do so, I will calculate the *interquartile range*: the number of years of attainment separating those at the third quartile point from those at the first quartile point, that is, the gap between the most-educated quarter and the least-educated quarter of the population. If the interquartile range has increased, this is evidence in favor of the polarization hypothesis.

Second, I will consider the full distribution of educational attainment. Is education evenly distributed, or does only a small proportion of the population achieve high attainment? An appropriate measure for assessing this is the *Gini index* of educational concentration. In a society where everyone completed just about the same number of years of school—say twelve years—the Gini index would take on its minimum value of zero, indicating that educational attainment was evenly distributed. In a society—perhaps an impoverished developing country—where the vast majority received no education but a very few individuals got the training needed to become doctors, lawyers, or statesmen, the Gini index would approach its maximum value of 100. Increases over time in the Gini index, indicating that the distribution of attainment is becoming more highly concentrated, would be evidence supporting the polarization hypothesis.

Figure 6.1 shows the interquartile range and the Gini index for black and white men for the period 1959–1982. In 1959 black men in the most educated quarter of the population completed about 6.7 more years of schooling than those in the least educated quarter; by 1982 their advantage declined to 4.1 years. The interquartile range among white men fluctuated narrowly and was lower in 1982 than at any previous date since 1959. For both races, the Gini index of educational concentration decreased, although educational attainment was more evenly distributed among whites than among blacks. Data for women (not shown) reveal a similar trend. Also, restricting this analysis to people who have recently completed their educations, those aged 25–29, shows a similar trend. The interquartile range decreased among blacks from 1959 through 1982, and the Gini index fell for both races. Beverly Duncan (1968) reported that between 1900 and 1960 the distribution of attainment became less concentrated. Apparently this trend has continued to the present, and thus evidence on educational

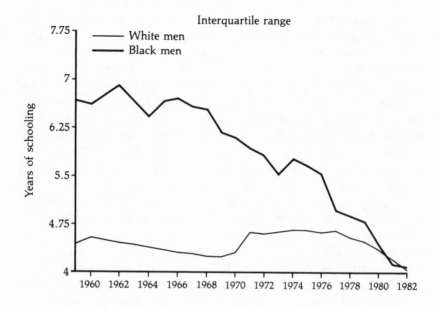

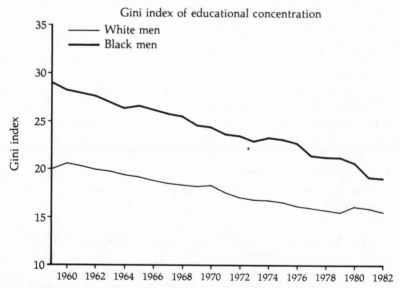

Figure 6.1. Interquartile range and Gini index of educational concentration for black and white men aged 25 and over, 1959–1982.

Source: U.S. Bureau of the Census, *Current Population Reports*, ser. P-20, nos. 99, 121, 138, 158, 169, 182, 194, 207, 229, 243, 274, 295, 314, and 356.

attainment refutes the polarization hypothesis. The gap between blacks at the top and at the bottom of the educational distribution is getting smaller, not larger.

The measures described thus far show that lower-class blacks are not falling further behind upper-class blacks in education, but they do not indicate whether lower-class blacks are falling behind lower-class whites, or whether blacks have caught up with whites at the upper end of the educational distribution. Table 6.1 reports the educational gap that separates blacks from whites in the most and least educated quarters of the population. The table concentrates on people in the age group 25–29; since changes in average educational attainment come about primarily because highly educated young people replace less educated older people who die, examining the attainment of young people is a good way to gain insight into overall trends.

The table shows that there is a continuing racial convergence at the first quartile point. This trend implies that the least educated quarters

Table 6.1. Comparison of blacks and whites aged 25–29 at the first and third quartile points of their distributions of educational attainment, 1960–1979.

	First quartile point		Third quartile point	
	Racial difference in attainment	Black attainment as % of white	Racial difference in attainment	Black attainment as % of white
Men				
1960	2.2 years	78%	1.4 years	90%
1970	2.1	82	2.5	83
1975	.7	94	2.3	86
1982	.2	99	1.2	90
Women				
1960	1.9 years	82%	.3 years	97%
1970	1.9	84	1.0	92
1975	.8	93	1.9	88
1982	.1	99	1.0	93

Source: U.S. Bureau of the Census, Current Population Reports, ser. P-20, nos. 158, 295, and 356; Census of Population: 1960, PC(1)-1D, table 173; Census of Population: 1970, PC(1)-1D, table 199.

of the black and white populations will soon have similar attainments. In education, lower-class blacks did not fall further behind lower-class whites in the 1970s. In fact they gained on whites and very nearly caught up with them.

The story is more complex at the upper end of the educational distribution. During the 1950s and early 1960s there was a convergence of enrollment rates at the elementary and secondary levels and differences between the races in high school completion decreased. College enrollment rates of whites accelerated more than those of blacks, and thus the racial gap widened at that level. Since the late 1960s, however, college enrollment rates of blacks have increased more rapidly than those of whites. (Indeed, enrollment rates have decreased among white men; see Chapter 2.) If this trend continues, there will eventually be a racial convergence of attainment at the upper end of the distribution. Indications of this can be seen in Table 6.1: the racial gap at the third quartile point is smaller for 1982 than for previous years. I conclude that the black population is becoming more homogeneous with regard to educational attainment and that blacks at both the top and bottom of their educational distribution are becoming more like whites who have similar positions in the white educational distribution.

Occupational Prestige

As noted in Chapter 2, the occupational prestige of blacks has risen more rapidly than that of whites. Data about occupational prestige can be used, with caution, to test the polarization hypothesis. Considering the occupations reported by all blacks who worked in a given year, I will treat occupational prestige much as I treated educational attainment and will look at its distribution. A variety of schemes have been proposed for coding occupational prestige. The scheme I use, first developed by Otis Dudley Duncan (1961), has become standard in the analysis of occupational stratification. In this system, for example, lawyers and judges are scored 93, mail carriers 53, bartenders 19, and stevedores 11.

Figure 6.2 shows trends in the interquartile range for the occupational prestige distribution of whites and nonwhites. This range is the number of prestige points separating those in the bottom quarter of the prestige distribution from those in the top quarter. Data for

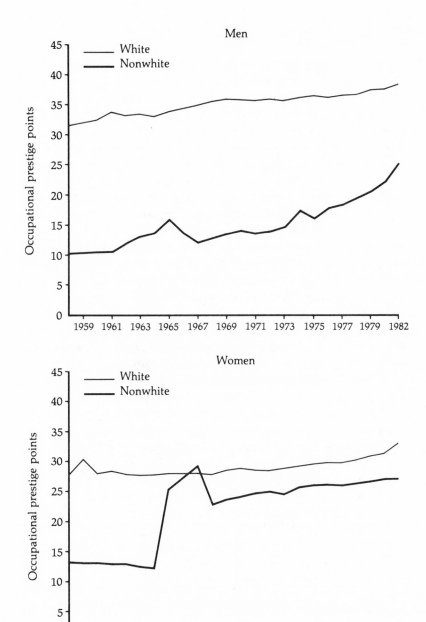

Figure 6.2. Interquartile range of occupational prestige distribution for whites and nonwhites, by sex, 1959–1982.

Source: U.S. Bureau of Labor Statistics, *Handbook of Labor Statistics: 1978*, table 18; *Employment and Earnings*, vols. 26–29, no. 1 for each vol.

nonwhites are used here because information about the occupations of blacks was not tabulated until recently.

Trends in this measure support the view that blacks are becoming more polarized by social class. For both men and women, the inter-quartile range of occupational prestige has grown larger, meaning that a greater gap in prestige separates those at the top and the bottom of the distribution. Among nonwhite women the bigger change took place in the 1960s; among nonwhite men it occurred in the 1970s. There is also evidence of growing polarization by social class among whites, although the changes have been much smaller than among nonwhites.

Occupational prestige increased much more for nonwhites than for whites throughout this interval. In the late 1950s a large proportion of employed nonwhites worked at jobs that scored very low on all prestige scales. More than one-third of employed nonwhite men were unskilled laborers or farm hands and nearly half of employed non-white women were domestic servants or farm laborers. Because most blacks were concentrated into a few low-prestige occupational cate-gories, there was no more than a meager black elite and the inter-quartile range of prestige was small—considerably smaller than among whites. Between 1959 and 1982 there were substantial increases in the proportion of blacks working as craftsmen and in the more highly esteemed white-collar jobs. The distribution of nonwhites across the occupational spectrum widened, resulting in a doubling of the inter-quartile range for both men and women.

Nonwhites at the bottom of their prestige distribution are definitely not falling any further behind those whites who are at similar points in their prestige distribution. An examination of the data used to compile Figure 6.2 shows that the first quartile point rose rapidly among nonwhites and by the early 1980s was just about equal to the first quartile point for whites. Blacks at the bottom of their distribution used to work at less prestigious jobs than similar whites, but a racial convergence has just about eliminated this difference.

The third quartile point—the prestige score that distinguishes the top 25 percent from all other workers—has moved up for both races. This change also has been much greater for nonwhites, leading to a smaller racial difference at the third quartile point. The gap between the races has not disappeared, nor will it soon be eliminated. Whites at the top of their distribution continue to work at jobs that are more prestigious than those of nonwhites in the upper ranks of their dis-tribution.

Family Income

The same measures can be applied to the distribution of family income. Figure 6.3 shows the interquartile range (in constant 1979 dollars) and the Gini index of income concentration for black and white families between 1959 and 1982. If Moynihan, Wilson, and others are correct in arguing that economic polarization is occurring among blacks, the gap between the rich and poor should be increasing as successful blacks move into the upper income categories.

The data in Figure 6.3 both support and refute the polarization hypothesis. On the one hand, the interquartile range grew larger for both races; that is, the economic gap between the poorest quarter and the richest quarter of families is greater than it used to be. Among blacks the interquartile range increased from about $8,600 in 1959 to $12,300 in 1970 and peaked at about $15,000 in 1978. On the other hand, the Gini index—the most widely used measure of income concentration—changed very little. As measured by the Gini index, income is somewhat more concentrated among black families than among white, but there was no substantial change in the degree of concentration for either race. Indeed, longer-run analyses report there has been very little change in the distribution of family income since the end of World War II (Henson, 1967; Merriam, 1968; Schultz, 1969).

How can two appropriate indexes give such different pictures of what is happening to the distribution of family income? Suppose that, from one year to the next, the rank position of every family in an income distribution remained exactly the same but the absolute amounts of their real incomes grew by 20 percent, so that each family was able to purchase 20 percent more goods and services in the second year. The basic shape of the income distribution would not change, since the rank order of every family with regard to every other family would be unaltered, and measures of income concentration such as the Gini index would remain constant. However, the interquartile range would grow by 20 percent; those at the top and bottom of the distribution would be further apart in terms of purchasing power. This type of change has occurred among both whites and blacks in recent years; hence the apparent contradiction.

I have repeatedly stressed that the conclusions drawn about economic trends depend upon whether the focus is on absolute differences or relative differences. In relative terms, the economic gap between rich and poor black families is not getting any larger. At least since 1960, the incomes of black families in the lowest quarter of the black

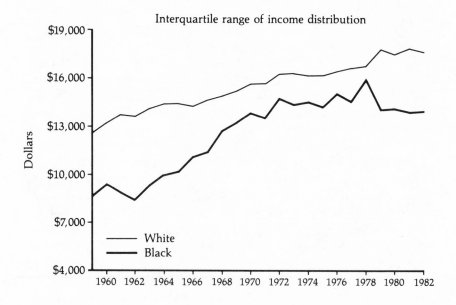

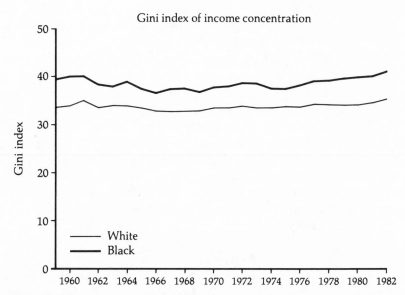

Figure 6.3. Interquartile range (constant 1979 dollars) and Gini index of income concentration, for black and white families, 1959–1982.

Source: U.S. Bureau of the Census, *Current Population Reports,* ser. P-60, no. 132, table 16; no. 134, tables 3 and A-2.

income distribution have been about 27 percent as large as those of black families in the highest quarter. This does not support the polarization hypothesis; in relative terms blacks at the bottom of the distribution are not falling further behind those at the top. But examining the absolute income gap (in constant dollars) yields a very different picture. The gap in purchasing power between those at the top and bottom of the income distribution is growing larger, a trend that supports the polarization hypothesis.

It is also difficult to find an unambiguous answer to the question of whether low-income black families are falling further behind low-income white families in terms of income. The incomes of black families in the lowest quarter of their distribution were about 45 percent as great as those of white families in the lowest quarter of their distribution in 1959 and about 50 percent as great in 1982. However, the dollar amount (in constant dollars) of the racial gap for this bottom quarter of the income distribution rose from $5,200 in 1959 to $6,900 in 1982. Thus in terms of actual purchasing power lower-income blacks fell further behind lower-income whites, while in relative terms blacks moved a bit closer to whites.

In making these comparisons of people who are at the lower end of the income distribution, it is important to note the gains in real income and the declines in poverty that occurred. The average income of black families in the lowest quarter was about $2,200 in 1959, $3,800 in 1982.

The income status of blacks at the upper end of the income distribution has also improved relative to that of similarly situated whites. Black families in the top quarter of their income distribution had incomes that were 57 percent of those of whites in 1959, 68 percent in 1981. Nevertheless, the gap in purchasing power between blacks and whites at the top of their respective income distributions increased during this period.

Dropping Out of the Labor Force

Many analysts of economic polarization contend that there are increasing numbers of men, often living in central-city ghettos, who lack the skills or motivation needed to get jobs. Supposedly these men give up the search for work and depend upon welfare benefits, transfer payments, or illegal activities to support themselves. I reported earlier that an increasing fraction of black men are moving into professional and managerial occupations. This implies that a type of economic polarization may be occurring as some black men drop out of the work force while others move into prestigious positions.

Figure 6.4 shows trends in the proportions of white and nonwhite men who reported they were neither working nor looking for a job. (Again, I use data for nonwhites because data on labor force status are not available for blacks for most of the period.) The age range is limited to 25–54 to exclude men who might be out of the labor force because of school attendance or retirement. The figure also presents trends in unemployment, to allow a closer analysis of nonparticipation. If nonparticipants in the labor force are primarily discouraged workers who cannot find jobs, then there should be a close correspondence between the rates of unemployment and of nonparticipation. During harsh economic times many men are unemployed, and many others may give up the search for work and drop out of the labor force.

But Figure 6.4 shows that the time trends in unemployment and nonparticipation are not at all similar. Unemployment rates decreased during the prosperous years of the late 1960s, rose sharply in the 1973–75 recession, and rose again in 1980–82. I reported in Chapter 2 that a real increase of one percent in the GNP lowers nonwhite unemployment rates by about six-tenths of a percent and white unemployment rates by about three-tenths of a percent. Unemployment rates are quite responsive to economic change. Being out of the labor force, however, is not at all responsive to economic change. There was a definite linear increase for both races throughout the 1960s and 1970s. Thus the data do not support the view that men who drop out of the labor force are mostly discouraged job-seekers.

We know very little about these men who are not participants in the labor force. Are they largely concentrated in central-city ghettos? Do they live on welfare? How long, on average, do they remain out of the labor force? Are they a "permanent underclass," as some suggest, or do they just spend unusually long intervals between jobs? Recent Census Bureau surveys have asked men not in the labor force what they are doing. The distribution of responses is just about the same among blacks and whites: about one in twenty claim they are not working because they have to keep house, about one in ten say they are students, and roughly three in ten report they are unable to work, presumably because of physical or mental disabilities. But the majority claim they are out of the labor force for "other" reasons—the category that probably includes those who have given up looking for work out of discouragement.

Unemployed

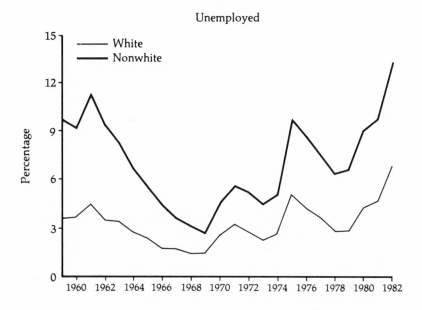

Out of the labor force

Figure 6.4. Proportion of men aged 25–54 unemployed or out of the labor force, by race, 1959–1982 (data standardized by age).

Source: U.S. Bureau of Labor Statistics, *Handbook of Labor Statistics: 1978,* tables 3 and 60; *Employment and Earnings,* vols. 26–29, no. 1 for each vol.

A growing proportion of adult men do not participate in the labor force. This shift is evident among both races, but the changes are more dramatic for blacks: by 1982 about one adult black man in eight was neither employed nor looking for work. This trend, combined with the fact that an increasing proportion of black men are working at high-paying white-collar jobs is consistent with the hypothesis that the black community is becoming increasingly polarized.

Polarization by Family Type

Since the time of Moynihan's report in 1965, observers have suggested that "stable" black husband-wife families are achieving economic parity with white families (Glazer, 1975) while families headed by black women are often impoverished. Commentators such as Martin Kilson (1981) argue that the rapidly growing number of female-headed families in the black community is extremely troubling because children who grow up in such circumstances will form the core of the next generation's underclass.

Cross-sectional data from Census Bureau surveys shed no light on the view that families headed by black women are largely responsible for the transmission of poverty from one generation of blacks to the next. However, they do allow an assessment of whether or not female-headed families are increasingly disadvantaged relative to husband-wife families. Families with a woman as head typically have much smaller incomes than do husband-wife families, but they also have fewer members. For this reason I will examine trends in per capita income. Figure 6.5 shows per capita income in female-headed families as a percentage of per capita income in husband-wife families for the period since 1959.

In the previous chapter I reported that during the 1960s and 1970s real incomes rose quite rapidly among husband-wife families of both races but only slightly among families headed by women. As a result, incomes in female-headed families fell further behind those of husband-wife families, as Figure 6.5 demonstrates. For blacks, per capita income in families headed by women was 63 percent that of husband-wife families in 1959 but only 50 percent in 1981. A similar trend is evident among whites, although female-headed families are not as far behind husband-wife families among whites as they are among blacks.

Families headed by women fell behind husband-wife families not

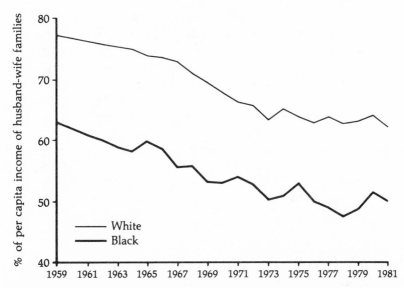

Figure 6.5.   Per capita income in families headed by women as a percentage of that in husband-wife families, by race, 1959–1981.
Source: same as for Figure 5.5. (Data for 1959 refer to whites and nonwhites. Data for 1960–1963 are estimates.)

only in relative income levels but also in absolute amounts. Recall from the previous chapter that the constant-dollar amounts separating husband-wife and female-headed families have grown larger (see Figure 5.12). Black families headed by women in 1959 had $870 less to spend per person per year than husband-wife families; in 1981 it was $2,580 less (in constant 1979 dollars). An increasing share of the black population—37 percent in 1982 compared to only 18 percent in 1960—live in families headed by women (U.S. Bureau of the Census, 1983d, table 1; 1963a, tables 156 and 187).

In an absolute sense, families headed by women are not getting any poorer over time. They made modest gains in per capita income in the 1960s and 1970s. However, their gains were small compared to those of families that included a married couple. Thus, relative to husband-wife families, female-headed families *are* getting poorer. Economic polarization by type of family is occurring among both blacks and whites.

These conclusions are based on data on cash income. If the value of noncash transfer payments were included in the calculations, the economic gap between female-headed and husband-wife families might be somewhat smaller. It appears that families headed by women are more likely to obtain noncash benefits even when income differences are taken into account. In 1981, for example, among families with cash incomes below $7,500, 27 percent of the husband-wife families received food stamps compared to 63 percent of the female-headed families (U.S. Bureau of the Census, 1982g, tables 2 and 3). The Census Bureau first gathered data about noncash benefits in 1980, so it is impossible to know how the trend toward greater economic polarization by family type has been altered by the expansion in the 1970s of transfer payments such as food stamps, school lunches, subsidized housing, and Medicaid.

Subjective Social Class Identification

Since the early 1970s the National Opinion Research Center (NORC) has included the following question in its General Social Survey: "If you were asked to use one of four names for your social class, which would you say you belong in: the lower class, the working class, the middle class or the upper class?" The results of these pollings are shown in Table 6.2. Observe, first, that there is a substantial racial difference in social class identity. Many more blacks claim they are members of the working class, and more whites than blacks say they are in the middle class. Each year about half of the whites but only one-quarter of the blacks said they were middle class. Blacks are more likely than whites to say they are in the upper class. Second, for both races the proportion choosing each of the four social classes remained pretty much the same from one year to the next, suggesting that there has not been much change since 1972 in social class identification.

The table also shows the index of dissimilarity, which measures how different the races are from each other by indicating the proportion of either blacks or whites who would have to shift their class identity for the two distributions to be equal. The value of this measure changed very little between 1972 and 1982, implying that whites and blacks were neither converging nor diverging in their social class identification.[1]

These subjective data are of limited import, since they pertain to just a few years and, for blacks, are based upon a small sample. Nevertheless, they do provide some evidence against the polarization

Table 6.2. Reported social class identification in General Social Surveys, by race, 1972–1982.

	1972	1973	1974	1975	1976	1977	1978	1980	1982	Mean	Standard deviation
Blacks											
Sample Size	260	92	169	163	129	175	158	139	155	160	45
Upper	2%	5%	5%	4%	2%	6%	3%	9%	7%	5%	2%
Middle	25	28	30	24	28	19	27	25	27	26	3
Working	56	59	55	59	58	61	58	56	56	58	2
Lower	17	8	10	14	12	14	12	10	10	11	4
Whites											
Sample Size	1,340	648	1,299	1,316	1,355	1,330	1,355	1,312	1,312	1,252	227
Upper	2%	3%	3%	3%	1%	4%	2%	3%	3%	3%	1%
Middle	48	48	48	46	50	46	48	47	46	47	1
Working	45	46	46	47	45	47	46	45	47	46	1
Lower	5	3	3	4	4	3	4	5	4	4	1
Racial Index of Dissimilarity[a]	23	20	18	22	22	27	21	22	21	21	

Source: National Opinion Research Center, National Data Program for the Social Sciences, General Social Surveys, 1972–1982.
a. The index of dissimilarity compares the four-category social-class distributions of whites and blacks.

hypothesis. At all dates, about one-eighth of the blacks said they were lower class, just under three-fifths working class, about one-quarter middle class, while the remaining few claimed they were upper class.

Hereditary Social Status

A different facet of the polarization hypothesis involves the intergenerational transmission of social status. Presumably, in a society with rigid class lines and large differences between the classes, those at the top will be able to pass on their advantages to their children while the offspring of people at the bottom will find it extremely difficult to move into the upper ranks of society.

In the United States, there has been less intergenerational transmission of status in the black community than in the white. In this sense, black social structure is more egalitarian than white. Otis Dudley Duncan, who studied social mobility in the United States using data gathered by the Census Bureau in 1962, reported that the relationship of son's occupational prestige to father's occupational prestige was weaker among blacks than whites. Similarly, the relationship of a man's income to his father's education or to his father's income was less among blacks than among whites. This and other evidence led Duncan (1969) to conclude that well-to-do blacks were much less able than similarly well-to-do whites to pass on their advantages to their children. However, it also demonstrated that blacks at the bottom of the educational and occupational scale were much less likely to pass on their disadvantages to their sons than were similar whites. A 1973 replication of this study similarly found that the intergenerational transmission of status—as measured by educational attainment, occupational prestige, and earnings—was less among blacks than among whites. However, the racial differences in this regard diminished between 1962 and 1973, as the patterns of intergenerational mobility of blacks became more like those of whites (Featherman and Hauser, 1978).

Conclusions

It is an oversimplification to claim that the black community is now split into an elite and an underclass. Some trends point toward such polarization, but others point in the opposite direction.

The trends in educational attainment do not show increasing polarization. On the contrary, the gap separating those at the bottom from those at the top of the black educational distribution is getting smaller, and at all points in the educational distribution blacks are catching up with whites.

A look at the occupational distribution leads to the opposite conclusion: polarization appears to be occurring among blacks. The gap in prestige levels between those at the top and bottom of the occupational distribution has grown larger. This conclusion comes from looking at the occupations of employed workers. There has also been a rather sharp increase in the proportion of adult black men who neither work nor look for jobs, and it is difficult to assign these men an occupational prestige score. Placing these men who are out of the labor force at the bottom of the prestige distribution would make the separation between those at the top and bottom of this distribution even greater.

The trends in income distribution yield mixed evidence. If blacks were becoming increasingly polarized by economic status, then the rich would receive a larger and larger share of total income and the poor would get less. In fact, however, the distribution of family income has changed very little in the last thirty years: ever since the end of World War II, the richest 5 percent of black families have received about 16 percent of all the income obtained by black families, while the poorest 20 percent of black families have received about 4 percent (U.S. Bureau of the Census, 1982e, table 19; 1983b, table 4). But it is also true that the actual gap in purchasing power between those toward the top and the bottom of the black income distribution expanded throughout the 1960s and 1970s.

One kind of polarization is certainly occurring: economic polarization by type of family. Income levels have gone up much more rapidly in husband-wife families than in those headed by women. As a result, families headed by black women are falling further behind husband-wife black families in both absolute and relative terms. This is particularly important because a large and increasing proportion of all blacks live in families headed by women.

It is possible that polarization is one stage in the process by which ethnic and racial groups become assimilated into the mainstream of American social and economic life. Perhaps when groups such as the Irish, Italians, or Russians came to the United States, their first-generation immigrants could obtain only the lowest-paying manual jobs. In such a situation there would be few social class differences within a group, since all its members would be at the bottom of the ladder. We know that later generations of all these groups have moved upward on the social scale. The question is how such social mobility occurs. If the members of each succeeding generation move up the occupational and income ladders pretty much as a group—so that the first generation of migrants has the worst jobs, the second generation gets somewhat better jobs, and the third generation moves into professional and managerial positions—then polarization by social class may not occur. At any point, all members of the group will occupy roughly similar positions.

Another pattern of social mobility is equally plausible. Perhaps a few members of the second generation move into better jobs while most remain in low-income, low-skill jobs like those of their parents. Perhaps in the third generation there is an even wider spread, with some members attaining positions of great prestige and high income while others remain at the bottom of the distribution. But in some later generation when the group no longer fills the niches at the bottom of the occupational hierarchy, polarization may decrease. If this process is the one that actually occurs in the history of assimilating groups, then polarization by social class is simply one stage of assimilation.

In most ways, the experience of blacks in unlike that of any other immigrant group to the United States. They arrived a century or more ahead of most European and all Asian migrants, and they crossed the ocean unwillingly. But blacks did not enter the industrialized urban economy in large numbers until World War II, and so in a way they resemble the immigrants of earlier decades. Perhaps many ethnic groups have become more polarized by occupation, income, and wealth as they have moved into the economic mainstream. Much of the polarization that is occurring among blacks may be part of a longer and larger process of social change. It is more difficult to account for the economic polarization by family type that is now occurring among both blacks and whites.

7

A Scorecard on Black Progress

What has the civil rights revolution accomplished? In the first chapter I outlined three different opinions about this issue. The optimists believe that racial progress has been great, that the practice of discrimination has declined or even been eliminated, and that skin color now has little to do with how much schooling, what kind of job, or what level of pay a person gets. The pessimists paint a very different picture. They consider many of the changes to be superficial, and they stress areas such as family income, poverty, and unemployment, in which progress during the 1970s was minimal. A third view is that blacks are increasingly polarized into a successful elite group and a downtrodden underclass.

I have examined many different indexes concerning the status of blacks. I have stressed that changes must be interpreted cautiously. Sometimes the requisite data are not available; sometimes the data are adequate but the interpretations are ambiguous. The differences between relative and absolute measures of change raise questions that do not have clear answers.

Looking at all these indicators has not made it possible to conclude that one of the three views is correct and the other two are wrong. The best way to summarize what the demographic measures reveal about racial change is to divide them into three categories: those which clearly show that the status of blacks relative to whites is improving, those which show no such improvement, and those which are mixed.

Indicators Showing Improvement

EDUCATIONAL ATTAINMENT

Racial differences in educational attainment are certainly decreasing. On the eve of World War II adult blacks averaged about three fewer years of schooling than whites, but by the early 1980s the racial difference declined to one and one-half years. In the period after World War II the black and white rates of secondary-school attendance converged, and by the mid-1970s racial differences in enrollment through age 17 had about disappeared. During the 1960s college enrollment rates increased more rapidly among whites than among blacks, but in the 1970s the college enrollment rates of blacks moved closer to those of whites. This trend seems to be continuing, bringing a further contraction of racial differences in educational attainment.

Despite the obvious progress for blacks, there is still a substantial difference in attainment. Among those who were in their early twenties in 1980, about 85 percent of the whites but only 70 percent of the blacks had finished high school. Among those in their late twenties, about one white in four but only one black in eight had four or more years of college (U.S. Bureau of the Census, 1980, table 1). This difference comes about partly because enrollment rates are still lower for blacks and partly because more blacks than whites are behind the grade level typical for their age. Grade retardation means that blacks spend more years getting to a given attainment level than do whites.

OCCUPATIONS OF THE EMPLOYED

Another area of obvious racial progress involves the occupations of employed workers. Without doubt blacks now hold more prestigious and higher-paying jobs than they ever did in the past. Since 1960 there has been only a little upgrading of the occupational distribution among whites and thus the proportion of whites with white-collar jobs has risen only slightly. Among blacks meanwhile, the proportion with white-collar positions has gone up rapidly. Back in 1960 the 10 percent of all workers who were black held only 3 percent of the professional and managerial jobs. In 1980 blacks still made up about 10 percent of the work force, but they held 6 percent of the managerial and professional jobs (U.S. Bureau of Labor Statistics, 1979, table 18; 1983, tables 23 and 48).

These changes are particularly impressive for black women. Traditionally, black women cleaned the homes of whites, cooked their food, and washed their clothes. As recently as 1963 a third of all employed black women were domestic servants (U.S. Bureau of Labor Statistics, 1979). This changed rapidly as black women moved into clerical work and the professions.

Despite several decades of impressive improvement, a large gap still separates the occupational distributions of blacks and whites, especially men. In 1982 about 30 percent of all employed black men held white-collar jobs; just about the same proportion of white men held such jobs on the eve of World War II. Thus, black men are four decades behind white men in occupational attainment. The occupational distributions of blacks and whites are unambiguously converging, but the substantial remaining difference will disappear only if this trend continues for several more decades.

EARNINGS OF EMPLOYED WORKERS

Another important area in which there has been progress is the earnings of workers. Several problems that arise in the analysis of earnings limit the dependability of the conclusions. Some types of earnings are probably underreported. Also, one major reason the annual earnings of black men fall below those of white men is that black men work fewer hours per year than white men. We cannot determine whether this difference in hours worked results from discriminatory practices on the part of the employers, whether black and white men prefer different amounts of work and leisure, or whether other reasons, such as the location of jobs and residences, are responsible.

In 1959 black men earned only 61 percent as much per hour as white men; twenty years later they earned 74 percent as much. An analysis of annual earnings reveals a larger difference between the races because black men work fewer hours than white men. But the annual earnings of blacks did clearly improve relative to those of whites. Black men earned 49 percent as much per year as white men in 1959, 55 percent as much in 1979.

The racial gap in earnings has all but disappeared among women. In 1959 black women earned only 61 percent as much per hour as white women; by 1979 they earned 98 percent as much. Since black women typically work more hours per year than white women, they caught up with them in annual earnings by the late 1970s. Women did not catch up with men, however. In 1980 both black and white women had annual earnings about 35 percent of those of white men.

Part of the reason blacks earn less than whites is that they complete fewer years of school and are more likely to live in the South where wages are low. I investigated whether, if black and white workers had the same characteristics, they would earn similar hourly wages. This type of analysis must be interpreted with caution, since not all factors that influence earnings can be precisely measured. The factors I assumed to affect a worker's hourly rate were the worker's educational attainment, years of potential labor force experience, and region of residence. I found that a black man who had the education, years of experience, and region of residence of the typical white man in 1959 would have earned only 81 percent as much per hour as the white man; in 1979 he would still have earned only 88 percent as much. This discrepancy between the wages paid to ostensibly similar workers of different races is sometimes called "the cost of being black," and it is one estimate of the dollar cost of discrimination. My findings indicate that this cost has decreased substantially since the 1950s but has not been eliminated.

Looking at annual earnings rather than hourly wages makes the situation of black workers seem worse, because black men work fewer hours per year than white men. If this racial difference in hours of employment is caused by discrimination by the employers—so that blacks are usually last hired and first fired—then the cost of being black is higher than the previous paragraph implied. A black man who had the characteristics of the typical white man, but who worked the number of hours typical for a black man and was paid at the rate of return for a black man, would have earned only 65 percent as much as the typical white man in 1959 and 76 percent as much in 1979. In other words, discrimination, according to this estimate, cost black men about 35 percent of the earnings of white men in 1959 and about 24 percent in 1979.

Black women in the labor market once suffered from the double burden of being both black and female, but this is no longer the case. An employed black woman who had the labor market characteristics of the typical white woman but was paid for those characteristics at the rates observed among black women would have earned 84 percent as much per hour as the white woman in 1959, but in 1979 she would have earned about 8 percent *more* than the white woman. For women there is no longer any evidence of racial discrimination in earnings.

Black women who are as well-qualified as white women earn at least as much as white women.

But black women have made only modest progress toward catching up with those with the highest earnings: white men. A black woman who had the labor market characteristics of the typical white man but was paid for them at the rates observed among black women would have earned 53 percent as much per hour as the white man in 1959, 64 percent as much in 1979.

I also investigated whether gains in the earnings of blacks were restricted to certain favored groups such as the highly educated, the young, or government employees. I found that the improvements were not limited in this fashion. For almost all segments of the population, the actual earnings of blacks rose faster than those of whites and the apparent cost of labor market discrimination declined. This was true in the 1960s, when the per capita Gross National Product increased at a high rate, and also in the 1970s, when the economy expanded more modestly. In all regions, for all occupational groups, at all levels of educational attainment, and in all sectors of the economy, the earnings of blacks moved closer to those of whites.

There were differences in the timing and rates of gain. Improvements were generally greater for blacks at the upper educational levels. In the North, blacks made greater economic progress in the 1960s than in the 1970s. By examining data for birth cohorts I found that the apparent cost of discrimination decreased very little as people grew older. That is, if the wages of blacks fall behind those of whites by a certain amount when they are at ages 25–34, this discrepancy continues as the workers grow older. However, racial differences are smaller for groups of workers who have entered the labor force more recently.

Some groups of black women reached earnings parity with white women by 1970; by 1980 most groups of black women had done so. The situation is very different for men. Despite the rapid gains in pay among blacks, the earnings of black men in all groups lag behind those of similar white men, implying the persistence of discrimination. For example, among college-educated black and white men who worked the same number of hours and had the same ages and the same regional distribution, blacks earned 90 percent as much as the whites in 1979. Among black and white men aged 25–34 who had the same educational attainment, regional distribution, and hours of work, the blacks earned 89 percent as much as the whites. The cost of discrimination is lower than it was twenty years ago, but it is still costly to be a black man.

Indicators Showing No Improvement

Not all indicators of racial change show progress. As measured by levels of unemployment, blacks were as far behind in 1979 as in 1959. The unemployment rate of black men was twice that of white men in the mid-1950s, and the ratio has changed little since then (Killingsworth, 1968). It did decline a bit in the prosperous years of the late 1960s, as black employment picked up more rapidly than white, but it rose again quite quickly during the recessions of the 1970s.

A related trend also indicates a lack of racial progress: a growing proportion of adult men are neither working nor looking for a job; they have dropped out of the labor force. The rise in non-participation has been much greater among blacks than among whites. In the 1970s the proportion of men aged 25–54 who were not in the labor force rose from 8 to 13 percent for nonwhites, from 3 to 5 percent for whites. The increase was even more dramatic for younger nonwhite men. There have been few investigations of how these men support themselves or spend their time, but what data are available from Census Bureau surveys show that the rise in nonparticipation is not attributable to more men staying in school, being unable to work, or keeping house.

Among women the unemployment rate has persistently been about twice as high for blacks as for whites. But there have been no major changes in labor force participation and employment. Traditionally, a higher proportion of black women than white women held jobs. Since 1960 the proportion employed has gone up for both groups but more sharply for whites; by the 1980s the proportion employed was higher for white women.

Mixed Indicators

INTEGRATION OF SCHOOLS

An example of an indicator on which the trends are mixed is the racial integration of public schools. In most rural areas of the South, in many small and medium-sized cities in all regions, and in those southern metropolises where schools are organized on a county-wide basis, the promise of the *Brown* decision has largely been achieved, and black and white children now attend the same schools. In addition, the majority of black college students, instead of attending the traditionally black institutions, now go to predominantly white colleges and universities.

But little progress has been made in integrating public schools in the nation's largest metropolises. In many central cities, efforts toward integration have been no more than modest, and white enrollments have fallen sharply because of declining birth rates and the migration of whites away from central cities. In cities such as Baltimore, Chicago, and Detroit, the central-city district has a predominantly black and Spanish enrollment, most suburban districts are largely white, and a few suburban enclaves are almost all black. A high proportion of the nation's black students attend school in these large metropolises, where persistent segregation effectively negates the *Brown* ruling. Black and white students go to separate schools just as they did when "separate but equal" was the guiding principle.

THE INCOMES OF FAMILIES

Another area of mixed trends is family welfare. Blacks made much progress in family income in the 1960s but little in the 1970s. Black families had median incomes about 52 percent as great as those of whites in 1959, 64 percent as great in 1970, and only 55 percent as great in 1982 (U.S. Bureau of the Census, 1963a, table 224; 1983b, table 2). At first glance it seems that the gains of one decade were largely wiped out in the next.

The two most common types of families are those which include a married couple and those headed by a woman who lives apart from her spouse, frequently with children. I examined income data—especially trends in per capita income—for these types of families and found that black families continued to gain on similar white families in the 1970s just as in the 1960s. The deterioration in the average economic status of all black families in the 1970s came about mostly because of changes in living arrangements.

Such changes are occurring rapidly. Between 1970 and 1982 the proportion of all black families headed by women rather than by husband-wife couples rose from 28 to 41 percent. An identical but less dramatic trend toward more separation, more divorce, and more childbearing before or outside marriage occurred among whites: the proportion of white families headed by women rose from 9 to 12 percent (U.S. Bureau of the Census, 1971, table 1; 1983d, table 1). These changes had a great impact on the overall ratio of black to white family income, because female-headed families, which tend to have much lower incomes than husband-wife families, are making up a larger and larger fraction of all black families.

POVERTY

Much progress was made during the 1960s in reducing poverty among blacks. In 1959, 55 percent of the black population lived in households whose cash income fell below the poverty line; in 1970 it was only 34 percent. From 1970 to 1979 the poverty rate changed very little; about one black person in three and one white person in eleven was impoverished. Poverty has become more common among both races since 1979; 36 percent of the black population fell below the poverty line by 1982. Because of both population growth and this higher incidence of poverty, the actual number of poor blacks, which was 7.1 million at the start of the 1970s, rose to 9.7 million by 1982 (U.S. Bureau of the Census, 1983b, table 17).

These are disturbing statistics. But considerable caution is needed in interpreting these recent trends. On the one hand, changes in family structure helped to keep the poverty rate high, since female-headed families are much more likely to be impoverished than husband-wife families. This is not to suggest that a statistical adjustment eliminates poverty. Obviously there are an increasing number of black women and children who have few financial resources. Nevertheless, it is important to note that the shift in family living arrangements explains much of the persistence of high rates of poverty among blacks in the 1970s.

On the other hand, the 1970s saw the expansion of federally sponsored noncash transfer programs such as food stamps, school lunches, subsidized housing, and Medicare. None of these noncash benefits are included in the Census Bureau's estimates of poverty rates, even though the majority of low-income households obtain such benefits (U.S. Bureau of the Census, 1982g, table 1). A poverty rate that includes noncash benefits will be lower than the official poverty rate based on cash income alone. In 1979 the official poverty rate for blacks was 30 percent. Including noncash benefits reduces that rate to between 21 and 25 percent, depending upon how you estimate the cash value of benefits (Smeeding, 1982). Without doubt, the poor of 1980 were, in some sense, better off than the poor of two decades earlier, since many of them had access to these benefit programs.

RESIDENTIAL SEGREGATION

Residential segregation of blacks from whites may also be a mixed indicator revealing progress in some locations and no change in others. There is a great deal of convincing evidence showing that blacks and whites seldom share the same urban neighborhoods, that black-white residential segregation is quite unlike the segregation of white ethnic groups, including Hispanics, and that economic factors account for little of the observed residential segregation of blacks from whites (Lieberson, 1963; Taeuber and Taeuber, 1965; Hermalin and Farley, 1973; Massey, 1979; Lieberson, 1980). Residential segregation is seemingly not a consequence of the desires of blacks; they prefer to live in racially mixed areas rather than all-black areas (Pettigrew, 1973; Farley et al., 1978). Numerous studies have found that similar black and white customers are treated very differently in the housing market, implying that discriminatory practices help to keep blacks and whites isolated in different neighborhoods (Saltman, 1975; Pearce, 1979; Wienk et al., 1979; Lake, 1981).

In large cities of all regions of the country, racial residential segregation decreased little between 1940 and 1970 (Taeuber and Taeuber, 1965; Sørenson, Taeuber, and Hollingsworth, 1975; Van Valey, Roof, and Wilcox, 1977). We do not yet know how extensively it declined between 1970 and 1980. The Civil Rights Act of 1968 banned discrimination in the sale or rental of housing, and the incomes of black husband-wife families rose more rapidly in the 1970s than those of similar white families. These changes, along with the continued liberalization of white attitudes, may have made it easier for blacks to enter formerly white neighborhoods. Detailed analysis of data from the 1980 Census will reveal just how much progress has been made since 1970.

Views of Racial Change

Based on all this evidence, which of the three views of racial change I outlined in Chapter 1 is most accurate? Is it true that progress has been widespread and that discrimination is rapidly fading? Or has the observed racial progress been superficial, so that the status of blacks relative to whites has hardly changed? Or is the black population becoming economically polarized, so that some blacks are much better off than they were in the past while a larger group have gained little from the civil rights revolution of the 1960s?

Blacks in the United States are a diverse group, larger than the total population of Argentina, Australia, Canada, South Africa, or Yugoslavia. No simple generalization can adequately describe racial trends. Each of the views contains some truth, but each also fails to capture the complexity of the changes that have occurred.

There is good reason to be particularly critical of the view that black gains are superficial. In the important areas of education, occupations, and earnings, racial differences declined substantially. This is not tokenism. Throughout the entire economy and in all regions, racial differences on the most important indicators are smaller now than before. And I presented strong evidence that discrimination in earnings has declined considerably.

There is also good reason to doubt that the black community is becoming increasingly polarized into an elite and an underclass. Some aspects of this perspective are accurate: there has always been a prosperous segment of the black community and a large impoverished group. In recent decades the black elite has grown larger and more visible, and the black poor have moved to cities where they are also more visible. The welfare of the poor apparently has improved because of the expansion of government services. Nonetheless, the indicators of social and economic polarization are mixed. One type of economic polarization is certainly occurring, but it is quite different from the polarization by social class that is described most frequently. That is, the income gap separating husband-wife families from those families headed by women is growing.

The view that black gains are widespread and significant is the most accurate of the three, but its optimism needs to be tempered. As I have stressed again and again, many more decades of change similar to the 1960s and 1970s will be necessary if racial differences are to disappear.

What Will Happen in the Future?

In the decade following the Civil War, Congress passed five major civil rights acts and funded the Freedman's Bureau to provide ex-slaves with education and economic opportunities. In the final quarter of the nineteenth century, however, the Supreme Court vitiated civil rights laws and permitted southern states to establish rigid systems of segregation, which kept blacks not only impoverished but in a type of bondage reminiscent of the pre-Civil War period. In the 1960s the Congress amended the Constitution to extend suffrage to blacks, passed four major civil rights bills, and funded numerous social welfare programs, including the War on Poverty. These efforts to improve the situation of blacks were successful: the economic status of blacks improved, poverty declined, and on many indicators differences between the races became much smaller. Will this racial progress continue? Or, just as the advances made by blacks after the Civil War were largely eliminated in the period following Reconstruction, will the gains of the 1960s and 1970s disappear in the coming decades?

The racial developments of the late twentieth century are unlikely to resemble those of the late nineteenth century. There has been a revolution in race relations in the United States. If a study similar to the one described in this book is carried out in 2010 or 2020, it will almost certainly find that racial differences have continued to shrink.

I offer this prediction for three reasons. First, the legal status of blacks has been fundamentally changed, and their political power has greatly increased. For seventy years following the Civil War, blacks were concentrated in the rural South, where they were politically and economically powerless. Demographic changes of the 1940s and 1950s—especially the black migration to cities in the North and West—and the civil rights laws of the 1960s made blacks an important force in the political arena. Black voters increasingly influence elections, and the number of black officeholders continues to rise. It is extraordinarily difficult to imagine that the nation might return to a system that would prevent blacks from voting, deny them the right to serve on juries, or ostracize them in public facilities as the Jim Crow laws did.

Second, black Americans will surely never again tolerate the racial discrimination that existed before the civil rights revolution of the 1960s. The changes in consciousness brought about by Martin Luther King, Malcolm X, and other leaders will be long lasting. Increasing numbers of blacks are succeeding in industry, education, and government. No one knows what shape the civil rights movement may take in the future, but it is unlikely that blacks will allow the gains of recent decades to slip away.

Third, whites have confronted the American dilemma described by Gunnar Myrdal and have accepted the principles that all should be allowed to vote and that blacks and whites should have equal opportunities for jobs and education. To be sure, racism is not dead. A small number of whites are still active in the Ku Klux Klan, crosses are still burned on the lawns of some blacks who dare to move into white neighborhoods, and proposals to build low-income housing or to integrate public schools still meet heated opposition. But no more than a small minority of whites would prefer to overturn the civil rights laws of the 1960s and go back to a legally segregated society.

Affirmative action programs that guarantee blacks jobs, appointments, or promotions largely on the basis of their color still arouse strong white opposition. Nathan Glazer (1975) contends that the United States is moving away from the traditional system in which achievement was based on ability and toward a system in which race or ethnicity plays a large role. Many whites probably have an image of their own ethnic history that is incompatible with a quota system. Perhaps their grandparents or great grandparents came to the United States penniless and were called Guineas, Micks, or Polacks; by working diligently, they gradually moved up the economic ladder. Whites whose own ethnic group overcame immense disadvantages through individual efforts may believe any group can achieve in a similar manner.

Recent national samples of whites suggest that they hold contradictory views of the problems blacks now face. About three-quarters of whites feel that racial discrimination still limits opportunities for blacks, and yet just about the same proportion believe blacks get preferential treatment that improves their chances to get ahead. Apparently the majority of whites think blacks simultaneously suffer from discrimination in some circumstances and benefit from preferential affirmative action in others (Kluegel and Smith, 1982).

The trends I have described—the increased political power of blacks, the lasting impact of the civil rights movement, and changes in the attitudes of whites—will all cause racial differences to diminish in the future. The speed with which these differences decrease may depend upon the rate of economic growth and the future strength of the civil rights movement. The greatest threats to further black gains may be an economic depression and a federal administration that assigns a low priority to civil rights issues.

If the economy prospers and many new jobs are created, unemployment rates will be low and the large occupational gap that still separates the races will diminish. High rates of economic growth should provide local governments with funds to improve educational opportunities, and this may lead to even smaller racial differences in enrollment and attainment. Economic growth will reduce the need for some types of income security programs but will improve the government's ability to support the ones that are required.

If the economy grows lethargically, the high unemployment rates of blacks will undoubtedly persist. Indeed, as more women of both races obtain advanced educations and enter the job market, competition for employment will be heightened and there may be a further rise in unemployment among black men. If the economy falters, tax revenues will fall and government employment will decline, a change that will have an unusually large impact upon blacks and women, who are overrepresented in this sector. Reductions in assistance programs for the poor will have greater consequences for blacks than for whites, since blacks are overrepresented among the beneficiaries.

It is probable that all future federal administrations will endorse the principles of civil rights, nondiscrimination, and equal opportunities. But the change in the actual status of blacks will depend upon whether an administration gives these issues high or low priority. This, in turn, may depend upon the strength and effectiveness of the civil rights movement.

In the 1960s President Johnson not only supported legislation protecting the rights of blacks but endorsed affirmative action programs and proposed that equality be made a national goal. Referring to the Voting Rights Act of 1965, which allowed all southern blacks to vote, he said:

> But freedom is not enough. You do not wipe away the scars of centuries by saying: "Now you are free to go where you want, do as you desire, and choose the leaders you please" . . .
>
> You do not take a person who, for years, has been hobbled by chains and liberate him, bring him up to the starting line of a race and then say, "You are free to compete with all the others," and still believe that you have been completely fair . . .
>
> We seek not just freedom but opportunity—not just legal equity but human ability—not just equality as a right and theory but equality as a fact and as a result . . .
>
> To this end equal opportunity is essential, but not enough (Johnson, 1970:560–561).

Five years later, in a different administration, a White House memorandum described the gains recently made by blacks and proposed a moratorium on further federal actions in the area of race. Its author, Daniel Patrick Moynihan, suggested that "the time may have come when the issue of race could benefit from a period of benign neglect" (Kihss, 1970:1).

Throughout the nation's history there has been a tendency to underestimate the magnitude of racial differences, to overestimate the progress that has been made, and to oversimplify the solutions to remaining racial problems. Many people probably believe that during the 1960s and 1970s enough effort was devoted to the struggle for civil rights and the numerous laws and court rulings solved racial difficulties. The evidence I have presented makes it clear that much has been accomplished. People may focus upon these gains and assume that the time has indeed come for a strategy of benign neglect.

But in congratulating ourselves as a nation for the real and impressive progress we have made toward racial equality, we should not lose sight of the distance that remains to be traveled. Black men are still twice as likely as white men to be out of work. A high—and growing—proportion of black families have incomes below the poverty line (35 percent in 1982, compared to only 11 percent of white families). And the public schools in New York, Chicago, Los Angeles, Philadelphia, and Washington were as racially segregated in 1980 as two decades earlier. Much remains to be done before we will be able to say unequivocally that the economic and social gap between the races has been closed.

Appendix
Notes
References
Index

Describing Racial Differences in Earnings

The approach I use to assess racial differences assumes that how much people earn is a result of their educational attainment, years of labor market experience, and region of residence. The data I analyze are from the Census Bureau. This source does not provide information about how long workers have been with their current employers, their health status, their scores on tests of learning or mental ability, or the characteristics of their families of origin. But this analysis includes those explanatory variables which have proved to be most important in previous studies of racial differences in earnings. I measured the variables as follows:

Hourly wage rate. I determined each person's earnings by summing wage, salary, and self-employment income including any obtained from the sale of farm products. The earnings figures refer to 1959, 1969, or 1979.

As indicated in Chapter 2, blacks are much more likely than whites to be unemployed, so whites typically spend more time on the job each year. This difference in employment—especially among men—accounts for some of the racial difference in annual earnings and must be taken into account in this investigation. There are two ways to do this. First, earnings in a year can be treated as the dependent variable and an independent variable measuring either weeks of work or hours of work during the year can be included. Second, the hourly wage can be used as the dependent variable. I chose the second approach because the hourly wage rate is an easily understood indicator of economic status. The question of why blacks generally earn less per hour than whites when they are at work is a separate issue—albeit a related one—from the question of why black men work fewer hours each year than white men. In this investigation, I focus upon racial differences in earnings rather than upon the supply of labor.

To determine the hourly wage paid to an individual, I divided his or her annual earnings by the number of hours of employment during the year. It was easy to calculate how many hours a person worked during 1979, because the March 1980 Current Population Survey asked respondents how many weeks they worked in the previous year and how many hours they usually worked per week when they were employed. It was more difficult to ascertain hours of work for 1959 and 1969. The Census of 1960 and the March 1970 Current Population Survey asked adults how many weeks they were employed in the previous year. Those who were working during the week prior to the census or survey were also asked how many hours they worked during that specific week. I multiplied their hours of work during that week by their weeks of employment in the previous year to estimate their annual hours (for an evaluation of this procedure, see Smith and Rytina, 1983).

In 1960 and 1970 about one-sixth of the people who were employed in the previous year were not working when the census or survey was conducted and thus did not report about their hours of work. Rather than delete them from the analysis, I imputed their hours of employment. I considered all those people in the 1960 and 1970 samples who worked during the previous year and reported their hours of employment for the week before the survey. I divided them into four groups—white men, black men, white women, and black women—and for each group I regressed hours of work during the week before the survey on years of education, age, occupational prestige, weeks worked in the previous year, earnings in that year, marital status (a dichotomy indicating whether a person lived with a spouse), and region (a dichotomy indicating whether a person lived in the South). For women, an additional variable was used indicating whether or not there was a child under age 6 in the household. Using results from these four regression equations, I estimated hours of employment for those who worked during the year before the census or survey but not in the week preceding the census or survey.

The dependent variable was not the hourly wage itself but its logarithm. This transformation was necessary because the distribution of wage rates is quite skewed: a small number of persons earn very high hourly wages. In statistical terms, the distribution of the log of hourly wages is closer to a normal distribution than is the distribution of hourly wages themselves, and thus the log transformation reduces the nonlinearity in the regression equations for earnings. The log transformation is used to reduce any positive skew in the distribution, but if wage rates are very low the transformation may introduce a negative skew (see Featherman and Hauser, 1978).

Educational attainment. Each adult in the census and surveys reported the number of years of schooling he or she had completed. I divided attainment into two variables: *elementary and secondary education*, the number of completed years of precollege education, ranging from 0 to 12 years; and *college education*, the number of years of postsecondary education, ranging from 0 to 6 years.

Years of labor market experience. The variable measuring labor market experience equals a respondent's current age minus his or her years of schooling minus 6 (because most people begin their enrollment at age 6). It measures years of *potential* labor market activity, but it is not an accurate indicator of how many years a person actually worked. The calculation assumes that all people begin school at age 6, attend continuously, and begin their careers shortly after they finish school. Although this is a fairly common pattern among men, there are numerous exceptions (see Hogan, 1981).

Years of labor market experience squared. Since job skills become obsolete as a person grows older, earnings do not increase linearly with age (Mincer, 1974; Mincer and Polachek, 1974). To take this into account, I include the square of the previous variable as an explanatory factor. (For an alternative approach, see Stolzenberg, 1975.)

Region (South). Wage rates have traditionally been lower in the South than in other regions, and blacks are more likely than whites to live in southern states. To include the effects of this regional difference, a variable was used that identifies people living within the region designated as South by the Census Bureau.

The sample. To analyze earnings for the broadest possible array of workers, I considered all black and white persons aged 25–64 who were in the 1960 Census sample or the samples from the March 1970 and March 1980 Current Population Surveys. Individuals under age 25 were excluded because many of them were just beginning their careers and combined schooling with employment, and those 65 and over were excluded because most of them were retired and many who did hold jobs had a different attachment to the labor force than did younger workers 25–64.

The Current Population Surveys are restricted to the noninstitutional civilian population: persons who were in institutions at the time of the census or survey were not included even if they had earned money during the previous year. The surveys were also limited to the civilian population, so the small proportion of people over 25 who were on active military duty were excluded.

Since I was interested in racial differences in *earnings*, I eliminated from the analysis anyone who did not work in a given year. In each year there were a few people—generally less than one-half of one percent—who worked but had negative earnings. This might occur if you trade commodities or speculate in real estate. A somewhat larger group, mostly white women, reported that they worked some number of hours but had no cash earnings. They might work in a family business or assist a spouse who is self-employed. Since people with negative earnings or no earnings differ in many ways from those who work for wages, they were also eliminated.

Table A.1 shows the number of individuals in the Census Bureau's samples and the percentages who were deleted for various reasons. Between 1960 and 1980 there was a slight drop in the proportion of white men included in the analysis and a larger drop in the proportion of black men, primarily because an increasing proportion of black men did not work in the year prior to the survey. Nevertheless, this analysis involves 90 percent of the white and 83 percent of the black men who were 25–64 when the 1980 survey was conducted. Because of their growing labor force participation, an increasing proportion of white women were included in the study; by 1980 about two-thirds of both white and black women reported earning money during the previous year.

The Census Bureau data files provide information about all variables for these respondents. In some cases the values have been allocated or have been assigned through editing procedures; for instance, if an individual failed to report earnings or educational attainment, the Bureau allocated values using information about other characteristics of the respondent; if a person claimed impossible characteristics such as an age of 245 years or 170 hours of work during a week, the responses were edited.

Data from the 1960 sample are self-weighting such that every observation represents exactly 1,000 persons. In the 1970 and 1980 Current Population Surveys, each observation represents a different number of respondents. As a result, weighting was used with all the statistical analyses for these years. The number of cases indicated in the tables

Table A.1. Sample size and sample selection.

	White men	Black men	White women	Black women
	1980 Current Population Survey			
Total in sample (unweighted count)	37,004	3,928	38,610	4,851
% deleted because:				
Did not work in 1979	8.50%	16.80%	34.65%	33.37%
Worked but had negative earnings	.60	.40	.41	.00
Worked but had zero earnings	<.00	.00	1.01	.10
% of sample included in analysis	90.09	82.79	65.35	66.60
	1970 Current Population Survey			
Total in sample (unweighted count)	27,751	2,791	29,418	3,336
% deleted because:				
In armed forces	1.70%	1.40%	.00%	.00%
Did not work in 1969	4.27	7.49	44.42	32.19
Worked but had negative earnings	.49	.18	.15	.12
Worked but had zero earnings	.13	.11	2.54	.51
% of sample included in analysis	93.41	90.83	52.88	67.18
	Census of 1960			
Total in sample	36,538	3,699	38,084	4,186
% deleted because:				
In armed forces	1.95%	1.41%	.03%	.00%
Did not work in 1959	1.72	7.52	52.79	38.10
Worked but had negative earnings	.13	.08	.02	.02
Worked but had zero earnings	1.06	.78	2.13	1.70
% of sample included in analysis	95.14	90.21	45.03	60.18

Sources: U.S. Bureau of the Census, *Census of Population: 1960,* Public Use Sample File; *Current Population Survey,* March 1970, Public Use Sample File; *Current Population Survey,* March 1980, Public Use Sample File.

is the actual number of respondents interviewed in these surveys.

Table A.2 lists the means and standard deviations of the variables used in this analysis. Table A.3 presents coefficients from the regression equations for employed persons aged 25–64 classified by sex and race. Since the dependent variable in each equation is the log of hourly earnings, the regression coefficients report the percentage change in earnings associated with a one-unit change in the independent variable.

Table A.2. Means and standard deviations of variables used in analysis of earnings for employed persons classified by race and sex, 1960, 1970, and 1980.

Variables	White men			Black men			White women			Black women		
	1960	1970	1980	1960	1970	1980	1960	1970	1980	1960	1970	1980
VARIABLES USED IN REGRESSION MODELS												
Log of hourly wage	.8548	1.3237	1.9736	.3627	.9381	1.6723	.3954	.7279	1.4024	−.1006	.4370	1.3841
	.7461	.7528	.8257	.8196	.8325	.8378	.7877	.8604	.9853	.9205	.9476	.6915
Elementary & secondary education (years)	9.85	10.68	11.25	7.53	9.04	10.46	10.35	10.95	11.46	8.34	9.79	10.99
	2.61	2.19	1.80	3.47	3.28	2.97	2.27	1.89	1.46	3.22	2.66	2.01
College education (years)	.73	1.02	1.54	.25	.37	.73	.63	.73	1.20	.36	.45	.85
	1.58	1.83	2.10	.96	1.17	1.69	1.42	1.53	1.85	1.12	1.23	1.76
Experience (years)	26.18	25.28	22.61	27.76	26.42	23.17	25.91	25.61	22.03	26.51	25.19	21.33
	12.14	12.27	12.38	12.30	12.99	14.28	11.53	11.75	11.92	12.03	12.14	12.82
Experience squared (years)	832.48	788.84	662.74	922.29	860.07	693.63	804.17	794.77	628.30	847.27	784.98	614.50
	681.41	655.40	625.76	735.12	752.03	757.01	635.24	621.99	588.34	694.42	672.81	665.80
Proportion in South	.26	.27	.30	.57	.52	.50	.26	.28	.30	.57	.54	.50
	.44	.45	.46	.50	.51	.57	.44	.45	.46	.49	.49	.54
RELATED VARIABLES												
Annual earnings (constant 1979 dollars)	14,820	18,846	18,780	7,399	10,984	12,439	6,258	7,488	8,066	3,618	5,815	7,961
	14,277	14,157	12,606	5,292	7,000	9,168	5,187	5,982	6,337	3,524	4,825	6,245
Log of annual earnings	8.4111	8.9429	9.5800	7.6998	8.3600	9.1394	7.3842	7.7428	8.4959	6.7222	7.4511	8.5930
	.8255	.8049	.9552	.9174	.9418	1.1006	1.1602	1.2856	1.4079	1.2128	1.3084	1.2127
Annual hours	2,076	2,189	2,151	1,780	1,890	1,925	1,431	1,458	1,561	1,283	1,434	1,636
	633	705	632	695	728	692	765	786	758	783	764	718
Hourly wage rate (constant 1979 dollars)	7.67	9.31	8.85	4.88	6.81	6.63	5.05	5.48	5.31	3.47	4.22	4.72
	8.94	8.85	6.33	5.53	11.54	12.61	6.62	5.94	7.07	4.77	3.70	3.09

Source: same as for Table A.1.

Note: For each variable, the first number listed is the mean; the second is the standard deviation.

Table A.3. Coefficients of equations regressing log of hourly earnings on independent variables, by race and sex, 1959, 1969, and 1979.

	White men			Black men			White women			Black women		
	1959	1969	1979	1959	1969	1979	1959	1969	1979	1959	1969	1979
Elementary & secondary education	.0569 (.0018)	.0577 (.0024)	.0619 (.0027)	.0361 (.0050)	.0301 (.0065)	.0653 (.0068)	.0498 (.0031)	.0472 (.0040)	.0534 (.0045)	.0487 (.0070)	.0748 (.0090)	.0581 (.0077)
College education	.0890 (.0027)	.0769 (.0027)	.0750 (.0023)	.1048 (.0148)	.0658 (.0144)	.0887 (.0101)	.1069 (.0045)	.1006 (.0046)	.0863 (.0036)	.1746 (.0164)	.1555 (.0155)	.1070 (.0074)
Experience	.0271 (.0015)	.0250 (.0016)	.0382 (.0016)	.0267 (.0051)	.0214 (.0055)	.0197 (.0050)	.0074 (.0023)	.0096 (.0025)	-.0043* (.0023)	.0121* (.0064)	-.0064* (.0067)	.0005* (.0041)
Experience squared	-.00041 (.00003)	-.00044 (.00003)	-.00063 (.00003)	-.00043 (.00008)	-.00038 (.00010)	-.00028 (.00010)	-.00007* (.00004)	-.00015 (.00005)	.00010* (.00005)	-.00019* (.00011)	.00006* (.00012)	-.00002* (.00008)
Region	-.1810 (.0088)	-.1630 (.0101)	-.0993 (.0095)	-.4999 (.0275)	-.3792 (.0326)	-.2092 (.0281)	-.1668 (.0136)	-.0911 (.0150)	-.0784 (.0134)	-.5604 (.0349)	-.3622 (.0376)	-.2380 (.0223)
Intercept	-.0920	.3875	.7434	-.0001	.6008	.7683	-.2773	.0358	.7451	-.4073	-.0522	.7769
R²	.1104	.0993	.0771	.1651	.1105	.1268	.0775	.0525	.0406	.2062	.1810	.1771
Number of cases	33,613	25,833	33,286	3,253	2,435	2,501	16,318	15,701	24,859	2,447	2,291	2,747

Source: same as for Table A.1.
*Coefficient not significantly different from zero at .025 level of significance.

Notes

2. Education, Employment, and Occupation

1. As a practical matter, schools could be integrated by shifting a smaller proportion of the total enrollment if black and white students were exchanged. The minimum proportion of total enrollment that would have to be shifted to produce an index of dissimilarity of zero is given by $2pqd$ where p is the proportion of students minority, q is $1-p$, and d is the index of dissimilarity (Farley and Taeuber, 1974). This is known as the replacement index and has a maximum value of 50 percent.

2. These data refer to the 243 Standard Metropolitan Statistical Areas (SMSAs) defined on the basis of the Census of 1970. The suburban ring is that portion of the SMSA which is outside the corporate limits of the central city or cities.

3. Let y_1 = year-to-year change in unemployment rate of white men; y_2 = year-to-year change in unemployment rate of nonwhite men; x = year-to-year percentage change in constant-dollar GNP. With 32 observations for the 1950–1982 period, we find:

$$y_1 = 1.15 - .32x \qquad r^2 = .83 \qquad \text{D.W.} = 2.67$$
$$(.03)$$
$$y_2 = 1.98 - .57x \qquad r^2 = .75 \qquad \text{D.W.} = 2.49$$
$$(.70)$$

(Figures in parentheses are the standard errors of the regression coefficient.)

3. Personal Income and Earnings

1. Since the statistical model uses the log of earnings as the dependent variable, the amounts shown in Figure 3.3 are the average of the log of

earnings of a group expressed in 1979 dollars. Average wage rates, based on the log of earnings, are ordinarily smaller than average hourly earnings themselves. This is because people with high hourly earnings raise the average of hourly earnings but have less effect on the mean of the log of earnings. In 1979 the mean of the log of hourly earnings for black men in this sample implied an average wage of $5.32 while the mean of actual earnings was $6.63. Means and standard deviations of both hourly earnings and the log of hourly earnings are shown in the Appendix, Table A.2

2. These estimates of dollar value were obtained by considering the average earnings of a group and their regression equation. The coefficients of these equations are shown in the Appendix, Table A.3. I determined the net change in hourly earnings that would result from one additional year of education, from one year of experience, or from living in the South. This assumes that all variables other than the one in question take on their observed mean value.

4. Who Benefited?

1. Statistical models were fit separately for men and women of both races within each attainment category. The log of hourly earnings was the dependent variable. Years of potential labor force experience, the square of that variable, and a dichotomous variable indicating whether the person lived in the South were the independent variables. The models were fit with the log of hourly wages as a dependent variable, but the text discusses racial differences in both annual earnings and hourly earnings.

2. To estimate these annual earnings I used the equation for blacks that regressed the log of hourly earnings on region, years of experience, and the square of years of experience, and inserted the mean values for whites for the independent variables. The estimated log of hourly earnings for blacks was then added to the log of hours actually worked by blacks to obtain the log of annual earnings. This was converted to actual dollars and compared to the earnings reported by whites.

3. Separate statistical models were computed within each occupational category for every race-sex group. The log of hourly earnings was regressed upon years of elementary and secondary schooling, years of college education, years of labor market experience, the square of that variable, and a variable indicating whether a person lived in the South. Adding the log of hourly earnings to the log of hours worked led to estimates of annual earnings.

4. Persons who worked during the previous year but were unemployed or out of the labor force at the time of the survey were classified by the longest job they held in the preceding year.

5. Separate regression models were fit for black and white men and women within each industrial sector. The log of hourly earnings was the dependent variable. Years of elementary and secondary education, years of college ed-

ucation, years of potential labor market experience, the square of years of experience, and the region variable (South or non-South) were the independent variables.

6. There are regional differences in the cost of living, but they are seemingly smaller than regional differences in hourly wage rates. In the mid-1970s, hourly wage rates in the South fell about 15 percent below those of other regions. Although it is difficult to determine precise regional differences in the cost of living, the available indexes suggest that the cost of living may be about 10 percent lower in the South than elsewhere (U.S. Bureau of Labor Statistics, 1979, tables 135–146).

7. The statistical model used in this section regressed the log of hourly wages upon years of elementary and secondary education, years of college, and the region variable. The measures of years of labor market experience were not used since they have a limited variance within age groups. To estimate annual earnings, the log of hourly earnings was added to the log of hours worked and the resulting sum was converted to dollars.

8. Butler and Heckman (1977) warn that cohort trends should be interpreted cautiously because there may be a good deal of selectivity about who remains at work when they get older. Individuals with the potential for high earnings may stay on the job while those who lack skills may drop out of the labor force. As birth cohorts age, a higher proportion of blacks than whites may find their earnings prospects poor and so leave the labor force. Thus, as cohorts grow older, the earnings of blacks and whites may become more alike because a larger proportion of unskilled blacks leave the work force.

It is difficult to test the selective attrition hypothesis with the data at hand. There are indications that selective attrition does not "cause" the improvement in the earnings of the birth cohorts of blacks. Using data from the 1950, 1960, and 1970 Censuses and from the March 1980 Current Population Survey, I calculated the proportion of cohorts of black and white men who worked at all during the previous year.

Birth cohorts of black men consistently have lower proportions working than similar cohorts of white men, and the racial difference gets wider with age. However, the decreases in labor force activity among black men are quite small until the age group 55–64. Consider men born between 1935 and 1944. At ages 25–34 the proportion employed was about six points greater for whites than for blacks; at 35–44 the white advantage was about seven points. Such a small change in employment could not produce the cohort gains in the relative earnings of blacks.

I also examined the incomes of *all* men in birth cohorts to see if racial differences increased with aging. If the selective attrition hypothesis is accurate, the relative economic status of blacks should decline as cohorts age when all members of a cohort are considered, because as they age a larger and larger share of blacks will be out of work and thus have no earnings.

Black per capita income, relative to white, stayed about the same as men grew older. Among those born in the decade 1925–1934, black men at ages 25–34 had average incomes 56 percent as great as those of whites. When these men were twenty years older, blacks reported 55 percent as much income as whites. There is no evidence that birth cohorts of black men substantially fall behind whites as they age, which would be expected if the selective attrition hypothesis were accurate.

5. The Welfare of Families and Individuals

1. Let:

x = year-to-year percentage change in constant-dollar GNP
y = year-to-year change in the ratio of median black family income to that of whites for the period 1950–1980
n = 31 observations of year-to-year changes for the period 1949–50 to 1979–80

Then:

$$y = .3596 + .0058x \qquad r^2 = .01 \qquad \text{D.W.} = 2.65$$
$$ (.1267)$$

2. Several minor adjustments were made in 1969; for details, see U.S. Bureau of the Census, 1982f:185–187.

3. Let:

y_b = year-to-year change in percentage of blacks below poverty line
y_w = year-to-year change in percentage of whites below poverty line
x = year-to-year percentage change in constant-dollar GNP
n = number of years (fourteen observations beginning with 1966–67 and ending with 1979–80).

Then:

$$y_b = .307 - .321x \qquad r^2 = .21 \qquad \text{D.W.} = .93$$
$$ (.181)$$
$$y_w = .590 - .233x \qquad r^2 = .70 \qquad \text{D.W.} = .69$$
$$ (.044)$$

4. Federal government spending for food stamps, school lunches, public housing, and Medicaid (in constant dollars) rose from $530 per poor or near-poor person in 1970 to $1,086 in 1980 (Smeeding, 1982; U.S. Bureau of the Census, 1983; table A-2).

6. Class Differences in the Black Community

1. I tested to see whether the reports of social class changed over time as the polarization hypothesis suggests. Year and class identification were statistically independent among both the black and white samples. That is, the probability that a person selected a given class did not vary significantly from one year to another, meaning that there was no time trend.

References

Anderson, Elijah. 1978. *A Place on the Corner.* Chicago: University of Chicago Press.
——— 1979. "Some Observations of Black Youth Employment," in Bernard E. Anderson and Isabel V. Sawhill, eds., *Youth Employment and Public Policy.* Englewood Cliffs, N.J.; Prentice-Hall.
Anderson, Martin. 1978. *Welfare: The Political Economy of Welfare Reform in the United States.* Stanford: Hoover Institution Press.
Auletta, Ken. 1982. *The Underclass.* New York: Random House.
Banfield, Edward C. 1970. *The Unheavenly City: The Nature and Future of our Urban Crisis.* Boston: Little, Brown.
Beck, Elwood, Patrick M. Horan, and Charles M. Tolbert, III. 1978. "Stratification in a Dual Economy: A Sectoral Model of Earnings Determination." *American Sociological Review* 43, no. 5 (Oct.):704-720.
Bell, Derrick A., Jr. 1973. *Race, Racism and American Law.* Boston: Little, Brown.
Bianchi, Suzanne M. 1980. "Racial Differences in Per Capita Income, 1960–76: The Importance of Household Size, Headship and Labor Force Participation." *Demography* 17, no. 2 (May) :129–144.
——— 1981. *Household Composition and Racial Inequality.* New Brunswick, N.J.: Rutgers University Press.
Bianchi, Suzanne, and Reynolds Farley. 1979. "Racial Differences in Family Living Arrangements and Economic Well-Being: An Analysis of Recent Trends." *Journal of Marriage and the Family* 41, no. 3 (Aug.):537–551.
Blau, Peter M., and Otis Dudley Duncan. 1967. *The American Occupational Structure.* New York: John Wiley.
Blaustein, Albert P., and Robert L. Zangrando. 1970. *Civil Rights and the Black American.* New York: Simon and Schuster.
Bluestone, Barry, W. M. Murphy, and M. Stevensen. 1973. *Low Wages and the Working Poor.* Policy Papers in Human Resources and Industrial

Relations no. 22. Ann Arbor: Institute of Labor and Industrial Relations, University of Michigan.

Bonacich, Edna. 1976. "Advanced Capitalism and Black/White Race Relations in the United States: A Split Labor Market Interpretation." *American Sociological Review* 41 (Feb.):34–51.

Bond, Horace Mann. 1934. *The Education of the Negro in the American Social Order.* New York: Prentice-Hall.

Brimmer, Andrew F. 1966. "The Negro in the National Economy." In John P. Davis, ed., *The American Negro Reference Book.* Englewood Cliffs, N.J.: Prentice-Hall.

——— 1970. "Economic Progress of Negroes in the United States: The Deepening Schism." Paper presented at Tuskeegee, Ala. March 22.

Brown, Michael K., and Steven P. Erie. 1981. "Blacks and the Legacy of the Great Society: The Economic and Political Impact of Federal Social Policy." *Public Policy* 29, no. 3 (Summer) :299–330.

Bullock, Henry Allen. 1973. *A History of Negro Education in the South.* Cambridge, Mass.: Harvard University Press.

Bumpass, Larry, and Ronald R. Rindfuss. 1979. "Children's Experience of Marital Disruption." *American Journal of Sociology* 85, no. 1 (July):49–65.

Burstein, Paul. 1979. "Equal Employment Opportunity Legislation and the Income of Women and Nonwhites." *American Sociological Review* 44. no. 3 (June):367–391.

Butler, Richard, and James J. Heckman. 1977. "The Impact of the Government on the Labor Market Status of Black Americans: A Critical Review of the Literature and Some New Evidence." In Leonard S. Hausman, ed., *Equal Rights and Industrial Relations.* Madison, Wis.: Industrial Relations Research Association.

Cherlin, Andrew J. 1981. *Marriage, Divorce, Remarriage,* Cambridge, Mass.: Harvard University Press.

Clague, Alice J., and Stephanie J. Ventura. 1968. *Trends in Illegitimacy: United States, 1940–1965.* Vital and Health Statistics, ser. 21, no. 15. Washington: National Center for Health Statistics.

Coleman, James S., Sara D. Kelly, and John A. Moore. 1975. *Trends in School Segregation, 1968–73.* Urban Institute Paper 722–03–01. Washington: Urban Institute.

Converse, Philip E., Jean D. Dotson, Wendy J. Hoag, and William H. McGee, III. 1980. *American Social Attitudes Data Sourcebook: 1947–1979.* Cambridge, Mass.: Harvard University Press.

Conway, Delores A., and Harry V. Roberts. 1983. "Reverse Regression, Fairness, and Employment Discrimination." *Journal of Business and Economic Statistics* 1, no. 1 (Jan.):75–85.

Corcoran, Mary, and Greg J. Duncan. 1979. "Work History, Labor Force Attachment and Earnings: Differences Between the Races and Sexes." *Journal of Human Resources* 14, no. 1 (Winter):3–20.

Cottingham, Clement. 1982. "Conclusion: The Political Economy of Urban Poverty." In Clement Cottingham, ed., *Race, Poverty, and the Urban Underclass*. Lexington, Mass.: D. C. Heath.

Darity, William A., Jr., and Samuel L. Myers, Jr. 1980. "Changes in Black-White Income Inequality, 1968–78: A Decade of Progress?" *Review of Black Political Economy* 10, no. 4 (Summer):354–379.

Doeringer, Peter B., and Michael J. Piore. 1971. *Internal Labor Markets and Manpower Analysis*. Lexington, Mass.: D. C. Heath.

Duncan, Beverly. 1968. "Trends in Output and Distribution of Schooling." In Eleanor Bernert Sheldon and Wilbert E. Moore, eds., *Indicators of Social Change*. New York: Russell Sage.

Duncan, Greg J., and Saul D. Hoffman. 1983. "A New Look at the Causes of the Improved Economic Status of Black Workers." *Journal of Human Resources* 18, no. 2 (Spring):268–281.

Duncan, Otis Dudley. 1961. "A Socioeconomic Index for All Occupations." In Albert J. Reiss, Jr., ed., *Occupations and Social Status*. New York: Free Press of Glencoe.

—— 1969. "Inheritance of Poverty or Inheritance of Race?" In Daniel P. Moynihan, ed., *On Understanding Poverty: Perspectives from the Social Sciences*. New York: Basic Books.

Farley, Reynolds. 1977. "Trends in Racial Inequalities: Have the Gains of the 1960s Disappeared in the 1970s?" *American Sociological Review* 42 (April):189–208.

—— 1978. "School Integration in the United States." In Frank D. Bean and W. Parker Frisbie, eds., *The Demography of Racial and Ethnic Groups*. New York: Academic Press.

Farley, Reynolds, Toni Richards, and Clarence Wurdock. 1980. "School Desegregation and White Flight: An Investigation of Competing Models and Their Discrepant Findings." *Sociology of Education* 53 (July):123–129.

Farley, Reynolds, Howard Schuman, Suzanne Bianchi, Diane Colasanto, and Shirley Hatchett. 1978. "Chocolate City, Vanilla Suburbs: Will the Trend Toward Racially Separate Communities Continue?" *Social Science Research* 7 (Dec.):319–344.

Farley, Reynolds, and Alma F. Taeuber. 1974. "Racial Segregation in the Public Schools." *American Journal of Sociology* 79, no. 4 (Jan.):888–905.

Featherman, David L., and Robert M. Hauser. 1978. *Opportunity and Change*. New York: Academic Press.

Franklin, John Hope. 1967. *From Slavery to Freedom*. New York: Knopf.

Freeman, Richard B. 1973. "Decline of Labor Market Discrimination and Economic Analysis." *American Economic Review* 63 (May):280–286.

—— 1976. *Black Elite: The New Market for Highly Educated Black Americans*. New York: McGraw-Hill.

Fuchs, Victor R. 1983. *How We Live*. Cambridge, Mass.: Harvard University Press.

Garrow, David J. 1978. *Protest at Selma*. New Haven: Yale University Press.

Gilder, George. 1981. *Wealth and Poverty.* New York: Basic Books.

Glascow, Douglas G. 1981. *The Black Underclass.* New York: Vintage.

Glazer, Nathan. 1975. *Affirmative Discrimination: Ethnic Inequality and Public Policy.* New York: Basic Books.

Glazer, Nathan, and Daniel Patrick Moynihan. 1970. *Beyond the Melting Pot: The Negroes, Puerto Ricans, Jews, Italians, and Irish of New York City.* Cambridge, Mass.: M.I.T. Press.

Gordon, David M. 1972. *Theories of Poverty and Underemployment: Orthodox, Radical and Dual Labor Market Perspectives.* Lexington, Mass.: D. C. Heath.

Groeneveld, Lyle P., Nancy Brandon Tuma, and Michael T. Hannan. 1980. "Marital Dissolution and Remarriage." In Philip K. Robins, Robert G. Spiegelman, Samuel Weiner, and Joseph G. Bell, eds., *A Guaranteed Annual Income: Evidence from a Social Experiment.* New York: Academic Press.

Grove, Robert D., and Alice M. Hetzel. 1968. *Vital Statistics Rates in the United States: 1940–1960.* Washington: Government Printing Office.

Hannan, Michael T., Nancy Brandon Tuma, and Lyle P. Groeneveld. 1978. "Income and Independence Effects on Marital Dissolution: Results from the Seattle-Denver Income Maintenance Experiments." *American Journal of Sociology* 84, no. 3 (Nov.):611–633.

Hannerz, Ulf. 1969. *Soulside: Inquiries into Ghetto Culture and Community.* New York: Columbia University Press.

Haworth, Joan Gustafson, James Gwartney, and Charles Haworth. 1975. "Earnings, Productivity, and Changes in Employment Discrimination During the 1960s." *American Economic Review* 65, no. 1 (March):158–168.

Harris, William. 1982. *The Harder We Run: Black Workers Since the Civil War.* New York: Oxford University Press.

Henson, Mary F. 1967. "Trends in the Income of Families and Persons in the United States, 1947–1964." U.S. Bureau of the Census, Technical Paper 17. Washington: Government Printing Office.

Hermalin, Albert I., and Reynolds Farley. 1973. "The Potential for Residential Integration in Cities and Suburbs: Implications for the Busing Controversy." *American Sociological Review* 38, no. 5 (Oct.):595–610.

Hill, Martha S. 1981. "Poverty Persistence and Its Associated Factors." Paper presented at the annual meetings of the Population Association of America, Washington, D.C., March 30.

——— 1983. "Trends in the Economic Situation of U.S. Families and Children: 1970–1980." In Richard Nelson and Felicity Skidmore, eds., *American Families and the Economy: The High Costs of Living.* Washington: National Academy Press.

Hill, Robert B. 1981. *Economic Policies and Black Progress: Myths and Realities.* Washington: National Urban League.

Hodson, Randy, and Robert L. Kaufman. 1982. "Economic Dualism: A Critical Review." *American Sociological Review* 47, no. 6 (Dec.):727–739.

Hogan, Dennis P. 1981. *Transition and Social Change.* New York: Academic Press.

Hyman, Herbert H., and Paul B. Sheatsley. 1964. "Attitudes toward Desegregation." *Scientific American* 211, no. 1 (July):16–23.

Jiobu, Robert M., and Harvey H. Marshall, Jr. 1971. "Urban Structure and the Differentiation between Blacks and Whites." *American Sociological Review* 36, no. 4 (Aug.):638–649.

Johnson, Lyndon B. 1970. "To Fulfill These Rights." Commencement address at Howard University, June 4, 1964. Rpt. in Blaustein and Zagrando, 1970.

Jordan, Vernon. 1979. "Introduction." In James D. Williams, ed., *The State of Black America, 1979.* Washington: National Urban League.

―――― 1980. "Introduction." In James D. Williams, ed., *The State of Black America, 1980.* Washington: National Urban League.

Kain, John F. 1968. "Housing Segregation, Negro Employment and Metropolitan Decentralization." *Quarterly Journal of Economics* 82, no. 2 (May):175–197.

Kain, John F., and John M. Quigley. 1975. *Housing Markets and Racial Discrimination.* New York: National Bureau of Economic Research.

Kerr, Clark. 1954 "The Balkanization of Labor Markets." In Paul Webbink, ed., *Labor Mobility and Economic Opportunity: Essays.* Cambridge, Mass.: M.I.T. Press.

Kihss, Peter. 1970. "Benign Neglect on Race is Proposed by Moynihan." *New York Times,* March 1.

Killingsworth, Charles C. 1968. *Jobs and Income for Negroes.* Ann Arbor: Institute of Labor and Industrial Relations, University of Michigan.

Kilson, Martin. 1981. "Black Social Classes and Intergenerational Poverty." *Public Interest,* no. 64 (Summer):58–78

Kluegel, James R., and Eliot R. Smith. 1982. "Whites' Beliefs about Blacks' Opportunity." *American Sociological Review* 47, no. 4 (Aug.):518–531.

Lazear, Edward. 1979. "The Narrowing of Black-White Wage Differentials Is Illusory." *American Economic Review* 69, no. 4 (Sept.):553–564.

Lake, Robert M. 1981. *The New Suburbanites: Race and Housing in the Suburbs.* New Brunswick, N.J.: Center for Urban Policy Research, Rutgers University.

Levitan, Sar A., William B. Johnston, and Robert Taggart. 1975. *Still A Dream: The Changing Status of Blacks Since 1960.* Cambridge, Mass.: Harvard University Press.

Lieberson, Stanley. 1963. *Ethnic Patterns in American Cities.* New York: Free Press of Glencoe.

―――― 1980. *A Piece of the Pie: Black and White Immigrants since 1880.* Berkeley: University of California Press.

Liebow, Elliot. 1967. *Tally's Corner.* Boston: Little, Brown.

Long, Larry, and Diane DiAre. 1981. "Suburbanization of Blacks." *American Demographics* 3, no. 8 (Sept.):16–44

Mallan, Lucy B. 1982. "Labor Force Participation, Work Experience, and the Pay Gap between Men and Women." *Journal of Human Resources* 17, no. 3 (Summer):437–448.

Masnick, George, and Mary Jo Bane. 1980. *The Nation's Families: 1960–1990.* Cambridge, Mass.: Joint Center for Urban Studies, MIT and Harvard University.

Massey, Douglas S. 1978. "On the Measurement of Segregation as a Random Variable." *American Sociological Review* 43, no. 4 (Aug.):587–590.

——— 1979. "Residential Segregation of Spanish Americans in U.S. Urbanized Areas." *Demography* 16 no. 4 (Nov.):533–564.

Masters, Stanley H. 1975. *Black-White Income Differentials: Empirical Studies and Policy Implications.* New York: Academic Press.

McCarthy, James. 1978. "A Comparison of the Probability of the Dissolution of First and Second Marriages." *Demography* 15, no. 3 (Aug.):345–359.

Meier, August, and Elliott Rudwick. 1975. *CORE: A Study on the Civil Rights Movement, 1942–1968.* Urbana: University of Illinois Press.

Merriam, Ida C. 1968. "Welfare and Its Measurement." In Eleanor Bernert Sheldon and Wilbert E. Moore, eds., *Indicators of Social Change.* New York: Russell Sage Foundation.

Mincer, Jacob. 1974. *Schooling, Experience and Earnings.* New York: National Bureau of Economic Research.

Mincer, Jacob, and Solomon Polachek. 1974. "Family Investment in Human Capital: Earnings of Women." In Theodore W. Schultz, ed., *Economics of the Family.* Chicago: University of Chicago Press.

Morgan, James N., Katherine Dickinson, Jonathan Dickinson, Jacob Benus, and Greg Duncan. 1974. *Five Thousand American Families: Patterns of Economic Progress.* Vol. 1. Ann Arbor: Institute for Social Research, University of Michigan.

Moynihan, Daniel Patrick. 1972. "The Schism in Black America." *Public Interest*, no. 27 (Spring):3–24.

Myrdal, Gunnar. 1944. *An American Dilemma: The Negro Problem and Modern Democracy.* New York: Harper & Row.

National Commission on Employment and Unemployment. 1979. *Counting the Labor Force.* Washington: Government Printing Office.

Parsons, Donald O. 1980. "Racial Trends in Male Labor Force Participation." *American Economic Review* 70, no. 5 (Dec.):911–920.

Pearce, Diana. 1979. "Gatekeepers and Homeseekers: Institutionalized Patterns in Racial Steering." *Social Problems* 26 (Feb.):325–342.

Pettigrew, Thomas F. 1973. "Attitudes on Race and Housing: A Social-Psychological View." In Amos H. Hawley and Vincent P. Rock, eds., *Segregation in Residential Areas*, 21–84. Washington: National Academy of Science.

Plotski, Harry A., and Warren Marr. 1976. *The Negro Almanac.* New York: Bellwether.

Polachek, Solomon. 1975. "Discontinuous Labor Force Participation and Its

Effect on Women's Market Earnings." In Cynthia B. Lloyd, ed., *Sex, Discrimination, and the Division of Labor.* New York: Columbia University Press.

President's Committee to Appraise Employment and Unemployment Statistics. 1962. *Measuring Employment and Unemployment.* Washington: Government Printing Office.

Preston, Samuel H., and James McDonald. 1979. "The Incidence of Divorce within Cohorts of American Marriage Contracted Since the Civil War." *Demography* 16, no. 1 (Feb.):1–25.

Priebe, John. 1980. "Occupational Classifications in the 1980s." Paper presented at the 1980 meetings of the Southern Sociological Society.

Rawlings, Steve W. 1980. "Families Maintained by Female Householders: 1970–79." U.S. Bureau of the Census, *Current Population Reports,* ser. P-23, no. 197.

Reich, Michael. 1981. *Racial Inequality: A Political-Economic Analysis.* Princeton: Princeton University Press.

Robins, Philip K. 1980. "Labor Supply Response of Family Heads and Implications for a National Program." In Philip K. Robins, Robert G. Spiegelman, Samuel Weiner, and Joseph G. Bell, eds., *A Guaranteed Annual Income: Evidence from a Social Experiment.* New York: Academic Press.

Robins, Philip K., and Richard W. West. 1980. "Labor Supply Response of Family Heads Over Time." In Philip K. Robins, Robert G. Spiegelman, Samuel Weiner, and Joseph G. Bell, eds., *A Guaranteed Annual Income: Evidence from a Social Experiment.* New York: Academic Press.

Rossell, Christine H. 1976. "School Desegregation and White Flight." *Political Science Quarterly* 92 (Winter):657–696.

Rytina, Nancy F. 1982. "Tenure as a Factor in the Male-Female Earnings Gap." *Monthly Labor Review* 105, no. 4 (April):32–35.

Sandell, Steven H., and David Shapiro. 1978. "The Theory of Human Capital and the Earnings of Women: A Reexamination of the Evidence." *Journal of Human Resources* 13, no. 1 (Winter):103–117.

Schultz, T. Paul. 1969. "Secular Trends and Cyclical Behavior of Income Distribution in the United States: 1944-1965." In Lee Soltow, ed., *Six Papers on the Size Distribution of Wealth and Income.* New York: National Bureau of Economic Research.

Sheatsley, Paul B. 1966. "White Attitudes toward the Negro." *Daedalus* 95, no. 1 (Winter):217–238.

Siegel, Paul M. 1965. "On the Cost of Being a Negro." *Sociological Inquiry* 35 (Winter):41–57.

Smeeding, Timothy M. 1982. *Alternative Methods for Valuing Selected In-Kind Transfer Benefits and Measuring Their Effect on Poverty.* U.S. Bureau of the Census, Technical paper 50.

Smith, James P. 1979. "The Convergence to Racial Equality in Women's Wages." In C. B. Lloyd, E. S. Andrews and C. L. Gibson, eds., *Women in the Labor Market.* New York: Columbia University Press.

Smith, James P., and Finis R. Welch. 1977. "Black/White Male Earnings and Employment: 1960–70." In F. Thomas Juster, ed., *The Distribution of Economic Well-Being*. Cambridge, Mass.: Ballinger.

Smith, Shirley J., and Nancy F. Rytina. 1983. "Testing a New Measure of Annual Hours of Work." Paper presented at the annual meetings of the American Statistical Association, Toronto, August.

Sørenson, Annemette, Karl E. Taeuber, and Leslie J. Hollingsworth, Jr. 1975. "Indexes of Racial Residential Segregation for 109 Cities in the United States, 1940 to 1970." *Sociological Focus* 8, no. 2 (April):125–142.

Sowell, Thomas. 1981. *Ethnic America*. New York: Basic Books.

Stack, Carol B. 1975. *All Our Kin: Strategies for Survival in a Black Community*. New York: Harper and Row.

Stolzenberg, Ross M. 1975. "Education, Occupation and Wage Differences between White and Black Men." *American Journal of Sociology* 81, no. 2 (Sept.):299–323.

Suter, Larry E., and Herman P. Miller. 1973. "Income Differences between Men and Career Women." *American Journal of Sociology* 78, no. 5 (March):963–974.

Taeuber, Karl E. 1983. "Racial Residential Segregation, 28 Cities, 1970–1980." CDE Working Paper 83–12. Madison: Center for Demography and Ecology, University of Wisconsin.

Taeuber, Karl E., and Alma F. Taeuber. 1965. *Negroes in Cities*. Chicago: Aldine.

Taylor, D. Garth, Paul B. Sheatsley, and Andrew M. Greeley. 1978. "Attitudes toward Racial Integration." *Scientific American* 238, no. 6 (June):42–50.

Taylor, Patricia A. 1979. "Income Inequality in the Federal Civilian Government." *American Sociological Review* 44, no. 3 (June):468–479.

Thornton, Arland. 1977. "Decomposing the Re-Marriage Process." *Population Studies* 31, no. 2 (July):572–595.

—— 1978. "Marital Instability Differentials and Interactions: Insights from Multivariate Contingency Table Analysis." *Sociology and Social Research* 62, no. 4 (July):572–595.

Thurow, Lester C. 1969. *Poverty and Discrimination*. Washington: Brookings Institution.

U.S. Bureau of the Census. 1918. *Negro Population: 1790–1915*.

—— 1943a. *Sixteenth Census of the United States: 1940, Population*, vol. IV, p. 1.

—— 1943b. *Sixteenth Census of the United States: 1940, Population*, vol. III, p. 1.

—— 1953. *Census of Population: 1950*, P-D1.

—— 1963a. *Census of Population: 1960*, PC(1)-1D.

—— 1963b. *Census of Population: 1960*, PC(2)-1C.

—— 1963c. *Census of Population: 1960*, PC(2)-7A.

—— 1963d. *Census of Population: 1960*, PC(2)-4A.

—— 1971. *Current Population Reports*, ser. P-20, no. 218.

—— 1973a. *Census of Population: 1970*, vol. 1, p. 1.

———— 1973b. *Census of Population: 1970*, PC(2)-7A.

———— 1973c. *Current Population Reports*, ser. P-23, no. 46.

———— 1975. *Historical Statistics of the United States: Colonial Times to 1970.*

———— 1976. *Current Population Reports*, ser. P-20, no. 289.

———— 1977. *Social Indicators: 1976.*

———— 1978a. Statistical Abstract of the United States: 1978.

———— 1978b. *Current Population Reports*, ser. P-20, no. 321.

———— 1978c. *Current Population Reports*, ser. P-20, no. 325.

———— 1980a. *Current Population Reports*, ser. P-20, no. 356.

———— 1980b. *Social Indicators III.*

———— 1981a. *Current Population Reports*, ser. P-20, no. 360.

———— 1981b. *Current Population Reports*, ser. P-20, no. 362.

———— 1981c. *Current Population Reports*, ser. P-60, no. 129.

———— 1981d. *Current Population Reports*, ser. P-20, no. 365.

———— 1981e. *Census of Population: 1980*, Alphabetical Index of Industries and Occupations.

———— 1981f. *Statistical Abstract of the United States: 1981.*

———— 1981g. *Current Population Reports*, ser. P-60, no. 130.

———— 1981h. *Current Population Reports*, ser. P-20, no. 366.

———— 1982a. *Statistical Abstract of the United States: 1982–83.*

———— 1982b. *Current Population Reports*, ser. P-25, no. 917.

———— 1982c. *Current Population Reports*, ser. P-23, no. 118.

———— 1982d. *Census of Population and Housing: 1980*, PHC80-S1-1.

———— 1982e. *Current Population Reports*, ser. P-60, no. 132.

———— 1982f. *Current Population Reports*, ser. P-60, no. 133.

———— 1982g. *Current Population Reports*, ser. P-60, no. 135.

———— 1983a. *Current Population Reports*, ser. P-60, no. 137.

———— 1983b. *Current Population Reports*, ser. P-60, no. 140.

———— 1983c. *Current Population Reports*, ser. P-20, no. 380.

———— 1983d. *Current Population Reports*, ser. P-20, no. 381.

———— 1983e. *Current Population Reports*, ser. P-23, no. 126.

U.S. Bureau of Labor Statistics. 1971. *Employment and Earnings* 17, no. 7 (Jan.).

———— 1979. *Handbook of Labor Statistics, 1978*, bulletin 2000.

———— 1980. *Employment and Earnings* 27, no. 1 (Jan.).

———— 1981. *Employment and Earnings* 28, no. 1 (Jan.).

———— 1982. *Employment and Earnings* 29, no. 1 (Jan.).

———— 1983. *Employment and Earnings* 30, no. 1 (Jan.).

U.S. Department of Health, Education and Welfare. 1966. *Equality of Educational Opportunity*, OE-38000.

U.S. Department of Health and Human Services. 1982. *Social Security Bulletin* 45, no. 7 (July).

U.S. Department of Labor. 1965. *The Negro Family: The Case for National Action.* Office of Policy Planning and Research. Washington: Government Printing Office.

U.S. National Advisory Commission on Civil Disorders. 1968. *Report of the*

National Advisory Commission on Civil Disorders. New York: Bantam Books.

U.S. National Center for Health Statistics. 1980. *Vital Statistics of the United States: 1977,* vol. II, p. A.

——— 1981a. *Monthly Vital Statistics Report* 30, no. 6, supplement 2.

——— 1981b. *Vital Statistics of the United States: 1977,* vol. I.

——— 1982. *Monthly Vital Statistics Report* 31, no. 8, supplement (Nov. 30).

——— 1983. *Monthly Vital Statistics Report* 32, no. 4, supplement (Aug. 11).

Van Valey, Thomas L., Wade Clark Roof, and Jerome E. Wilcox. 1977. "Trends in Residential Segregation: 1960–1970." *American Journal of Sociology* 82, no. 4 (Jan.):826–844.

Wallace, M., and A. L. Kalleberg. 1979. "Economic Organization, Occupations, and Labor Force Consequences: Toward a Specification of Dual Economy Theory." Paper presented at the annual meetings of the American Sociological Association, Boston.

Wallace, Phyllis A., ed. 1976. *Equal Employment Opportunity and the A.T.&T. Case.* Cambridge, Mass.: MIT Press.

Wattenberg, Ben J., and Richard M. Scammon. 1973. "Black Progress and Liberal Rhetoric." *Commentary* 55, no. 4 (April):35–44.

Weed, James A. 1980. *National Estimates of Marriage Dissolution and Survivorship: United States.* U.S. Department of Health and Human Services, Vital and Health Statistics, ser. 3, no. 19.

Weiss, Leonard, and Jeffrey Williamson. 1972. "Black Education, Earnings and Interregional Migration: Some New Evidence." *American Economic Review* 62 (June):372–383.

Welch, Finis. 1973. "Black-White Differences in Returns to Schooling." *American Economic Review* 63 (Dec.):893–907.

Wienk, Ronald E., Clifford E. Reid, John C. Simonson, and Frederick J. Eggers. 1979. *Measuring Racial Discrimination in American Housing Markets: The Housing Market Practices Survey.* Washington: Department of Housing and Urban Development, Office of Policy Development and Reseach.

Williams, Walter E. 1981. "Legal Barriers to Black Economic Gains: Employment and Transportation." In *The Fairmont Papers.* San Francisco: Institute for Contemporary Studies.

——— 1982. *The State Against Blacks.* New York: McGraw-Hill.

Wilson, William J. 1978. *The Declining Significance of Race.* Chicago: University of Chicago Press.

Wurdock, Clarence, and Reynolds Farley. 1980. "School Integration and Enrollments in the Nation's Largest Cities: An Analysis of Recent Trends." *Proceedings of the Social Science Section of the American Statistical Association* 1979:359–363.

Zoloth, Barbara S. 1976. "Alternative Measures of School Segregation." *Land Economics* 53 (Aug.):278–298.

Index